The New Americans
Recent Immigration and American Society

Edited by
Carola Suárez-Orozco and Marcelo Suárez-Orozco

A Series from LFB Scholarly

Transnational Messages
Experiences of Chinese and Mexican Immigrants in American Schools

Carmina Brittain

LFB Scholarly Publishing LLC
New York 2002

Library of Congress Cataloging-in-Publication Data

Brittain, Carmina.
  Transnational messages : experiences of Chinese and Mexican immigrants in American schools / Carmina Brittain.
      p. cm. -- (The new Americans)
  Includes bibliographical references (p.) and index.
  ISBN 1-931202-29-X (alk. paper)
    1. Children of immigrants--Education--Social aspects--United States. 2. Chinese American students--Attitudes. 3. Mexican American students--Attitudes. I. Title. II. New Americans (LFB Scholarly Publishing LLC)
  LC3746 .B75 2002
  371.829'6872'073--dc21

2001006811

ISBN 1-931202-29-X

Printed on acid-free 250-year-life paper.

Manufactured in the United States of America.

Dedication

To my beloved husband, Jason Alan Brittain, whose immense love, support, and patience have been pivotal to the completion of this project. The present volume is the testimony of our true partnership in this endeavor and our life together. My endless gratitude and love to you, Jason, for sharing your time and expertise by providing the database for this study and for being with me every step of the way of this process.

Contents

vii

Tables

ix

Acknowledgements

I want to thank all the participants in this study and their families who graciously shared their experiences. I would also like to express my gratitude to the members of my dissertation committee, Dr. Patricia Gándara, Dr. Carola Suárez-Orozco, and Dr. Yvette Flores-Ortiz. *Muchisimas gracias a todas por el apoyo brindado y por compartir su invaluable experiencia conmigo.*

I am also indebted to Drs. Carola and Marcelo Suárez-Orozco from Harvard Immigration Projects who with good grace included my main questionnaire in the *Longitudinal Immigrant Student Adaptation Study Student Interview* in 2000. Along with Drs. Suárez-Orozco, I would like to express my appreciation to their staff, both in Cambridge and in Northern California.

This study could not have been completed without the emotional and intellectual support of my friends and colleagues Teresa Huerta, Joanna Abbott, Ann Go, and Rena Ilasa.

A special acknowledgement to the open source Java software community for creating the software that served as the foundation for the database and the web application for this study and for making it available for free to everyone.

My endless gratitude to my dear husband, Jason Alan Brittain, whose technical expertise as a software engineer provided me with an incredibly efficient custom database web application software package that was pivotal in the completion of this project in a timely manner. But most importantly, I thank him for motivating me to be as determined to fulfill my dreams as he is. He has been a true role model of courage and determination.

Finally, I want to thank "Grandma" Elena Sorensson for embracing me into the family and for being proud of my accomplishments.

Introduction

Since the establishment of the United States as an independent country, immigrant student populations have drawn the attention of several scholars and reformers in the educational arena (Kloss, 1977). The long history of immigration to the U.S. has witnessed the influx of major waves of immigration at different points (Joppke, 1999; Rose, 1997). While the first major wave of immigrants, at the turn of the 20th century, came from Europe, in the last 20 years the United States "have experienced large-scale immigration from new source areas, particularly from Asia as well as from Latin America" (Castles & Miller, 1998, p. 6).

The assimilation model emerged as a construct that explained the way European immigrants of the early 20th century lived their lives in their new locality, the United States (Cornell & Hartmann, 1998). Assimilation assumed that as different cultural groups came in contact with one another, the immigrant group would learn and adopt the culture of the majority group in the receiving country in order to participate in the new locality (Spindler & Spindler, 1990; Keefe & Padilla, 1987). Some critics of assimilation suggest that this model failed to represent the experience of non-White immigrants who arrived during the second half of the 20th century (Castles & Miller, 1998; Schuck & Münz, 1998). Because most immigration after 1945 was comprised of non-White groups, immigration increased ethnic diversity in most receiving countries (Castles & Miller, 1998). Further, transportation and communication advances have contributed to the formation of a new global economic order, where intercultural and international encounters are more prevalent than before (Appadurai, 1996).

These changes in diversity, technology, and communication have contributed to the globalization of migration "the tendency for more and more countries to be affected by migration movements at the same time" (Castles & Miller, 1998, p. 8).

Some scholars have argued that immigrants in their new localities present more complex patterns of social interaction than traditional assimilation theory assumes (Itzigsohn et al., 1999; Rose, 1997). Some scholars have recognized the existence of transnational social spaces within which immigrants interact with each other (Glick-Schiller, Basch, & Szanton, 1994; Faist, 1998; Portes, 1996a; Smith, 1998b; Smith & Guarnizo, 1998). Far from the assimilation model, which claims that immigrants cut their ties to their country of origin, the notion of transnational social spaces proposes that immigrants in fact create social spaces that allow them to establish and maintain productive ties between their country of origin and their receiving country (Besserer, 1998; Portes, 1996a; Smith, 1998a, 1998b). That is, immigrants tend to form human collectivities with their co-nationals (people from the same country of origin). Defined as transnational social spaces (Faist, 1998), these human collectivities of co-nationals cross and overlap boundaries between the sending and receiving localities as everyday activities link the two localities in a social exchange.

Most scholars in the transnational literature argue that these transnational social spaces are instrumental in nature, allowing immigrants to exchange economic, social, and cultural capital between the sending and the receiving localities (Crisp, 1998; Faist, 1998; Guarnizo, 1998; Hannerz, 1996; Pessar, 1996). Immigrant groups create networks to facilitate the exchange of economic, social, and cultural capital as well as to ensure political and social participation in both sending and receiving communities (Besserer, 1998; Portes, 1996a; Smith and Guarnizo, 1998; Smith, 1998b). The flow of economic, social, and cultural capital within the transnational social spaces provides opportunities for certain immigrant groups, opportunities that might have been denied by the social apparatus of the receiving country (Dirlik, 1996). One of the key elements in the establishment of a transnational social space is the exchange of information (Portes, 1996a).

Much of the research on transnationalism has been directed to the institutionalized or organized efforts of the immigrants in the U.S. (e.g., transnational committees) and to the macro social systems that are involved in the process of globalization (e.g., transnational corporations; Alvarez, 1998; Ribeiro, 1998). For example, a number of studies (Guarnizo, 1998; Kastoryano, 1998; Smith, 1998b) have concentrated on how the governments of the sending countries (e.g., Mexico, Colombia, Dominican Republic) have adopted policies to promote institutionalized links with their nationals in the U.S. Dual-nationality policies have been adopted as a way to create a *national consciousness* among those nationals abroad in order to include them in the political and economic processes of the countries of origin (Guarnizo, 1998). Also, some studies have focused on how immigrants in the U.S. have become organized in transnational grassroots movements by creating committees that aim to provide political participation in both the U.S. and the country of origin (Smith, 1994). Most of this research, however, is directed to adult activities, and not to children. In this study, I aimed to contribute to the understanding of transnational social spaces in two areas that have not been strongly explored—education and immigrant children.

Borrowing from the research done on the creation of transnational social spaces, I investigated whether members of two immigrant student groups—Mexican and Chinese—interacted with other students from the same country (co-nationals) and exchanged information about their experiences in American schools that shaped their schooling experience. My focus on information about American schools is rooted in the fact that in transnational social spaces the exchange of information is one of the major resources available to participants (Portes, 1996a). This study provides information about how perceptions of U.S. schools are constructed among transnational human collectivities of co-nationals and how they reflect specific values or expectations that Chinese and Mexican immigrant children have with respect to American schooling. The main research questions of this study are:

1. What are the messages that immigrant students of Chinese and Mexican origin receive about American schools from their co-nationals residing in their country of origin and in the U.S.?
2. How do these messages affect the way these students perceive the American school experience?

3. What are the messages that immigrant children of Chinese and Mexican origin construct about U.S. schools after living in the U.S. that could be transmitted to potential new immigrants?
4. How are these transnational messages different for the two groups under investigation?

In the next section, I present an overview of the educational research focused on immigrant students—specifically the theory of segmented assimilation by Alejandro Portes (1995). Then, I provide a rationale to expand this concept to include transnational connections.

IMIGRANTS' EXPERIENCES IN AMERICAN SCHOOLS

Numerous works have addressed issues of immigrant students in American public schools (Olsen, 1988, 1997; Portes, 1995; Rumbaut & Cornelius, 1995; Suarez-Orozco & Suarez-Orozco, 1995). Researchers who have investigated how immigrant students experience American schools have reached similar conclusions. First, in general, regardless of country of origin, scholars conclude that immigrant students face some cultural discontinuities due to the differences between home and school cultures (Olsen, 1997; Rumbaut, 1995). Second, research has shown different paths of assimilation and academic achievement among different immigrant groups (Portes, 1995; Rumbaut, 1995). On one hand, some research studies have documented the high academic achievement of immigrant groups such as the Chinese (Rumbaut, 1995) and Punjabi (Gibson, 1995). On the other hand, in Mexican immigrant groups there is evidence of a decline in academic achievement in relation to the number of years that the students have been living in the U.S. (Suarez-Orozco & Suarez-Orozco, 1995). That is, some researchers suggest that for some immigrant groups (e.g., Mexican) the longer immigrant students stay in the United States, the less academically inclined the students become. While these conclusions need to be considered within the context of the samples analyzed and the multiple factors that may account for differences across and within groups, the literature on immigrant students leads us to the conclusion that there are multiple paths of assimilation of immigrant students.

Some of the factors that influence immigrant adaptation are individual, such as socioeconomic status or level of education.

However, research suggests that the demographic concentration of immigrants reflects how immigration is a network-driven process (Rumbaut, 1995) where the assimilation patterns immigrants take are in part based on the social networks they establish upon arrival. This suggests that immigrants' adaptation is influenced not only by individual factors (e.g., human capital) but also by social forces such as the ability of individuals to interact in social networks of co-immigrants.

Individual characteristics and social network influences need to be analyzed in the context of how these play out in the receiving community. Rumbaut (1995) suggests that the presence of immigration policies, ethnic enclaves, and employers that prefer migrant labor, as well as racial discrimination, can influence different paths of assimilation among immigrants. The presence of factors both micro (e.g., social networks) and macro (e.g., government policies) makes it imperative that any research on immigrant adaptation take into consideration the interplay between individual and social factors and their influence in assimilation patterns.

It is clear that the literature on immigration acknowledges the influence of social factors in assimilation of new immigrants (Cornell & Hartman, 1998; Rumbaut, 1995). However, how do these social factors come into play in the context of the school? These influences affect the assimilation of immigrant children in the public education system because the school often acts as a mirror of society (Suarez-Orozco, 2000). Social scientists have recognized that schools often reflect a *mirror image* of society (Apple, 1996, 1997; Giroux, 1993; Giroux & McLaren, 1989; McLaren, 1988; Suarez-Orozco & Suarez-Orozco, 1995). In other words, "the classroom is a microscopic version of the larger socioeconomic power structure, where teachers from the dominant majority culture and minority students miscommunicate and interact in an environment of social inequality" (Suarez-Orozco & Suarez-Orozco, 1995, p. 59). Carola Suarez-Orozco (2000) suggests that immigrant children are indeed aware of the negative social images reflected in the school context, and under these negative reflections it is "extremely difficult to maintain an unblemished sense of self-worth for very long" (p. 213). Others argue that the school provides youth with institutionalized identities that reflect educational stratification and an awareness of class position (Rothstein, 1991). These institutionalized identities also create awareness of the social position of ethnic minority students, as these identities validate perceptions of ethnic minority students as inferior (Welch & Hodges, 1997).

An understanding of the cultural, economic, and political influences of society allows the educational researcher to contextualize school experiences within a framework that accounts for the interplay of these multiple factors. If we accept the role of the school as a social mirror (Suarez-Orozco, 2000), then investigating the social factors affecting immigrant adaptation is key to a more complete understanding of immigrant children's participation in American schools.

The interplay of individual, social, cultural, and political factors in the assimilation of immigrants in general presents a complex task for the researcher who aims to understand what accounts for the divergent paths of different immigrant groups. However, one theoretical framework that considers the interplay of social factors in the receiving community and helps explain the differences in immigrant students' adaptation to American schools is Alejandro Portes' idea of segmented assimilation.

THE SEGMENTED ASSIMILATION VIEW

While immigration results from a number of causes (e.g., political), the creation of labor market opportunities abroad has been a major factor in the promotion of immigration (Castles & Miller, 1998; Espenshade, 1997; McCarthy & Vernez, 1997). Some argue that immigration is pushed and pulled by the emergence of transnational capital and labor markets (Besserer, 1998; Castles & Miller, 1998). As technological advances promote faster and more effective travel and communication, international trade and investment grow, narrowing the differences between regions and countries and expanding the opportunities and possibilities for international migration (Castles & Miller, 1998). In other words, globalization facilitates individuals' access to emerging labor markets abroad (Appadurai, 1996). However, the array of labor market opportunities offered to immigrants is sharply segmented into a bipolar mode. While there are some high-skilled professional immigrant workers, immigrants also include a large number of low-skilled workers who become trapped into insecure, low-paid jobs (Castles & Miller, 1998).

Participation in different labor market sectors depends in part on the legal residence status of the immigrants. Cornelius (1998) suggests the existence of "immigrant-dependent firms" (p. 118) in the U.S. These firms show high levels of reliance on immigrant labor (Cornelius, 1998, Pessar 1994). Often these immigrant-dependent firms rely "more heavily on illegal immigrant workers" (Cornelius, 1998, p. 122) because most of the jobs offered by these firms are not very attractive to native-born applicants due to low wages, absence of fringe benefits, and poor working conditions (Cornelius, 1998). Therefore, undocumented immigrants end up in the low-skill jobs within these immigrant-dependent firms. Further, immigrant-dependent firms tend to rely on social networks to recruit new workers (Cornelius, 1998). These social networks are highly influenced by the existence of ethnic enclaves, where it is common that undocumented individuals find assistance in securing employment via word-of-mouth.

Due in part to the segmentation of the migrant labor market, many immigrants experience what Alejandro Portes (1995) has called "segmented assimilation." According to Portes, the newcomer immigrant has roughly three major paths of assimilation. One option for some immigrants is to acculturate and assimilate into the mainstream social space of the receiving community, which in the U.S. case would be the White middle class. A second option in Portes' model is that the immigrant is assimilated into the underclass, experiencing severe economic disadvantages. The third path is to assimilate into immigrant communities (ethnic enclaves) as a resource to achieve economic capital and the preservation of the home culture.

According to Portes, while individual and family resources play a role in influencing the patterns of assimilation, a number of *vulnerabilities* and *resources* in the receiving community affect the patterns of assimilation for immigrants. Portes identified three major vulnerabilities: color, location, and absence of mobility ladders. Portes concluded that immigrant children's assimilation into different segments of American society depends in part on the children's racial background, the relationships and resources within the community where they reside in the U.S., and the presence of macro-economic factors that block opportunities for upward social mobility, especially for immigrants. Portes also identified three kinds of resources that are present for certain immigrant groups: the availability of government programs for immigrant groups, the absence of prejudice towards certain immigrant groups, and resources made available via networks in the ethnic community.

The segmentation of the market promotes the assimilation of immigrants into specific labor markets where co-nationals are most likely to participate. The presence of other co-nationals might promote the formation of ethnic enclaves that facilitate the entry to specific labor markets. According to Portes, these ethnic enclaves can become either vulnerabilities or resources, depending upon the economic conditions of the ethnic community and the resources they are able and willing to provide to members of the community.

Portes' view of segmented assimilation focuses on the receiving community. I agree that factors such as color, mobility ladders, government programs, and social prejudice are conditional to the social context of the receiving community (e.g., racial discrimination patterns, legal status as a barrier to mobility, or lack of economic opportunities in the U.S.). However, I propose that the *location and ethnic community resources* factors might emerge within the context of transnationalism. That is, I suggest that these factors can be localized not only in terms of experiences that immigrants have in the receiving community, but also in the influences (e.g., resources and vulnerabilities) that their sending communities have as immigrants continue to nurture relationships with their communities of origin.

Portes' notions of *location and ethnic community resources* are linked to the concentration of immigrant households in the receiving community. His discussion focuses on the relationship and socialization between immigrants and native-born minorities (e.g., children of immigrants born in the U.S.). However, these concepts of locality and ethnic enclave resources can be expanded to include the assimilation of immigrants into human collectivities, not only with individuals living in the ethnic enclave in the U.S., but also with individuals living in their community of origin. Transnational theory is a framework that has been developed to understand the activities and experiences of immigrants across borders and the influence of these activities in their lives in the receiving community. Basch, Glick Schiller, and Szanton Blanc (1994) define transnationalism as:

> The processes by which immigrants forge and sustain multi-strated social relations that link together their societies of origin and settlement. We call these processes

transnationalism to emphasize that many immigrants today build social fields that cross geographic, cultural, and political borders. (p. 7)

In this study, I took the notion of segmented assimilation as my theoretical framework. However, I expanded Portes' idea of vulnerabilities and resources to include the influence of social relations, not only from within the ethnic enclave in the U.S., but also from the community of origin, transforming the idea of location and ethnic communities into transnational influences. My intent is to use a transnational theoretical framework to investigate whether immigrant children establish social relations with co-nationals in the school, in a way that emulates what the literature on transnationalism has described as transnational social spaces

CHAPTER 1
Transnationalism

Because the current literature on transnationalism has not expanded significantly to the issues of children and education, the following discussion may not specifically describe issues of schooling. The purpose of this chapter is to present an overview of the concepts and frameworks under transnational theory that have explained how immigrants organize their lives in ways that create links between the receiving and the sending communities. In chapter 2, the discussion on transnationalism focuses on the applicability of this theory to explain the experiences of immigrant students in the school context.

Transnationalism is a theoretical perspective that, while not a discipline in itself, is a field to which many disciplines have contributed (Albrow, 1998; Chen, 1996; Portes, Guarnizo, & Landolt, 1999). The idea of transnationalism emerged first from the study of international relations as a new term to account for the continued social and physical crossing of boundaries by individuals from different nation-states (Albrow, 1998). Transnational theory aimed to capture the complex economic, social, cultural, and political processes that emerged in the world as a result of globalization. Waters (1995) defines globalization as a "social process in which the constraints of geography on the social and cultural arrangements recede and in which people become increasingly aware that they are receding" (p. 3).

In other words, globalization refers to the existence of economic, cultural, political, and social exchanges beyond the territorial boundaries of a nation-state because of the individuals' abilities to cross and overlap boundaries between nation-states.

As a result of globalization, a new framework was needed to understand social phenomena—beyond the configuration of the "nation-state."

THE EMERGENCE OF TRANSNATIONALISM

Albrow (1998) argues that in order to understand the concept of transnationalism, it is important to contextualize its emergence within the framework of a nation-state.

The nation-state is the unit that represents the establishment of a nation, under the territorial control of a given state (Castells, 1997). While *trans*-national is different from *national*, it is a variant of national (Albrow, 1998). Castells (1997) proposes that as economic interdependence grows among nation-states, the ability of the state to maintain control is diminishing, because in order to survive economically, the nation-states have to comply with the demands and requirements of global capitalism. This diminishing control of the nation-state results in a re-configuration of the concept of nation, as individuals participate in new social spaces that transcend territorial boundaries. "Transnationalism" is the product of this reconfiguration of the nation-states in an era of globalization that redefines "nation" beyond the boundaries of a nation-state (Albrow, 1998).

The meanings of *nationalism* and *nation* are important because globalization allows the concept of nation to be expanded beyond the territorial boundaries of a specific nation-state. A nation can exist across different "nation-states," not in the physical sense, but in a social and cultural sense. This concept of nation as transcending territorial boundaries is a key element in the formation of transnational social spaces because under this view a nation might exist across different nation-states if the individuals who feel they belong to the nation adopt this transnational perspective.

Some argue that even if we reject the idea of the declining importance of the nation-state, a transnational perspective is still needed to understand the reality of the nation-state and the reality of social phenomena across different nation-states (Kastoryano, 1998; Sklair, 1998; Wahlbeck, 1998). This is because "the social relations emerging from contemporary developments are not easily confined within the borders of nation-states" (Wahlbeck, 1998, p. 3). Sklair (1998) explains:

My argument is that individuals, groups, institutions, and even whole communities, local, national, or transnational, can exist, perhaps even thrive, as they have always done outside the orbit of the global capitalist system, but that this is becoming increasingly more difficult." (p. 2–3)

Kastoryano (1998) suggests that while the processes of globalization in general are an "obvious challenge to the nation-state, they do not lead necessarily to its erosion" (p. 4). However, he acknowledges that globalization and immigration movements raise the issues of a redefinition of the nation-state's political structure and of the balance between nation and state. In other words, a perspective that accounts for the influence of globalization and immigrant populations in the understanding of social phenomena is needed.

DEFINING TRANSNATIONAL

But what is the meaning of transnational? Transnational studies focus on three major elements: the unit (nation-state), the boundaries around units, and the ties between units (Albrow, 1998). While relations between "units" can also be seen in *intra-* and *inter-*national relations, *trans-*national relations are of two kinds—ties *across* boundaries, and *overlapping* boundaries (Albrow, 1998). If we consider nation-states to be the "units," transnationalism refers to the relations across nation-state boundaries and the overlapping of boundaries between nation-states.

While transnationalism has explored the macro-systems that cross and overlap boundaries between nation-states (e.g., transnational corporations, political agreements, and migrant labor markets), some argue that transnational activities also occur within the context of micro social units (Albrow, 1998; Cohen, 1998; Smith and Guarnizo, 1998). These micro social units represent the individual activities of people who cross boundaries and create overlapping boundaries across different nation-states. Albrow (1998) refers to these social units as human collectivities to the extent that they refer to the activities of individuals, rather than cities, firms, or nations. These human collectivities are transnational in nature because "they contain nations [e.g., people from the same country] and they spread across nations [people residing in different countries]" (Albrow, 1998, p. 13). Some argue that the emergence of these transnational human collectivities "challenges the accepted boundaries in the study of political participation, social mobility, and identity formation as these processes take place across national boundaries rather than within them" (Itzigsohn et al., 1999, p. 317).

The transnational exists in the context of relations across national units, whether in the shape of nation-states or in the shape of human collectivities (Albrow, 1998). Albrow explains that human collectivities can "materialize as aircraft or concerts, as software or banknotes, as clothing or food, and where a few persons, at a minimum two or three, are gathered together in the name that they find a community" (1998, p. 13). The recognition of the dual source of transnational activities—from nation-states and from human collectivities—has given rise to the distinction between transnationalism from "above" and from "below." *Transnationalism from above* pays attention to the dynamics at the macro level of the society (e.g., financial markets, transnational corporations, or labor movements; Castles & Miller, 1998). *Transnationalism from below* refers to the activities of human collectivities, where individuals engage in activities that cross boundaries and create social spaces that overlap boundaries between different nation-states (Smith and Guarnizo, 1998).

These two forms of transnationalism co-exist in an interdependent relationship. While some transnational activities at the human collectivity level are the product of the reconfiguration of macro-systems (e.g., transnational corporations, advances in technology, and labor markets), some of the human collectivities' activities also create reactions in nation-state governments, labor markets, and so forth. For example, Mexican migration has been highly motivated by the emergence of labor markets in the U.S. (Cornelius & Bustamante, 1989). However, Mexican migrant workers have maintained links with their communities of origin, mostly in terms of remittances, ties to families in Mexico, and participation in the local politics in their communities of origin (Besserer, 1998; Portes, 1996b; Smith, 1998a). This pattern of emigration with continuity of home-community involvement has motivated Mexico's federal government to institutionalize programs, such as the Mexican Communities Abroad, that aim to address the needs of Mexican immigrants in the U.S. (Guarnizo, 1998). Similarly, in the 1950s the Chinese communist government established Overseas Chinese Investment Corporations to attract and control the remittances of Chinese living abroad (Pan, 1999).

In these cases, transnational activities at the human collectivity level emerged from transnational labor market opportunities (transnationalism from above). However, the transnational activities at the level of human collectivity (e.g., remittances and community/political involvement) also influenced the Mexican and Chinese nation-states to create transnational programs. That is, individual transnational activities (transnationalism from below) influenced activities in a nation-state (transnationalism from above).

HUMAN COLLECTIVITIES IN TRANSNATIONAL SPACES

Within the transnational literature, terms like transnational social space, transnational social field, transnational circuit, or transnational social formation have often been used loosely or interchangeably (Faist, 1998; Sklair, 1998). Faist (1998) argues that the literature on transnationalism often fails to make clear distinctions between transnational community, circuit, network, and space, and that *transnational* has "become a catch-all phrase for sustained border-crossing ties" (p. 3). Because of this, I think it is important to reflect on the distinctions between these terms.

This book has discussed the nature of the term "transnational." Something is "transnational" if it involves the crossing of boundaries between two localities in two different nation-states and it creates an overlap between these boundaries (Albrow, 1998). Faist (1998) explains that all of the transnational terms in the literature refer mostly to the "sustained ties of persons, networks, and organizations *across* the borders of multiple nation-states, ranging from weakly to strongly institutionalized forms" (p. 2). Faist's definition acknowledges the "crossing" of boundaries, and affirms that the activities that establish this "crossing" might take different forms, from very formal to informal. While the terms "transnational community" and "transnational social space" have often been used synonymously, Faist makes a distinction. In his view, transnational community is a form of transnational social space. He considers the transnational social space as the basic unit, whereas transnational circuits, networks, communities, and such are *forms of transnational social spaces.*

Borrowing Albrow's definition of transnational activities, we could say that all these forms of *transnational social spaces* are also forms of human collectivities. These human collectivities can take many forms—from a small group or social network to a well-established community that expands across multiple nation-states. For the scope of this book, transnational social space is defined as a form of human collectivity where individuals engage in activities and processes (e.g., social exchanges) that link the individuals to multiple localities across boundaries, thus overlapping these boundaries.

Faist (1998) has identified four major characteristics of what constitutes a transnational social space, and Sklair (1998) has identified a fifth:

1. The spaces are socially dynamic, not static forms of ties and localities.

2. These spaces are instrumental in nature because they involve processes and activities that lead to the accumulation, use, and effects of economic, social, and cultural capital.

3. These spaces include mobile and relatively immobile persons and collectives as long as they maintain strong transnational links. The "crossing" of boundaries is not necessarily a physical one.

4. Transnational links within social spaces can be either informal (e.g., intra-household or family ties) or formally institutionalized (e.g., political parties, transnational committees or NGOs) (Faist).

5. Transnational practices operate in three spheres—the economic, the political, and the cultural-ideological (Sklair).

Faist has recognized three major variations in the transnational spaces: transnational ethnic/kinship groups, transnational circuits/networks, and transnational communities.

Forms of Transnational Spaces

Faist (1998) proposed a typology of transnational social spaces that includes transnational kinship groups, transnational circuits, and transnational communities. Faist's typology is based on three major forms in which social ties provide resources for the human collectivity. According to Faist, transnational social spaces involve the accumulation and use of resources based on reciprocity, social exchange, or solidarity. *Reciprocity* refers to the social norm of "what one party receives from the other requires some return" (Faist, 1998, p. 5). *Social exchange* refers to the mutual expectations and obligations associated with social ties. Finally, individuals in transnational spaces might be bound by *solidarity* sentiments towards others who share similar positions such as community membership, or ethnic or national ties (Faist, 1998). Faist proposes that what distinguishes a transnational kinship group from a transnational circuit or community is the type of *link* by which primary resources are exchanged within the human collectivity—on the basis of reciprocity, social exchange, or solidarity factors.

Mahler (1998) provides another way to map the differences in transnational practices. Like Faist, Mahler recognizes that transnational practices can take very formal, institutionalized forms or very informal forms. She also agrees with Faist that transnationalism may involve different degrees of mobility. That is, transnational practices do not necessarily involve the frequent movement of people between two localities. Mahler (1998) suggested two concepts—*broad* and *narrow*—to describe the levels of formality, institutionalization, and degree of mobility in transnational practices.

Broad transnational practices are those economic, political, social, and cultural practices that involve regular movement within two localities, a high level of institutionalization, and constant personal involvement (Mahler, 1998). *Narrow* refers to economic, political, social, and cultural practices that involve only sporadic physical movement between two countries, a low level of institutionalization, and just occasional personal involvement (Mahler, 1998). I consider Mahler's typology of transnational practices to be useful but limited. It is useful because it counts both formal and informal practices as transnational and recognizes that the crossing of borders is not necessarily a physical one. However, grouping high and low degrees of three characteristics (mobility, institutionalization, and personal involvement) into broad or narrow practices is problematic since characteristics classified by degree into opposite categories may not be mutually exclusive. For example, practices that display low levels of institutionalization may indeed involve high levels of mobility or personal involvement. I will discuss some of the characteristics of the different types of transnational spaces of Faist's typology.

Transnational Kinship Groups

Transnational kinship groups are small human collectivities (e.g., extended families) where a sense of reciprocity is shared between the family members residing in multiple localities. However, it is important to note that these reciprocity sentiments may be influenced by cultural elements and that not every transnational family shares these reciprocity sentiments.

Typically, in transnational kinship groups, social and economic capital is transferred from one locality to another by way of remittances, goods, job contacts, information, and so on. Kinship groups become transnational when they involve people (e.g., family members) residing in at least two localities (crossing borders) and the concept of the "family" is extended to include people in two localities (overlapping boundaries). Transnational practices are often not institutionalized since they occur within the context of family units. However, they can involve either high or low levels of personal involvement and physical mobility.

An example of a kinship group activity is the reciprocal exchange of goods and remittances. For example, many immigrants from the Dominican Republic (Itzigsohn et al., 1999; Torres-Saillant & Hernandez, 1998), Central America (Landolt, Autler, & Baires, 1999; Popkin, 1999), Mexico (Roberts, Frank, & Lozano-Ascencio, 1999) and even China (Pan, 1999) send goods that are more expensive or not available in their home countries (e.g., appliances and electronics) to family members. In exchange, family members usually send items and goods that are not available in the new locality, such as comestibles, beverages, or cultural artifacts from the home country, to their relatives living abroad. The exchange of goods between the two localities within the context of family ties has given rise to courier services that specialize in providing door-to-door deliveries, even to remote areas of the home countries. For example, Salvadoran people in Los Angeles and Washington, D.C. usually contract *viajeros* (travelers) who travel between El Salvador and the U.S. delivering cash, letters, gifts, and Salvadoran goods such as comestibles and pharmaceutical products between Salvadoran families in the U.S and families in El Salvador

(Landolt, Autler, & Baires, 1999). Ruben Hernandez (1997) found truck drivers who specialized in delivering money, food items, medical supplies, and commercial products between Monterrey, Mexico and Houston, Texas—again within the context of family-to-family exchanges (as cited in Roberts, Frank, & Lozano-Ascencio, 1999). The use of *viajeros* or transnational truckers usually means that the family members themselves are involved in low movement between the two countries, but the personal involvement is still significant to maintaining the family ties across boundaries.

Transnational Circuits/Networks

Transnational circuits are larger human collectivities than kinship groups, usually involving several families or individuals. They are characterized by a frequent circulation of goods, people, and information across the borders of sending and receiving states, which also implies a high level of mobility between the two localities (Rouse, 1991). According to Faist, transnational circuits are motivated more by a sense of social exchange than by reciprocity. That is, social ties establish mutual expectations and obligations between the participants. Social relationships become instrumental as immigrants established them for mutual economic, social, or political gains.

Transnational circuits often take the form of trading networks, which involve the capitalization of culture in the form of "insider" advantages (Faist, 1998). People become involved in the circuit because they know the language, culture, or have contacts with co-nationals. For example, Chinese businessmen in North America, often called "astronauts," are part of transnational circuits. They establish business in Singapore, Hong Kong, and other localities in Asia, while their families reside in the U.S. or Canada to maximize educational opportunities for their children or to escape from political instability (Faist, 1998). These entrepreneurs keep strong transnational ties with other entrepreneurs (both in Asia and North America) to capitalize on business connections. Because both business and family ties are involved, the circulation of social and cultural capital between two localities is more regular than in kinship groups. Their business and family ties cross boundaries between Asian and North American countries. Their conceptions of family and business transcend the boundaries of Asia and North America (overlapping boundaries).

Because these relationships are based mostly on economic exchanges, they are characterized by high levels of physical mobility, as well as personal involvement. The personal involvement is motivated mainly by economic gain, making the relationships more instrumental than reciprocal. Some transnational circuits may display a low level of institutionalization because they still rely on social networks. However, the emergence of transnational entrepreneurial organizations and programs can provide transnational networks with a level of institutionalization.

For example, Mexican transnational entrepreneurial activities range from large-scale to small-scale ventures (Roberts, Frank, & Lozano-Ascencio, 1999). Some Mexican entrepreneurs still rely on their transnational, ethnically based ties, while other large-scale Mexican entrepreneurs negotiate directly with banks, corporations, and the Mexican government (Roberts, Frank, & Lozano-Ascencio, 1999). Some argue that the penetration of transnational capital from these large-scale Mexican entrepreneurs in the U.S. has forced many smaller entrepreneurs into bankruptcy because of their inability to compete or to invest the capital and take advantage of the Mexican government's incentives for investment and trade (Roberts, Frank, & Lozano-Ascencio, 1999).

Transnational Communities

A transnational community is a more sophisticated form of human collectivity where shared ideas, beliefs, evaluations, and symbols are represented within a collective identity (Faist, 1998). The distribution of resources within transnational communities is based on solidarity sentiments rooted in religion, ethnicity, or nationality (Besserer, 1998). This solidarity goes beyond kinship ties or instrumental relationships.

Transnational "villages" where a majority of the town's population migrate from one locality to another, or where a history of migration is present in the community, are examples of transnational communities (Portes, 1996a). Social and cultural capital is exchanged between the two communities and a strong sense of solidarity is present in the emergence of committees or other formal organizations that aim to provide economic aid and support to the community of origin.

Federico Besserer (1998) explains the case of San Juan Mixtepec, a Mixtec community in the State of Oaxaca in Mexico, which historically has been involved in transnational migration due to participation in agricultural labor markets in the United States, specifically in California and Florida. Besserer claims that the transnational condition of this community (e.g., migrant labor crossing from Mexico to the United States) has influenced individuals to accept that their "nation" or "community" transcends the territorial boundaries of San Juan Mixtepec (overlapping of boundaries). When Besserer visited San Juan Mixtepec, he asked the Municipal President how many inhabitants the community had, and he got this response: "Well that depends. In terms of the census, the community has a total of 11,500 inhabitants. But for us, in the municipal presidency, the population is 25,000" (Besserer, 1998, p. 2). The municipal president was including as part of the San Juan Mixtepec community all of the individuals who reside outside Mixtepec, and their descendants (who quite possibly were not born in and have never been to San Juan Mixtepec). Part of this inclusion of the San Juanenses residing abroad is because these individuals provide a great source of capital to San Juan Mixtepec. Remittances and organized fund-raising activities of San Juanenses in the U.S. have provided the town of San Juan Mixtepec with improvements to its infrastructure, such as potable water and schools. Further, San Juanenses in the U.S. have provided political support for local politicians in San Juan Mixtepec (Besserer, 1998). Therefore, the residents of San Juan Mixtepec feel a sense of solidarity towards those residing abroad because of their monetary help and political involvement. Similar fund-raising activities have been documented in other immigrant groups such as Mexican Ticuani (Smith, 1998a), Salvadoran (Landolt, Autler, & Baires, 1999), Guatemalan (Popkin, 1999), and Haitian (Glick-Schiller & Fouron, 1999).

While "nation-state" indicates the establishment of a territorial unit under the control of a government (state), for some scholars the idea of "nation" has a less territorial nature. A *nation* may reside in multiple localities as long as the individuals who conform to the human collectivity of a nation recognize themselves as part of the nation (Albrow, 1998; Armstrong, 1998; Vertovec, 1999). Even nation-states are reconstructing the idea of nation to extend beyond the national boundaries. For example, in 1995, Mexican President Ernesto Zedillo established the National Development Plan 1995–2000, which promoted the concept of *Nación Mexicana* (Mexican Nation). This concept proclaimed that the "Mexican nation transcend its territory within its borders" (http://www.presidencia.gob.mx). In Haiti, President Jean-Bertrand Aristide in a symbolic way expressed that Haitians living abroad constituted the 10th department [state] of Haiti, a recognition of their contribution to the country (Glick-Schiller & Fouron, 1999). While the Constitution of Haiti does not provide for dual nationality (Glick-Schiller & Fouron, 1999), the President's recognition of Haitians abroad as part of the nation reflects a re-conceptualization of the Haitian nation beyond geographical boundaries. In China, the government has attracted the remittances and investments of overseas Chinese by providing economic incentives (Pan, 1999), but this does not seem to be tied to a "reclamation" of nationals overseas, as other countries such as Mexico seem to emphasize.

The reconceptualization of nation as transcending territorial boundaries has contributed to the resurgence of nationalistic sentiments among transnational people and the establishment of transnational communities. By adopting an identity along national or ethnic lines, transnational people may gain access to the human collectivities that can be considered transnational social spaces (Portes, 1996a). For example, Glick-Schiller and Fouron (1999) found that Haitian immigrants in the U.S. often "declare themselves to be part of Haiti" (p. 345). Armstrong (1998) argues that the emergence of transnational communities challenges the nation-states' more homogeneous definitions of what constitutes a distinctive society.

The reconstruction of nation beyond territorial boundaries has often been cited as the emergence of the *imaginary community* (Anderson, 1991; Appadurai, 1996). Some criticize the definition of communities that transcend territorial boundaries as "imagined" because the term might lead to the belief that these communities are not localized, when in fact they are specifically situated within a locality (Cohen, 1998; Smith and Guarnizo, 1998). The expression *re-territorialized community* (Besserer, 1998; Wahlbeck, 1998) might be more appropriate to define a community that is bound by common histories, values, and belief systems but that has expanded into multiple localities (Cohen, 1998).

Besserer (1998) argues that transnational communities become re-territorialized not only because their members travel beyond the community's territorial limits, but also because they establish new settlements of the community in other regions. What makes these communities transnational is the fact that the activities of the re-territorialized members of the community are linked to the community of origin. Under Besserer's definition, a transnational is an individual who has crossed the boundaries of two countries by the assimilation into a re-territorialized community. Members in this re-territorialized community identify themselves with the community of origin and establish new settlements (outside the territory of the community of origin) that they claim as part of their "community of origin." By virtue of the existence of these new settlements, the community of origin becomes transnational (Besserer, 1998; Caplan, 1998).

The transnational practices of these communities might be highly institutionalized if done within the context of a transnational committee or club. However, the ascription to the "nation" or "transnational community" does not necessarily need a formal ratification from the State, as long as individuals socialize within human collectivities created along national origin lines. In terms of the levels of personal involvement and mobility, these may vary among the members of the community. It is possible that people in leadership positions within the community become more personally involved, and travel more across the multiple spaces where the community expands, than non-leader members. For example, Salvadoran clubs in Los Angeles and Washington, D.C. often require their leaders to travel between these cities in the U.S. and their hometowns in El Salvador, but other community members often stay in one locality (Landolt, Autler, & Baires, 1999).

Characteristics of Transnational Social Spaces

People in transnational social spaces become involved in practices that cross and overlap boundaries. Michael Peter Smith (1994) defines people within a transnational space as *borderless people*. The borderless people live "here" and "there", not just in the physical sense, but also at the cultural, social, and ideological levels (Appadurai, 1996; Hannerz, 1996; Smith, 1994; Hall, 1990). The exchange of social and cultural capital, and the mutual influence that actions in the receiving and sending communities have upon each other, bridge the physical distance and create transnational social spaces, even when a physical crossing does not occur (England, 1999; Schein, 1998; Smith, 1998a). Smith and Guarnizo (1998) define the actions of transnational people as "translocal" because the actions that occur in one locality (e.g., receiving community) affect the actions in another locality (e.g., sending community).

> In these [translocal] social fields, transnational practices are vested with particular meanings. Translocal relations are constituted within historically and geographically specific points of origin and migration established by transmigrants. Such relations are dynamic, mutable and dialectical. They form a triadic connection that links transmigrants, the localities to which they migrate, and their locality of origin. (Smith and Guarnizo, 1998, p. 13)

While transnational social spaces cross and overlap boundaries between nation-states, they emerge within specific social contexts. In the next section, I will address some characteristics that the transnational literature has identified as part of the transnational social spaces.

Localized Experiences

People in transnational social spaces cross and overlap boundaries, but they are still located in one particular geographical area at any specific point in time. It is their actions that transcend their geographical location. Life in the transnational social space is a set of localized experiences that link people together to multiple localities—from the family which sends remittances back to relatives in the country of origin, to the political committee that supports campaigns for local politicians in the country of origin.

Instrumental Exchanges of Capital

One of the major characteristics of the transnational social spaces is that they have an instrumental role in the exchange and accumulation of resources in the form of economic, social, and cultural capital (Faist, 1998; Portes, 1999). Alejandro Portes (1996a) recognizes that communities and social spaces that span national borders have instrumental value to the extent that immigrants utilize these transnational social spaces to exchange money, material goods, cultural influences, and even political interests. Some authors have described transnational practices in terms of the type of benefit they provide—economic, political, cultural, and social (Itzigsohn et al., 1999). The instrumentality of transnational social spaces can be linked to Portes' idea of ethnic community resources, but these resources may be distributed among people in both the sending and the receiving communities.

The literature on Mexican (Roberts, Frank, & Lozano-Ascencio, 1999), Dominican (Itzigsohn et al., 1999), Guatemalan (Popkin, 1999), Salvadoran (Landolt, Autler, & Baires, 1999), Haitian (Glick-Schiller & Fouron, 1999) and Chinese (Pan, 1999) immigration has documented the instrumental nature of transnational social spaces in terms of capital exchanges. Research has shown that immigrant groups have vested interests in coming together as a community (both in the home country and the new locality), or in establishing networks that support their economic, social, and political interests (Dirlik, 1996). Immigrants often become involved in transnational social spaces to promote their economic welfare in the new country. But people in the home country also seek to include co-nationals abroad in their human collectivities (e.g., kinship groups or transnational communities) because of the economic support that immigrant co-nationals often provide to the home community, as well as the link to potential job markets in the U.S. for new immigrants from the community of origin.

While the mobilization of financial resources is significant within transnational social spaces, Portes (1996a) has identified that most of the resources that flow within transnational social spaces are social and cultural in nature. Peggy Levitt (1998) has described these forms of social and cultural capital as *social remittances*. These sociocultural resources in turn can provide access to economic and political benefits in terms of social and cultural capital required to access these benefits (Portes, 1996a).

Social Capital

The instrumentality of transnational social spaces resides mostly in the establishment of social networks that provide a source of social capital—usually in terms of information—for the new immigrants as well as for people in the home country (Crisp, 1998). Social capital is often defined as "networks" but it also includes the "know-how" (information) that is necessary to access participation in society (Hall & Neitz, 1993). In the context of the adult immigrants' participation in transnational social spaces, social capital is often used to achieve economic advancement or political participation.

Jeff Crisp (1998) identified information as a significant source of social capital among immigrant groups in transnational social spaces. Crisp's findings are based on a review of a number of studies of Asian immigrants and refugees in Western Europe, but similar characteristics have been found with other immigrant groups in the U.S. (Itzigsohn et al., 1999; Landolt, Autler, & Baires, 1999; Portes, 1996a, Smith, 1998a). The transnational social space acts as an important source of information to prospective asylum seekers and immigrants by providing specific details on issues such as transportation, entry requirements, asylum procedures, detention and deportation policies, and more (Crisp, 1998; Portes, 1996a). Crisp explains that access to this information, which is exchanged in transnational contexts (both in the receiving and the sending communities), became a determining factor in asylum-seekers' decision to immigrate.

This information is not only provided at the points of entry in the receiving country, but also in the sending country. Networks of co-nationals abroad and smugglers or other contact people provide information about life in the U.S. to the potential immigrants (Castles, 1998; Crisp, 1998; Smith, 1997). While some immigrants have relied on family or friends to obtain information (Cassagnol-Chierici, 1991), others rely on established business or brokers in the country of origin who provide key information about the immigration process for potential immigrants. These services have been described as the growing *migration industry*, which includes a number of services from travel arrangements to loan providers to pay-for-smuggling services (Castles, 1998; Itzigsohn, et al., 1999). The migration industry provides, besides information, an organizational structure that helps to maintain a constant flow of migration between the sending and the receiving country (Castles, 1998). In addition, Crisp (1998) found that transnational social spaces could also become instrumental in promoting economic and business exchanges between sending and receiving communities, and in promoting the participation of immigrants abroad in the political arena of their sending communities.

While information can be a source of social capital, Faist (1998) argues that the controlling power of a few people within the transnational space (e.g., holders of information and contacts) might restrict the degree of freedom and benefits that individuals have within the transnational social space. The "holders of information" often play a monitoring and controlling role within the transnational social space, which places them in positions of authority and power (Faist, 1998). That is, in a way, holders of information have the power to encourage or discourage immigration according to the messages they give to potential immigrants. Further, because individuals in some transnational social spaces base their relationships on reciprocity, the spaces might lead to cooperation, but also to retaliation (Faist, 1998). In other words, the transnational social space might become a vehicle to distribute or to withhold forms of social capital from the members of the human collectivity.

Guarnizo (1998) argues that the access to social capital within transnational social spaces might be unequally distributed among participants, creating the establishment of a "transnational elite" (e.g., entrepreneurs and politically active participants). The "transnational elite" in a sense is composed of people in already-powerful positions (e.g., entrepreneurs and politicians). This makes the establishment of a transnational social space a good move to promote the agendas and meet the needs of the transnational elite, but not necessarily those of other immigrants (e.g., working class immigrants). The agendas of the transnational elite may seek to reproduce the inequalities in the social structure of the community of origin because this structure aids in securing economic and political opportunities for those in powerful positions, but not for those outside the transnational elite (Guarnizo, 1998).

Cultural Capital

Besides social capital, transnational social spaces have been involved in the production of culture by creating a space where individuals can be exposed to the cultural heritage of their communities of origin. The transnational social space can be a vehicle for the country-of-origin's cultural diffusion and collective identity development (Faist, 1998). For example, Hmong immigrants in the U.S. have discovered their roots in Miao culture in China thanks to "travel videos" that depict Chinese Miao and are heavily marketed in American Hmong communities (Schein, 1998). Some transnational communities in the U.S. of

Mexican and Salvadoran backgrounds have established media forms (e.g., radio, magazines, and newspapers) to maintain the cultural links between the country of origin and the new locality (Besserer, 1998; Landolt, Austler, & Baires, 1999). Radio stations in the Central Valley of California promote regional music and the Mixtec language to the re-territorialized San Juanenses in California (Besserer, 1998). Another example is found in the "Mayan cultural experts" from Guatemala who are often invited to Mayan migrant communities in Los Angeles to help organize cultural events in Los Angeles such as religious festivities and ceremonies (Popkin, 1999). These Guatemalan cultural experts are considered pivotal to maintaining the cultural heritage of the U.S.-born Mayan youth in Los Angeles, and preventing the assimilation into the Latino culture of Los Angeles, which is often viewed as negative by the Mayan Guatemalan immigrants (Popkin, 1999; Vlach, 1992).

While the focus of the analysis of transnational social spaces is usually on the practices of individuals within human collectivities, it is important to clarify that these transnational spaces do not emerge solely from the initiative of the individuals within the human collectivity. Transnational spaces operate within situated social influences from macro-social systems in both the receiving and the sending communities.

Contributing Factors in Transnational Social Spaces

This book has argued that different forms of transnational spaces (e.g., kinship groups, networks, and communities) exist in part because they have an instrumental value in the accumulation and use of social and cultural capital. Therefore, we can argue that immigrants within the transnational social space exercise *agency* by organizing their lives within these transnational connections. However, the formation of these transnational social spaces is also stimulated by factors that facilitate the creation and maintenance of such spaces, not only by the individual agency of immigrants. Faist (1998), for example, suggests that international migration often is the result of prior economic, cultural, and political exchanges between two localities. Faist concludes that "activities in transnational social spaces do not create such transnational linkages *ex nihilo*, but usually evolve within pre-existing linkages, build new ones, and challenge existing arrangements" (p. 13).

Further, many of these linkages are facilitated by economic, social, and political structures of the receiving and sending communities.

Socioeconomic and Political Factors

Improvements in travel and communication technologies provide necessary, yet not sufficient elements for the emergence of transnational human collectivities (Hannerz, 1996). Media and communication technology play a major role in the diffusion of information and cultural production. But the flow of capital across boundaries, stimulated by migrant labor markets and remittances that immigrants send to their country of origins (Portes, 1996b), has also created the need for social networks that link people from different locations with one another (Faist, 1998). However, while transnational social spaces are the result in part of the agency of immigrants, they are still subject to the political regulations and cultural influences from the receiving and the sending countries (Faist, 1998). Smith (1998b) argues that in order to understand the dynamics of the transnational space, it is important to recognize the three major sets of institutions and practices within which these transnational spaces emerge and operate:

1. The domestic political institutions and strategies of the receiving community towards immigrants, and the presence of serious obstacles to socioeconomic integration of ethnic/immigrant groups into the receiving community.
2. The relationship of the sending state in the global capitalist expansion as supplier of low-wage labor for the receiving state and the hegemonic presence of the receiving state, in terms of capital investment, consumption patterns, and popular culture, in the sending country.
3. The autonomous political and economic activity of migrants abroad and the sending state's ability to control such activity. This includes the rise of the transnational enterprise and social spaces and the ability of sending states establish institutionalized practices to control such activities (e.g., via dual-nationality incentives).

Initiatives such as offering dual nationality (Colombia, Mexico) and voting rights (Dominican Republic) are enacted by state governments to control the autonomous activities of their compatriots abroad in transnational social spaces (Guarnizo, 1998). The Chinese government with its investment incentives has attracted large amounts of foreign investment from the "Overseas Chinese" in key "open-economy" regions such as Guangdong and Fujian (Pan, 1999). However, it is important to recognize the political and economic interests that the government had in attracting co-nationals living abroad to become involved with their "nation" of origin. Smith (1998b) argues that many of these government incentives aim to institutionalize and control activities that had already started at the autonomous, human collectivity level of the transnational social spaces. The interest of several foreign governments in their co-nationals abroad has prompted an evolution of the transnational social sphere into a transnational civic society (Smith, 1998a).

The Role of Media

Another force that might help maintain a transnational social space is the media. The term globalization has usually included the vision of a world that becomes closer and more global due to the technological advances in communication (Appadurai, 1996). The media bring images of distant places to diverse localities around the world (Hannerz, 1996). However, the emergence of "transnational" media that directly address the needs of immigrant communities for entertainment and information demonstrates the media response to the emergence of transnational social spaces. (Glendhill, 1998). Media influences in the transnational social spaces take three forms:

North-South Media

Information and media messages transferred from the immigrant receiving countries (e.g., the United States) to sending countries (e.g., Latin America and Asia) constitute the North-South media. These media provide hegemonic messages of life in the United States and Europe, usually in the context of "cultural imperialism" (Karim, 1998). Media in this context are a major vehicle for the diffusion of hegemonic messages that Smith (1998b) discusses as part of the sending state's relationship to the global capitalist system and to the receiving state.

South-North Media

Developing countries (sending countries) are producing film, television, and news that are being marketed and promoted worldwide (Karim, 1998). These productions from immigrant sending countries provide cultural "hubs" for members of transnational collectivities residing abroad (Karim, 1998). For example, the expansion of Mexico's major television network, Televisa, into the U.S. Spanish-speaking market allows Mexicans and other Hispanics residing in the U.S. to maintain a transnational link with Mexico through its programming.

Ethnic Media in Receiving Countries

Ethnic and immigrant groups have established a number of media operations in the receiving countries (e.g., United States and Canada; Karim, 1998). For example, in Vancouver, B.C., 46 ethnic newspapers (including 2 Chinese dailies) have a larger combined circulation that the two main English-language papers (Grescoe, 1994). In the United States, the fast growth of Spanish networks is the result of the recognition of Hispanic-American consumers' growing purchasing power, which was expected to surpass 400 billion dollars by the year 2000 (Collins, 1996). These networks produce programs with the Latino immigrant in mind. While some of these media directly address the immigrant communities in the receiving countries, some forms of ethnic media become transnational when they are also promoted in the sending countries.

For example, Spanish-speaking networks in the U.S., like Univision, are producing programs that diffuse news and cultural messages about life in the United States, often in relation to immigrant life (e.g., news magazine shows). These programs are also marketed in Latin America:

> The picture that Latin Americans see of American society is very different from that presented by mainstream U.S. television like CNN or by global TV news agencies like the World Television Network and Reuters Television. Univision and Telemundo adhere to Latin American news values that favor greater analysis than that offered by mainstream

American television. The Spanish-language networks also seek out Hispanic perspective on national news stories. (Karim, 1998, p. 7)

In Canada, Chinese versions of mainstream networks' programs have been produced to target the Chinese community, especially in Toronto (Karim, 1998). Also, some governments of sending states (e.g., Mexico) engage in the distribution of publications via their consulates in the U.S. These publications are aimed to provide a link between the country of origin and the transnational human collectivities. For example, Mexico publishes the magazine *La Paloma*, which is distributed in U.S. Consulates and aims to provide information about Mexican culture, politics, and other news that might be of interest to the Mexican nationals residing in the U.S. (http://www.presidencia .gob.mx). Immigrants' access to the Internet can help maintain links with their country of origin and other co-nationals in other countries (Rheingold, 1993). Newsgroups, for example, have given rise to virtual communities where individuals bonded by language or national origin come to discuss topics of interest (Mitra, 1997; Rheingold, 1993). However, it might be the case that not all immigrant groups have access to this form of media.

CONSTRAINTS IN THE TRANSNATIONAL FRAMEWORK

Before discussing how the inclusion of a transnational perspective in identifying influences in immigrant students' adaptation into American schools may yield important knowledge about the processes of adaptation, I would like to address some limitations in the use of transnational theory and its application in the study of social phenomena. One of the limitations of the transnational perspective has been the ambiguity of the term "transnational." In this chapter, I have addressed this issue by providing a more concrete definition of what constitutes a transnational social space for the scope of this book. A transnational social space is a form of human collectivity where the instrumental actions of the participants cross and overlap boundaries between multiple localities in different nation-states. These transnational social spaces can be informal or highly institutionalized, from kinship groups to transnational communities.

Besides the ambiguity of the term "transnational," there are still some considerations to keep in mind when approaching the study of social and educational phenomena from a transnational perspective.

Diversity in Immigration Patterns

While transnational social spaces are one way in which immigrants organize their lives, not all immigrants are part of these human collectivities. For example, according to Portes' theory of segmented assimilation (1995), some immigrants assimilate into the mainstream social space or into an underground economy that may not have any ties with the country of origin. Roberts, Frank, and Lozano-Ascencio (1999) found that immigrants from urban areas of Mexico (e.g., Mexico City) were less likely to be involved in transnational social spaces than were immigrants from rural areas of Mexico. They found rural immigrants, especially in transnational communities (e.g., from San Juan Mixtepec), often relying on transnational connections because of their close kinship ties and more homogeneous backgrounds (Roberts, Frank, & Lozano-Ascencio, 1999). Mexico City immigrants, on the other hand, were a more heterogeneous group in terms of socioeconomic status and education, and they hardly had access to social networks to support their immigration process and therefore established low group bonds with other people from Mexico in the new locality. Most of these urban immigrants migrated as individuals for short periods of time, during periods of economic recession in Mexico. In contrast, rural immigrants migrated as extended family units for longer periods of time, sometimes permanently. Roberts, Frank, and Lozano-Ascencio (1999) considered that "Mexico City migrants do not constitute a transnational migrant community. The weakness of their group bonds means that they do not see themselves collectively as a transnational migrant community" (p. 258).

Diversity within the Transnational Social Space

It is important not to fall in the trap of creating universal categories around the formation and participation of immigrants in transnational social spaces. The literature provides theoretical frameworks based on empirical data that depict characteristics of different transnational spaces (e.g., they are instrumental, formal/informal, etc.). However, because transnational social spaces are sustained by a number of contextual factors in society and within the groups, the experiences and forms that the transnational social space may take in terms of organization and practice may be very different across different immigrant groups. That is, not all immigrant groups involved in a transnational human collectivity may experience the transnational space in the same way.

This is because each immigrant group has unique cultural, social, and historical characteristics, along with unique economic and political relationships between the sending and receiving countries, that influence how transnational social spaces may be organized (from kinship groups to transnational communities). These differences will also create differences in the actual transnational practices across different groups (e.g., broad vs. narrow). Immigrant populations are highly heterogeneous, and factors such as gender, race, and socioeconomic status almost certainly have roles in the patterns of integration that different individuals experience in a specific social space—transnational or not. Issues of proximity between sending and receiving communities can also affect transnational mobility.

It is important to reflect on the fact that if transnational social spaces are "instrumental" in nature, different individuals might have different needs and find no instrumental value in the participation of a transnational social space. For example, immigrants who have already established employment contracts might be less motivated to seek the assistance of co-national networks to find jobs. However, undocumented workers might rely on co-nationals to locate potential employers (Crisp, 1998; Walhbeck, 1998). Besides jobs, the transnational social space can also provide access to other forms of support and social structures that sustain immigrants and co-nationals' lives (e.g., child-care, documentation, etc.). Further, the transnational social space is not the only form of social space in which individuals might participate. Other forms of social spaces in the workplace, school, and other sites might also influence the lives of immigrants. In other words, the participation in a human collectivity that is transnational in nature might not necessarily imply the exclusion of participation in other human collectivities.

Recognizing the Limitations of the Agency of Transmigrants

The level of interdependence between macro and micro social systems suggests that immigrants in transnational social spaces do have agency. On one hand, macro forces (e.g., global labor markets) influence the establishment of transnational spaces (e.g., formation of human collectivities). But on the other hand, the existence of transnational spaces also influences social and political institutions in both the receiving and the sending communities. However, there are limitations on the agency that participants in a transnational social space can exercise.

While the transnational space might provide economic, social, and cultural capital for their members, immigrants are still subject to the inequalities of society at large. That is, the potential benefits of the transnational space may not compensate for the inequalities and lack of opportunities that immigrants face in the receiving locality. Individuals within the transnational space are still subject to the social institutions and forces in their community of residence. As mentioned before, actions transcend the boundaries, but people still reside within one location and are bound and influenced by the social, economic, and political institutions of that location. This includes relations of power that might place some immigrant groups in disadvantaged positions relative to the majority group—e.g., immigrant groups as minority groups in the receiving community. Therefore, it is also important that the analysis of transnational social spaces does not neglect the role of the receiving community and the power structures involved in the majority-minority relations (Wahlbeck, 1998).

Transnational Social Spaces as Sources of Vulnerabilities

It is important to clarify that while the transnational spaces have been described as instrumental in the literature, the benefits of such participation might not exist or not be equally distributed among all members. In other words, the existence of a transnational space does not indicate that all individuals involved have access to social and cultural capital.

For example, it has been documented that the immigration experience is highly influenced by gender, including the participation in transnational communities (Malkin, 1998; Stivens, 1998). Smith

(1998a) reports that in the case of the transnational activities of the Ticuani Committee in New York City, the participation in the Committee was highly dominated by males. The Ticuani is an ethnic group from Puebla, Mexico with a history of migration to New York. Similar patterns of low female participation have been found within transnational grassroots organizations of Central American origin (Landolt, Austler, & Baires, 1999; Popkin, 1999).

Further, some argue that the distribution of benefits within the transnational space is not only unequal, but it also perpetuates the reproduction of inequalities that existed in the sending country (Guarnizo, 1998). Guarnizo's view on the emergence of a *transnational elite* suggests that transnational social spaces have served to support those who were already well established economically and politically. Guarnizo concludes that the creation of transnational social spaces, in this case, has actually led to the "transnational reproduction of inequality" (p. 69) where those already in power generate more power, while those who have no access to political and business connections are left out of the game. Ong and Nonimi (1997) also argue that transnational social spaces might indeed revive old forms of oppression in the new setting by assimilating the immigrants into segments of society that place the immigrants in disadvantaged positions. In this sense, the transnational social space may indeed become a source of vulnerabilities, rather than resources, for the immigrants.

Participation in the transnational space does not guarantee that individuals might accomplish positive economic, social, or political outcomes. The literature is inconclusive with respect to a particular "quality" or "direction" of the participation of individuals in a transnational human collectivity or social space. This study aims to identify and analyze the participation of children and adolescents in transnational social spaces in the context of school and education

CHAPTER 2

Transnational Social Spaces in American Schools

In chapter 1, five major elements from the transnational perspective and the study of transnational social spaces have been discussed:

1. Transnational social spaces are human collectivities where individuals engage in actions (e.g., social exchanges) that establish crossings between multiple localities in different nation-states.
2. Transnational social spaces also create an overlap of boundaries when individuals within these social spaces reconceptualize the notion of a social unit (e.g., family, community, or nation) to expand beyond the territorial boundaries of the locations of residence and origin.
3. Transnational social spaces are instrumental in nature to the extent that the actions of the individuals participating in the transnational social space lead to the accumulation, use, and exchange of economic, social, and, cultural capital.
4. Actions in the transnational social spaces transcend the boundaries of multiple localities, but the individuals are still acting from a specific locality. Therefore, these actions are still subject to the economic, social, cultural, and political influences of the location of residence.
5. Individual and autonomous actions within the transnational spaces are interdependent with transnational macro-social influences such as transnational capital flows, improvements in communications, and nation-states' initiatives.

Revising Portes' ideas of segmented assimilation under a transnational perspective, I propose that we could include these transnational social spaces as an influencing factor in the segmented assimilation of immigrants and their children in the United States. That is, these transnational social spaces are formed by human collectivities not only of individuals in the receiving community (as Portes suggests), but also of individuals in the sending community. Further, these human collectivities that engage in practices that cross and overlap boundaries can also be constructed as sources of resources and vulnerabilities for their participants.

The literature on transnationalism indicates that these transnational social spaces can be instrumental, offering *resources* to the participants. However, these forms of social capital (e.g., information) may not equate to the forms of social capital required to access social mobility in the receiving community—thus leading the immigrants to assimilate in disadvantaged sectors of American society, as Portes suggests, and becoming sources of *vulnerabilities* for the immigrants. Further, Wahlbeck (1998) argues that while transnational social spaces can provide economic, social, and cultural capital to their members, they may not provide them with the "same services and opportunities that are provided by a state to its citizens" (p. 12). Also, the distribution of "social capital" among transnational social spaces may not be equal, as Guarnizo (1998) exemplified with the emergence of the transnational elite.

Now, how are these characteristics of transnational social spaces present in the experiences of immigrant students within American schools? Do immigrant children also assimilate into transnational social spaces? What are the results of this participation, if it does exit? The empirical research on transnationalism has not expanded significantly towards the inclusion of immigrant children and adolescents. Only a few studies have described the experiences of youth in transnational spaces. These studies have focused mostly on the influence of young immigrants returning to the country of origin in the Americanization of their communities. For example, Miller, Matthei and Smith (1998) describe the experience of the exportation of gang culture from South Central Los Angeles to Garifuna communities in Belize. The Garifuna is an ethnic group of black racial heritage that has settled in many Central American countries including Belize and Honduras (England, 1999). Matthei and Smith report that Garifuna immigrant parents usually send their adolescent children back to Belize when the youngsters become involved in gangs. In fact, there is a growing *foster care* industry in Belize to service these repatriated adolescents (Miller, Matthei & Smith, 1998). Local residents in Belize often foster the children of migrant kin for a fee. However, contrary to the belief that the home country environment will "reform" these children, these youngsters have established gang affiliations in Belize, bringing gang culture to the streets of Belize. Tom Hayden in his article *L.A.'s Third World Export: Gangs* explains "while Belize exports people to Los Angeles, it imports Bloods and Crips" (as cited in Miller Matthei & Smith, 1998, p. 284–285). While this is an interesting transnational phenomenon, in the transnational literature addressing the impact of transnational ties for the immigrant children living in the U.S. discussion is limited, especially regarding education.

Studies of immigrant students in American public schools (Olsen, 1997, 1988; Rumbaut & Cornelius, 1995; Suarez-Orozco & Suarez-Orozco, 1995; Valdes, 1996;) have often highlighted students' assimilation processes into the school culture and their academic achievement compared to other groups (Rumbaut, 1995). However, I pose the question that if it has been documented that adults participate in transnational social spaces, are their children also involved in these human collectivities? Do immigrant children create their own transnational social spaces with other co-national children? I will review some of the characteristics of transnational social spaces and how they may operate within the context of immigrant students in American public schools.

CROSSING AND OVERLAPPING BORDERS IN SCHOOL

Research in numerous public schools in America has documented the existence of immigrant student groups at the social level of school interactions (Kretovics & Nussel, 1994; Olsen, 1997, 1988). One argument that explains the formation of these student groups has been the notion of resistance. Hunt (1990) argues that while students are the largest group involved in schooling, they seem to be the weakest actors in the school site to make specific changes that may fulfill their personal and collective educational needs. Lack of maturity, political organization, legal rights, and other skills and competencies have been cited as reasons for the inability of the students to have influence in school policies (Hunt, 1990). Without any political influence to change school policy at the institutional level, some students perceive that the school vision of society does not reflect their own (Carnoy, 1989). Some researchers have concluded that these contested perspectives result in resistance (Giroux & McLaren, 1989). Martin Carnoy (1989) argues that students from subordinate groups (e.g., ethnic minorities and working-class students) learn to perceive the school as a barrier to cultural expression because school prevents them, as members of a subordinate group, from obtaining learning experiences that reflect their culture (Carnoy, 1989). However, the motivation for the formation of a subculture might not be limited to resistance practices, and it is important to be aware of other factors that might motivate immigrant students to construct their own subculture within the social settings of schools. Further, it is not clear if this resistance is the result of each individual student's realization that the school is not the place for her or him, or a form of acculturation into a social group that collectively has concluded that the school is not the place for them. The diffusion of messages at the collective level might be an important area to investigate for the sources of resistance. The important point here is that it has been documented that student groups along national or ethnic lines are formed in American schools, and the assimilation in these co-national student groups may be a significant source of influence in the experiences of immigrant children in American public schools. I use the term co-national to describe individuals from the same country of origin. In order to understand how immigrant children experience school, we need to understand the nature of the social spaces that they encounter in the school context, including the interactions within co-national student groups. Could this experience be transnational?

Olsen (1997), in her ethnographic study of a high school with a high concentration of immigrant students, finds that immigrant children often socialize with co-nationals because of the language and cultural links that bring these students together. She concludes that the social life of the school is created around immigrant and racialized groups (Olsen, 1997). Students form human collectivities based on their ethnicity, race, or national origin. The co-national student is a familiar face in a strange setting (the school), an individual who shares the same language and culture. The presence of some co-nationals in the school, especially other recent immigrants, might provide newcomers with opportunities to establish a human collectivity that "crosses" boundaries and to maintain a link between the new locality and the country of origin.

In many studies of immigrant students, ethnic identity has been considered a major factor in the establishment of student groups—ethnic collectivities (Olsen, 1988; 1997). Students choose to socialize with co-ethnic students (students that share the ethnic background, not necessarily their national identity) because they provide "comfort from shared experiences and a protective shelter against the racism and prejudice of others, as well as pride and loyalty" (Olsen, 1997, p. 74). Immigrant students in American schools expand their ideas of nation, family, and community to include those students that come from the same region or those who share their culture. Often, students are welcomed into social groups because they come from the same region or the same country (Olsen, 1997).

When immigrant students embrace a collective identity based on their nationality or ethnicity, they are creating social links that overlap boundaries between nation-states if the collective identity expands across nation-states (e.g., national identity). Further, for families that assimilate into more organized transnational communities such as the San Juanenses in California and Florida, the question arises as to whether this sense of "community" prevails among the children who attend the same school.

INSTRUMENTAL VALUE

Transnational social spaces in adult contexts are instrumental in nature. Individuals seek to participate in human collectivities that are transnational in nature because of the flow of economic, social, and cultural capital that is exchanged within the space. In the case of immigrant students, the instrumentality of human collectivities is experienced mostly in terms of the benefits of assimilation into a reference group within the school site. Because children and adolescents are not considered a major part of the labor supply in the U.S., the social capital that a transnational space could provide them would most likely be in the form of information and means to assimilate into the school culture and perhaps academic support. These might include both academic and social "know-how" of how to participate in the school context. For example, Olsen (1997) reports that newcomers socialize with co-nationals because they speak the same language and the bilingual co-nationals serve as interpreters for the newcomers, allowing more participation and integration of newcomers into the school life. She explains, "networks of family members and friends from the same homelands serve as guides, advisors, and key sources of information to newcomers about survival at Madison High" (Olsen, 1997, p. 54).

The co-nationals also might play a role in providing cultural capital that might lead to the development of alternative identities that are more valuable within the students' social space. This is the result in part of the school serving as a social mirror (Suarez-Orozco, 2000) as it was discussed previously. For immigrant children who perceive that their national groups are viewed negatively in the school setting, a human collectivity that values their ethnicity or national origin can be appealing, especially for adolescents for whom a reference group is of keen importance for identity development (Marcia, 1966). Olsen (1997) argues that students view strong identification with the ethnic or national group as a resistance to forces that would make students invisible or denigrate them.

CONTRIBUTING FACTORS

From the literature on immigrant children in American schools, we could conclude that indeed some immigrant students establish human collectivities within school. These may be considered to some extent transnational when co-nationals are involved and these instrumental interactions with co-nationals somehow cross and overlap boundaries.

However, as mentioned in chapter 1, transnational social spaces and other human collectivities are not formed exclusively out of the autonomous actions of their participants. Many of these actions are promoted, influenced, and maintained by economic, social, political, and cultural factors. While students' lives may be influenced by the labor markets in which their parents participate, the general state of the economy, and the political climate, these effects are not easily established in the school context. In the context of immigrant students' collectivities in schools and their influence in immigrant students' educational experiences, I identified four major factors that may affect the construction and the nature of transnational social spaces in the U.S. schools.

School Context as Social Mirroring

School as a social mirroring (Suarez-Orozco, 2000) refers to the way school social life provides a context where negative or positive images about different immigrant student groups are projected. Educational researchers have suggested that many of these societal views reflect themselves in the school context (Apple, 1996, 1997; Giroux, 1993; Giroux & McLaren, 1989; McLaren, 1988; Suarez-Orozco & Suarez-Orozco, 1995)

Carola Suarez-Orozco (2000) suggests that while some immigrant children may benefit from positive expectations (e.g., Asians considered a model minority), other students may be subject to negative expectations. Further, Suarez-Orozco (2000) advises that false images may be promoted among immigrant groups, resulting in what she calls "false good" and "false bad" phenomena. According to Suarez-Orozco (2000), immigrant children experience a "false good" phenomenon when they are unaware of negative images of their immigrant group that may prevail in society, or when they are over-praised because they are viewed as members of model minorities, creating a "distorted view of their ... own abilities and accomplishments" (p. 213). On the other hand, some immigrant children may experience the "false bad" phenomenon where societal views are predominantly negative towards immigrants, creating low expectations based on stereotypical views of immigrant groups (Suarez-Orozco, 2000).

This reflection of societal views in the school may influence the creation of transnational spaces in the school as immigrant students socialize with co-nationals in an attempt to create or maintain a positive collective identity and/or to resist the negative images promoted in the school about their groups. Therefore, any messages or perceptions of American schools that are shared within transnational social spaces will reflect the specific characteristics of the school context the children assimilate into.

Media Messages and Cultural Promotion

Immigrant children's exposure to different sources of media (mainstream and ethnic) may provide messages about American schools that are distinct from those received by non-immigrant populations. Immigrant children might be exposed to media that transcend nation-state boundaries (e.g., TV productions from country of origin or forms of ethnic media in the United States). Therefore, media become a source of information that to some extent might provide images about life in the United States, specifically school life. Media can also provide cultural images about their country of origin, creating crossing and overlapping of boundaries between two localities and influencing the development of national or ethnic identities in immigrant children.

Ethnic Community Involvement

For adults in transnational human collectivities, the participation in ethnic communities to gain access to social services, networking, and other kinds of social capital has been documented (Portes, 1996b; Smith, 1998a, 1998b). Are these communities being involved in the schooling of their children? Some transnational social spaces in the community might be responsive to the educational needs of students. For example, ethnic and nationalistic community agencies might provide tutoring and homework help for immigrant children (Olsen, 1997).

The Role of the Home Country

For people residing in the home country, the instrumentality of the transnational social space is rooted in its ability to produce cultural capital for the co-nationals abroad. Usually, co-nationals abroad provide economic support to their communities of origin, while their compatriots in their country of origin provide resources to sustain the production of the home culture abroad.

Transnational literature has yet to address the involvement of home countries in the education of immigrant children. I speculate that co-nationals in the home country could provide cultural capital in terms of sending cultural artifacts and images that reflect the home culture of the children. For children, co-nationals in the home country are more likely to be members of a kinship group. Because this relationship may be sustained by affective ties, the role of the co-national in the home country may be expanded from a source of cultural capital to a more personal role that provides the children with moral and emotional support. Also, co-nationals in the home country can provide meaningful interpersonal relationships—relationships that children may not have in their new locality.

Another important influence from the home country in the educational experience of immigrant children may be the involvement of the government of the home country. Governments in immigrant-sending countries (e.g., Mexico) have established programs that are aimed to support the educational needs of their co-nationals. I have introduced the Mexican Communities Abroad Program (PCME) earlier, in chapter 1. This program established education as a priority, and it has created several programs that aim to "support the education of Mexicans and Mexican-Americans who live in the United States" (S. Orozco-Aguirre, personal communication, April 14, 1999). The PCME considers that by supporting the education of Mexican nationals in the U.S., the living standards of Mexicans in the U.S. will improve. In the area of education, the PCME provides training programs for U.S. bilingual teachers, teacher exchange programs between Mexico and the U.S., adult basic education programs, distribution of free Mexican textbooks, and programs for youth. Programs like the PCME might actually institutionalize a "transnational social space" within American schools where immigrant children are taught in native languages, with textbooks from their country of origin.

TRANSNATIONAL THEORY IN EDUCATIONAL RESEARCH

The discussion above has led to the proposition that immigrant students and their co-nationals in and outside of school might form instrumental collectivities that could become transnational. Crossing and overlapping boundaries between the U.S. and the country of origin might take place when immigrant children become assimilated into a human collectivity with other co-nationals that links them with their country of origin based on a nationalistic collective identity within the social life of an American public school. Bringing the transnationalism theory into the context of the school, I argue that the creation of student subcultures along national origin lines may resemble the transnational processes and practices that have taken place in other settings that have been defined as transnational social spaces. Further, I ask whether other co-nationals, not necessarily in the school site, may also directly influence immigrant children's assimilation to American schools, or their academic interests, by presenting vulnerabilities and resources to other co-nationals.

Educational research on immigrant and ethnic groups in schools has focused on race, ethnicity or cultural differences, but not particularly on their formation as a transnational phenomenon. Studies of immigrant students in the U.S. have paid attention to the cultural discontinuities between the home and the school culture, focusing on the cultural differences between the country of origin and the U.S. practices (Ogbu & Matute-Bianchi, 1986). However, some argue that this comparison between the two cultures where the immigrant child apparently lives (home and U.S. culture) yields a narrow understanding of the dynamics of immigrant life. For example, in her ethnographic work, "Writing Chinese Women Out of Context," Aihwa Ong (1995) suggests that immigrant Chinese women must be understood outside categories typically linked to the cultural, national, and geographical characterizations of China. Ong proposes that the mere experience of migration changed the way these women experienced and lived their "Chinese" identity in the United States. Therefore, their lives cannot be understood by analyzing the home culture per se. Ong argues that many of these Chinese women's actions are triggered by their immigration experience and their identity as immigrant women rather than by their Chinese cultural heritage (Ong, 1995).

Borrowing Ong's thoughts, I argue that immigrant children in American schools must be understood outside categories conventionally associated with the cultural, national, and geographical spaces of their country of origin. That is, understanding immigrant student adaptation requires more than a simple comparison/contrast exercise between their lives in their country of origin and their lives in the new locality. If these immigrant children are involved in the creation of the "transnational social space" where practices in both the sending and receiving communities affect their everyday lives, it is important to take these transnational influences into consideration when studying the patterns of adaptation in immigrant children in American schools.

The long history of immigration to the United States has prepared the path, for the newcomers who use these social networks to migrate, to have an understanding of how life could be for them in the United States (Smith, 1994; Smith 1998a). Diffusion of information within these transnational social spaces seems to be pivotal for the immigrants to succeed in their new life in America (Smith, 1994). Often immigrants and potential immigrants talk about their expectations and their visions of what America is (Cassganol-Chierici, 1991). When immigrant children in the U.S. actually move, they may already have envisioned a particular image of their lives in the U.S., even specific ideas about schools in this country. Further, when these students come to the American schools, they may assimilate into the familiar and socialize exclusively with co-nationals within the school (Olsen, 1997).

Understanding immigrant children in American schools requires more than just looking at how they experienced school in their native countries and how they experience it now. We need to contextualize these experiences within the social space that these children create within the school setting when these immigrant children become *the immigrant students* in the school. This social space might be transnational in nature if it places children in connection with their country of origin and their new locality.

The quest for an understanding of how immigrant children experience schooling does not mean that we could arrive at just one model. One factor that complicates the study of immigrant students is defining who they are according to ethnic, national, and racial categories. For example, some researchers have described Mexican immigrants as poor and with low levels of educational attainment (Bean & Tienda, 1987; Jasso & Roosenzweig, 1990; Portes & Bach, 1985; Portes, MacLeod, & Parker, 1978). However, Durand and Massey (1992) affirm that within the Mexican migration, there are clear class differences.

My focus on the transnational space and the diffusion of information about U.S. school within transnational social spaces does not mean the rejection of other influences. Because the actions within a transnational space are localized within one place and time, the creation of a transnational space might indeed be the response of these immigrant students to the other social forces they encounter in different schools.

CHAPTER 3

Methodology

My investigation aimed to gain an understanding of the extent to which immigrant students of Chinese and Mexican origin become involved in a transnational social space within the school context. A transnational social space in the school might be defined as a human collectivity of immigrant students from a particular country where students engage in activities that cross the boundaries of two nation-states (e.g., U.S. and country of origin) and create a sense of belonging that overlaps these two nation-states. Remember that the "crossing" does not refer exclusively to a physical crossing, but rather a crossing of a flow of social and cultural capital between the two localities.

In order to establish the existence of a transnational social space, I framed this concept around three elements. First was students' awareness of co-nationals in school sites, in the receiving community, and in the country of origin.

Second, because transnational social spaces are defined to be instrumental in nature, students' perceptions of the influence of information received from co-nationals were considered. Within the scope of instrumentality, scholars have considered the flow of information as one of the main instrumental assets of transnational social spaces (Crisp, 1998; Portes, 1996a). I focused the investigation on the information that children received from co-nationals about U.S. schools and identified this information as "transnational messages." However, the qualitative nature of the data collection instruments allowed for the exploration of other forms of social and cultural capital (besides information) that could have been at play within immigrant students' collectivities.

Third, the existence of media factors that could link the flow of information about American schools between the immigrant students' country of origin and their new locality in the United States was also investigated.

In this study, a transnational social space refers to immigrant students participating in a human collectivity that is considered to be transnational in nature if the following factors are present:

1. Students interact with co-nationals in the school and/or their community in the U.S., and/or they maintain contact with co-nationals in their country of origin. For the scope of this investigation, I focused on the interaction with co-nationals in terms of the exchange of information about American schools among co-nationals. Co-nationals refer to other individuals from the same country; it does not include U.S.-born co-ethnics.
2. Students are aware of media or other sources that promote messages about American schools between their country of origin and their new locality in the U.S.

RESEARCH QUESTIONS

I focused this investigation on four main research questions on how immigrant children interact within transnational social spaces and exchange of information about U.S. schools:

1. What kind of information (transnational messages) about U.S. schools is shared with immigrant children of Chinese and Mexican origin within the context of transnational social spaces in both the country of origin and the new locality in the United States?
2. To what extent do immigrant children of Chinese and Mexican origin perceive that these messages influence their experiences in and perceptions of the U.S. schools?
3. What are the messages that immigrant children of Chinese and Mexican origin construct about U.S. schools after living in the U.S. that could be transmitted to potential new immigrants?

4. How are these transnational messages different for the two groups under investigation?

These immigrant groups—Chinese and Mexican—have been the top two sending countries of U.S. immigration since 1994. According to the Immigration and Naturalization Service (INS), in 1998, Mexico held the first place with the highest number of immigrants admitted legally to the U.S. China had the second place. These statistics do not reflect the growing flow of undocumented immigrants from each of these countries. In terms of undocumented immigrants, by 1996 Mexico led the list with over 54% of all undocumented immigration in the United States. While there is undocumented immigration from China, this country is not among the top twenty sending countries for undocumented immigration according to INS data. Table 3.1 summarizes the data from the INS for both legal and illegal immigration from Mexico and China.

Table 3.1.
Legal and Undocumented Immigration from Mexico and China

Country	Undocumented Immigration	Legal Immigration		
	1996	1996	1997	1998
Mexico	2,700,000 (54%)	163,572 (17.9%)	146,865 (18.4%)	131,57 (19.9%)
China	Data not available	41,728 (4.6%)	41,147 (5.2%)	36,884 (5.6%)

Percentage figures represent percentage of total immigrant population in the U.S.
Source: Immigration and Naturalization Service (1998) http//: www.ins.usdoj.gov

By focusing on these two immigrant groups of diverse backgrounds, I sought to gain an understanding of the cross-cultural differences in transnational social spaces. That is, can the elements of transnational social spaces cited in the literature (e.g., instrumental) prevail across different immigrant groups? What do differences between the transnational messages reveal about the schooling experiences of these two immigrant groups?

Because of the limited participation of children and adolescents in more organized and formal forms of transnational spaces, I anticipated that the transnational social spaces in schools would take the form of informal student groups based on national/ethnic origin (a variation of the kinship group). While I recognized that multiple forms of social capital are involved in these informal collectivities, I investigated social capital in the form of information about U.S. schools and life in the U.S. If immigrant students participate in a transnational space, I was interested in knowing the extent to which immigrant student populations became instrumental in facilitating or supporting school experiences of other co-nationals in the school. I investigated whether transnational social spaces (both in the U.S. and in their country of origin) provided social, academic, and affective benefits to the immigrant students (e.g., support in adaptation to the school environment, help with homework and English communications, friendships, protection, and a sense of belonging). A number of activities that take place within these transnational social spaces can help immigrant students survive in a school context that otherwise could be very difficult to adapt to due to cultural, language, ethnic, and racial differences. However, at the same time, some practices within the transnational space may be actually reproducing the marginalization of these immigrant students within the school context (e.g., isolation, confrontation and conflict with other groups).

One important clarification is my exclusion of U.S.-born co-ethnics (children who share the ethnic background of immigrants but were born in the U.S.) as sources of information about American schools. I recognize that this approach may leave some important influences out of the scope of this investigation. However, I chose to define co-nationals as individuals who are born in the country of origin as a way to filter, to an extent, the influence of co-nationals from the influence of U.S.-born co-ethnics. In a sense, U.S.-born co-ethnics might become involved in transnational social spaces (e.g., the San Juan Mixtepec example). However, immigrant students' relationships with U.S.-born co-ethnics might not always lead to the formation of instrumental human collectivities that link the country of origin with the new locality in the U.S. For example, it has been documented that the relationship between Mexican immigrants and Mexican-Americans has been at times more conflictive than integrated in the name of one common national origin (Bernal & Martinelli, 1993; Browing & De la

Garza, 1986). Further, the relationship between immigrants and U.S.-born co-ethnics is a very complicated phenomenon that might not be rooted specifically in transnational elements, but rather historical and cultural elements between the two nation-states (more inter or intra-national in nature; Bernal & Martinelli, 1993). For simplification purposes, the scope of the investigation is focused on the information received from co-nationals. However, it is clear that the presence of co-ethnics in the school may have an important influence in the construction of transnational practices because these are localized within the school context and some children's responses in this study reveal theses influences.

While the focus of my investigation is the transnational social space, it is important to recognize this does not imply that the transnational social space is the only contributing factor in the assimilation of immigrant students into American schools. Remember that transnational social spaces involve activities that cross and overlap boundaries but which occur in very specific times and locations. This means that immigrant students are still influenced by forces that might not be "transnational" in nature, such as the context of the school, relations with peers that are not co-nationals. Further, because of differences in culture, socioeconomic status, reasons for immigration, assimilation patterns, political relationship of the country of origin with the U.S., and other factors, immigrants from different countries may experience the transnational space (if they experience it at all) in unique and distinctive ways. That is, my focus on the transnational space does not imply that all immigrant groups experience it, or that all groups experience it in the same way. However, I believe that using a transnational perspective might add to our understanding of immigrant student assimilation to American schools.

RESEARCH DESIGN

My interest in the transnational space in American schools is the result of my ethnographic research done in an inner-city middle school in California during 1998. In this middle school, I came into contact with a group of seven Mexican students who participated in human collectivities based on national origin and/or ethnic affiliation.

These children were participating in an intervention program that I designed entitled *Learning Goals Training*. The purpose of this intervention was to generate discussion among recent Mexican immigrant children regarding factors in school and family contexts that facilitated and hindered their academic and English language acquisition progress. One of the recurrent themes in the discussion was the participation in human collectivities of co-national peers (children from the same country of origin) and how these associations often became either opportunities or impediments to learning and assimilation into school life. I was able to triangulate these experiences with an ethnographic investigation in the school.

Having learned of the transnational perspective in my graduate coursework, I started to recognize that many of the activities that my group of seven Mexican immigrant students engaged in brought them into a social space that crossed and overlapped boundaries. I came to realize that many of the daily activities that these children engaged in involved the exchange of social and cultural capital among co-national peers. For example, these students shared information about school, helped co-nationals with translations, built solidarity to fight against other ethnic groups in school, and exchanged cultural items from Mexico (e.g., soccer shirts).

While I do not imply that the experience of these seven Mexican immigrant students is typical or representative of other immigrant students, this research directed my interest into the area of transnational social spaces in U.S. schools. In a sense, the theme of this present investigation is *grounded* in my ethnographic and intervention data. With the present study, I wanted to inquire more systematically and with a larger sample about the way human collectivities of immigrant students in American schools operate.

Subject Selection and Field Sites—The LISA Project

From 1997 to 2001, I was a research assistant for the Longitudinal Immigration Student Adaptation study (LISA), which is conducted by the Harvard Immigration Projects. The principal investigators of LISA are Drs. Carola and Marcelo Suarez-Orozco from the Graduate School of Education at Harvard University. The LISA study has the major purpose of investigating the changes over time that immigrant students experience in American schools. Student informants in the LISA study are interviewed once during each school year, for a period of five years (1997–2002). Each year, some questions are repeated to assess changes over time. In addition, the LISA study focuses on a specific topic for investigation and new questions are developed each year for the focus topic. For the Year 3 (1999–2000), the principal investigators assigned *School Context* as the focus area. The scope of this study about transnational social spaces and their influences in the experiences of immigrant students in American schools fit well within the scope of the focus area of the LISA study for Year 3. Given the alignment between the research questions of the LISA study and my study, Drs. Suarez-Orozco agreed to include the questions related to my investigation in their Year 3 Student Interview.

The subjects in the LISA study (about 400 participants) are immigrant children from Central America, China, the Dominican Republic, Haiti, and Mexico. All children were recruited during the school year 1997–1998 based on specific criteria: age 10–14, less than three years of residence in the U.S., and both child and parents born in the same country. Since the inclusion of my study took place in the Year 3 of this longitudinal study, at the time of the implementation of this study, participant students were between 12–17 years of age. Students were recruited from selected school districts that had high concentrations of immigrant students. Mexican and Central American subjects were recruited from schools in the San Francisco Bay Area in California. Chinese, Dominican, and Haitian subjects were recruited from schools in Boston, Massachusetts. There are more than 60 schools participating: 29 in Boston and 32 in California, including elementary, middle, and high schools.

While data were collected on all subjects (the five immigrant groups) to fulfill the requirements of the LISA study, the scope of my investigation focused on the Chinese and Mexican samples. I obtained and analyzed data from 74 Chinese students and 78 Mexican students. I opted to focus on these two groups because of their demographic significance in the immigrant population of America. I also embraced with enthusiasm the opportunity to embark on a bi-coastal, comparative investigation with two groups that have a significant presence in American schools today and the possibility of establishing rewarding intellectual partnerships with Chinese and Mexican scholars, graduate students, and community members.

Data Analysis

Because the data collected from the interviews were qualitative in nature with a sizeable sample, I used both quantitative and qualitative methods of data analysis. My epistemological perspective is based on an interpretative approach, where I considered the potential emergence and existence of transnational social spaces in the school context as a complex social phenomenon—one that needs to be investigated while taking into consideration the social context in which the experience took place. While I used the transnational perspective to guide and frame my study, this does not imply that the outcome of my investigation became exclusively anchored in the transnational theory as it has been conceptualized in the literature to date. As I collected data, I considered non-transnational elements that I identified as major sources of influence (e.g., school characteristics).

Grounded Theory: The Emergence of the Theme

Since this project emerged from my ethnographic data from a middle school, I would like to note that the scope of this investigation around transnational social spaces has been "grounded" in empirical data. I used a grounded theory approach to construct the focus of the present investigation. Grounded theory is an approach to studying social phenomena that leads to the "development of theory, without any particular commitment to specific kinds of data, lines of research, or theoretical interest" (Strauss, 1996, p.5). During my ethnographic work in this middle school, I followed a grounded theory approach where I collected data from open-ended interviews, participant observations, and ethnographic notes from my intervention session, as well as from other classroom and school interactions, and informal encounters with students. I followed a systematic, intensive analysis of the data. Because my sample size at the time was only seven students, I was able to use the different coding stages—open, axial, selective, and core categories (Strauss, 1996). I should note that these seven students were not informants in the LISA study, but attended one of the schools participating in the LISA study. From this work, I found that these seven Mexican immigrant children created a transnational space by creating:

1. Friendships along national lines
2. Support networks for the newcomers (e.g., translators)
3. A strong force to face the rivals in school (usually non-Mexican student groups)
4. Exchanges of cultural icons (e.g., Mexican teen culture) within the school context.

These daily practices of Mexican immigrants created a transnational social space that not only linked them with their country of origin (cultural artifacts) and their new locality (helping newcomers to assimilate), but also reaffirmed their national identity as a source of power and stability. My data also revealed some major factors that contribute to the creation of this transnational space. These included:

1. The large population of Mexican students in the school (53% Latino, mostly of Mexican origin)
2. The promotion of Mexican culture in the ESL and Bilingual classrooms where these children were placed
3. The need to consolidate forces to face other ethnic/racial groups in the confrontations
4. The possible acculturation into the formation of these networks that Mexican immigrant children might have learned from their parents (e.g., their parents using transnational networks or belonging to a transnational community).

Based on these findings, my interest in transnational social spaces grew. In this current study, I explored with a larger sample the existence and function of transnational social spaces in other school contexts with two immigrant groups—Chinese and Mexican.

Qualitative Methods: Open-ended Interviews

Because I was working with a sample size of 152 children—74 Chinese and 78 Mexican—continuing to use a grounded theory approach was not feasible at this stage. Instead, still using an interpretative approach, I used an open-ended interview as my primary data collection method, rather than ethnographic observations. To address the four basic research questions, I developed an interview protocol that was included in the Year 3 Student Interview of the LISA project. The interview was carefully translated into Cantonese, Mandarin, Haitian Creole, and Spanish by selected research assistants who were native speakers of the language. An English version was also available for those children who may have suffered language attrition in their native language and had become fluent English speakers. A team of research assistants (including myself), who are proficient in the culture and language of the participant students administered this protocol as an in-depth interview. Many of the research assistants were members of the immigrant group under investigation (e.g., Chinese research assistants working with the Chinese informants) and they were immigrants themselves. The questions were piloted before final inclusion in the questionnaire, with children (not participating in the LISA study) from all of the five immigrant groups. The questionnaire included questions that addressed the four major research questions regarding the nature of transnational messages about U.S. schools, the instrumentality and influence of these messages in students' school experiences, and the children's perception of U.S. schools. Appendix A includes the questionnaire.

Children were asked questions regarding messages they received from their co-nationals about American schools at three particular points in time. First, messages prior to immigration, when the child lived in the country of origin. Second, messages upon entry to the U.S., when he or she just arrived to the U.S. and found co-nationals in the school. Third, messages that the informants themselves have constructed about American schools after living in the U.S. for a number of years. This retrospective approach aimed to assess the nature of perceptions about American schools that can in turn become potential transnational messages when these children share these messages with newcomers. Is there a reproduction pattern involved in the construction of messages about American schools within transnational contexts? Are there changes over time?

Because I recognized the constraints of using a retrospective instrument with children—issues of maturity and memory—I triangulated the primary data from the open-ended interview with data already collected by the LISA study that was relevant to my main research questions. The secondary data that I used to triangulate my primary data included:

1. Parents' and students' perceptions of the U.S. held prior to immigration (from interviews conducted in 1997–1998)
2. Students' positive and negative perceptions of U.S. schools over time (from interviews conducted in 1997–1998, 1998–1999, and 1999–2000)
3. Parents' positive and negative perceptions of U.S. schools (from interviews conducted in 1997–1998).

Also, ethnographic notes from school site observations, structured school descriptions, and some demographic data were used for triangulation and illustration purposes. In this book, the secondary data will be identified as LISA data in the text (e.g., LISA 1997–1998 data).

Qualitative Approach with Large Samples

Some may argue that because of the large sample size (152 informants), a survey approach could be more feasible for this study. However, I chose to use qualitative methods (open-ended interview) for four main reasons. First, I acknowledge the complexity of social phenomena. While I was interested in testing the hypothesis that transnational spaces exist in the context of American schools, I was more interested in finding out the nature of such relationships and the factors or motivations that may create such transnational social spaces. Therefore, committing my study to a specific definition of the construction of transnational social spaces (e.g., using a survey) could have led my study to take a narrow view that might overlook important elements. While the literature guided me into the construction of preconceived categories regarding the forms of a transnational social space, I opted for a qualitative approach that allowed me to identify forms of transnational practices that might not be constructed by the informants in the way they are constructed in the literature. This was necessary because the literature is limited about the experiences of children in transnational social spaces. An open-ended interview provided the flexibility to reconceptualize the transnational social spaces in the school context beyond a preconceived definition imposed by the literature. It allowed the informants to relate their personal experience rather than fitting their experiences into a prescribed set of categories (e.g., a survey).

Second, I recognize that this study may not be generalizable to a number of other immigrant groups, or even to other individuals within the immigrant groups under investigation. However, qualitative methods of data analysis often view that theory at different levels of generality is important for deeper knowledge of social phenomena (Strauss, 1996). In other words, research that might not yield a high degree of generalizability is still valid to the extent that it contributes to our further understanding of social phenomena in a particular setting. Because my sample is not a random sample, I needed to contextualize the findings into the social realities of each school and each geographical area (San Francisco or Boston).

Third, I agree with the notion found in qualitative research of grasping the actors' viewpoint for understanding social phenomena (Strauss, 1996). As a researcher I believe research might also be used to give the informants a voice so they might share their understanding of their own reality via the research study. In order to give informants a "voice," instruments of data collection should be carefully designed to allow informants to speak truly, honestly, and with authority. I believe that my informants are the "true experts" in the sociological and educational phenomena that I am trying to investigate. I approach them with respect for their knowledge and experience. As a researcher, I am a vehicle to develop theory based on the data that my "expert informants" share with me in terms of their experiences and their view of their social reality. I did not collect data to prove a specific theoretical perspective, but rather to understand the reality of social and educational phenomena that a group of immigrant children might experience in some U.S. schools.

Fourth, some may argue that my sample size is problematic—that it is not large enough to make solid statistical inferences (high power), but it is too large to produce deep, rich descriptions in the way that a small sample size could provide when fewer individuals are involved like in an ethnographic study. However, having sample sizes of 72 (Chinese) and 78 (Mexican) allowed me to create "sub-groups" of students by student and school characteristics to identify patterns within these sub-groups, and yet still have a manageable sample size to use qualitative analysis. The qualitative responses, along with the information I gathered from research assistants, and the triangulation of data from other sources, allowed me to depict a more complete, contextualized picture of the students' responses than if the information was collected via surveys. Further, it provided a sizable sample to identify patterns within the sub-groups.

The reflective nature of the questions and the quality of the staff that administered the interview elicited authentic accounts of the students' experiences. I communicated with these research assistants regarding the content of the questionnaire and the administration procedure in order to provide consistent standards for administration. In California, a training session was conducted with the research assistants. For the Boston team, I prepared a training tape that contained the same information presented to the California team regarding the theoretical framework of the study, the scope of the questions, and administration procedures.

As a researcher, I am aware of the methodological constraints of embarking on cross-cultural research. In order to confirm my findings from the Chinese group, I secured the guidance and collaboration of my fellow research assistants in the LISA study to help me with the coding and analysis processes for the Chinese group. Because I am not as familiar with the Chinese group as I am with the Mexican group, I wanted to seek the language and cultural expertise of the research assistants working with Chinese participants. Their participation basically involved their assistance regarding the meaning and interpretation of words and phrases from the data, providing information about the students' school experiences and Chinese culture in general, and corroborating my findings within a framework that considered the repercussions of cultural differences. Because I received translated texts from the data, I planned three working sessions with the Chinese research team as an analytical exercise, as well as extensive communication via e-mail with research assistants who helped me contextualize the interview data in the Chinese sample. I also sought the advice of faculty members who specialized in Chinese social issues such as Dr. Min Zhou from the University of California, Los Angeles. Also, Chinese graduate students at U.C. Davis and Harvard University offered assistance in the data analysis process and the final manuscript of this book.

Quality of Data Collection and Data Analysis

With interpretive research, quality of data is usually based on dependability, credibility, and confirmability. Guba and Lincoln suggested that these elements are the respective parallel constructs to reliability, validity, and objectivity in positivist research (as cited in Merterns, 1998).

Dependability

Dependability is the interpretative approach's parallel standard for reliability. Within this perspective, change is expected and stability is not viewed as an element to evaluate the quality of the data. However, the researcher has the responsibility to track the change and provide documentation on the change process. This "change" element is usually present when the researcher conducts several interviews with the same subject and some changes occur. This was not possible in this study because I was not able to personally "go back" to the subject and ask more questions. However, in this study, changes across groups and differences within groups were documented and contextualized by triangulation with secondary data. Also, communication with research assistants regarding specific students provided an element of dependability in order to trace changes over time.

Credibility

Credibility is the equivalent of validity in interpretative research. This refers to the correspondence between the way the respondents actually perceive social constructs and the way the researcher portrays these viewpoints. In this case, the involvement of competent research assistants, who have cultural and linguistic knowledge of the informant's groups, as well as immigrant experiences, increased the credibility of this study. Further, the already established relationship between the research assistants and the informants (after three years of participating in the study) also increased the credibility of the informants' responses because of the level of trust and rapport already established between research assistants and the informants. The participation of research assistants, graduate students, and faculty specialized in Chinese studies allowed me to corroborate my analysis and representation of findings.

Confirmability

In interpretative research, confirmability is the parallel for objectivity in a positivistic perspective. Interpretative research acknowledges that reaching objectivity is not possible because values are present in every paradigm, as research paradigms are *human constructs* (Merterns, 1998). However, the interpretative researcher also seeks to "confirm that the data and their interpretations are not the product of the researchers' imagination" (Guba & Lincoln, as cited in Merterns, 1998, p. 229). To accomplish this, the data should be traced to "its original sources to confirm the process of synthesizing data to reach conclusions using a chain of evidence" (Merterns, 1998, p. 299). In this study, the communications with the research assistants served as an important link to the original source—the students—not only regarding specific answers, but also in contextualizing the answers in relation to the children's experiences in the school context. The assistance of research assistants helped me to achieve higher levels of confirmability, as the research assistants (those who had contact with the source of information) guided me to accurate interpretations of the data.

CODING PROCEDURES

In order to answer the four primary research questions, I took a qualitative approach to data analysis. As a first step, I established a *coding paradigm* which reflected some preliminary inquiry elements to code the data (Strauss, 1996). Strauss (1996) recommends including in the coding paradigm four elements: conditions, interaction among the actors, strategies and tactics, and consequences. For the scope of my investigation, I used these four elements of the coding paradigm as a starting point to understand the data in the following way:

- What are the conditions (sources and location) under which the transnational messages among co-nationals take place?
- What is nature of the messages among co-nationals regarding American schools? (content of message)
- What are the strategies and tactics that students use in assimilating/responding to transnational messages about U.S. schools? (instrumentality of messages)

- What are the consequences of the messages and the role of co-nationals in the school? (influence and reaction to message)

These questions were a preliminary structure for approaching the data as they were collected, and coding categories were revised and defined as data were collected. However, before any solid analysis of data could be carried out, it was important for me as a researcher to organize data in a way that could enable the coding process. Because I was interested in using qualitative data, it was important to me to track answers to specific students, rather than working with aggregated data. That is, I wanted to organize data in a way that I could trace each particular answer to a specific student's profile, which could allow me to analyze the reality and experiences of each child and its relations to his or her answers. I was also interested in creating sub-groups or sub-samples according to variables that depicted characteristics of students (e.g., age, gender) and schools (e.g., ethnic school composition).

Hard copies of the interviews were collected from the archives at Harvard University. From these hard copies, both primary and secondary data were entered verbatim from the interview text into a database that was customized for this purpose by Jason Brittain, a software engineer. The database not only included the answers, but also information regarding student characteristics (e.g., age, gender) and school information (e.g., free lunch participation). A profile for each student was created based on these descriptive data. The database allowed me to link each one of the students' answers to the particular student's profile. It also allowed me to link students' answers over time, for longitudinal analysis and triangulation purposes. The data were archived in a Structure Query Language (SQL) compliant, relational database, which allowed me running multiple queries across sub-samples by single or multiple variables (e.g., answers to question 1, organized by children's entry age). The database was electronically archived in a password protected web application (http://www .brittainweb.org/carminadb).

The advantage of having custom-made software is that the software was developed to meet my analytical needs in this study and my research design was not constrained by limitations in applicability and functions of commercial software. In consultation with Mr. Brittain, I was able to conceptualize analytical tools that I needed to organize and analyze my data. Mr. Brittain wrote the software code accordingly to my specifications, which were based on my research design. Once the database contained all of the data collected, I started the coding process. However, during the data entry process, I wrote data memos—theoretical, methodological, and interpretative—in order to start to identify patterns and compare and contrast responses across and within groups.

My analysis was based on Miles and Huberman's (as cited by Merterns, 1998) approach to qualitative data analysis. However, I expanded this model to include a hierarchical approach to coding. My data analysis process evolved as follows.

Preliminary Coding

I generated preliminary codes for my first round of analysis of the interview data, consulting my data memos generated during the data entry process. These general codes usually represented "key words" or themes that the answer represented (e.g., curriculum issues). I also noted the direction of the answer—positive, negative, or neutral. I wrote another set of theoretical, methodological, and interpretative memos as I was doing the first round of coding. Key quotes from answers were identified and organized into separate files by question number, tagged by student number.

Emerging Coding Categories

I engaged in a second round of coding where I refined the major categories and identified more specific key themes. This second coding allowed me to merge or eliminate major categories according to the distinctive nature of the theme. From the key words or themes, I generated a list of tentative major categories. For example, curriculum, instruction, and schoolwork fell under the *Academic* category. At this stage, I revised my choices for codes that indicated the direction of the answer (negative/positive/neutral), and nature of the answer (e.g., what was the specific nature or comment the child made about Academic issues?). From this exercise, a preliminary hierarchical tree of categories emerged. Again, I used memos to record important insights from the data.

Hierarchical Coding Tree

From the second round of coding, I created a tentative hierarchical coding tree. Potential coding categories were organized in different levels (e.g., Level 1 was the top category) from top to bottom. Some answers were coded from Level 1 to Level 4. For example, a specific answer regarding an academic theme was coded as follows:

- Academic (Level 1 coding)
  - Negative (Level 2 coding)
    - Curriculum (Level 3 coding)
      - Less demanding in the U.S. (Level 4 coding)

Each lower level category was embedded into a higher level category (e.g., Level 3 category was embedded into its corresponding Level 2 category). This hierarchical organization of categories allowed me to identify core themes and describe the nature of those themes (e.g., negative or positive) as well as specific sub-themes under the higher level categories.

Using the Coding Tree

The preliminary coding tree allowed me to engage in a third round of more careful, detailed coding. As I was coding the data, new codes were incorporated to the coding tree and existing codes were modified or refined to accurately assign a code that reflected the meaning of the answer. The hierarchical coding tree allowed me to generate codes until all potential codes were exhausted. Five different coding trees were established for the qualitative analysis:

- Transnational Messages (What did children hear about U.S. schools from co-nationals and media sources?)
- Sources of Messages (Who/What provided the information?)
- Reaction to Messages (How did children react to this information about U.S. schools?)
- Instrumentality of the Transnational Message (In which way did students find these messages useful or instrumental?)

- Peer Choice (Who constitutes the children's circle of friends? Co-nationals?)

Each of these coding trees was used for a specific set of questions, often organized in a longitudinal arrangement to analyze the subjects' answers regarding a specific theme over time.

The Final Coding

The hierarchical coding tree allowed me to map out the patterns and processes regarding the construction of messages about American schools among immigrant children. The same hierarchical coding tree in its final version was used to code the data for both groups—Mexican and Chinese. This allowed me to identify commonalties and differences based on the coding categories as mapped out in the hierarchical tree. The hierarchical tree allowed me to conceptualize major themes and the specific nature and quality of the multiple variations that a theme could comprise.

Generating Data Patterns

I began elaborating a small set of generalizations that cover the consistencies discerned in the data (Miles and Humberman, as cited by Marterns, 1998) based on the analysis derived from the hierarchical coding tree, and organized by the top category, such as Academic Messages.

Generating Knowledge

From the analysis, I generated some generalizations to establish a knowledge base (Miles and Humberman, as cited by Marterns, 1998) regarding the construction and influence of transnational messages about U.S. school in immigrant children's assimilation to school life.

The hierarchical coding tree was used to code both primary and secondary interview data. Structural school descriptions were utilized to categorize schools, and this information was used as a variable for quantitative analysis. School and community ethnographies were used to contextualize the answers in the discussion of the findings.

DESCRIPTIVE STATISTICS AS ROAD MAP TO THE DATA

Because most of the data generated from the open-ended questionnaire was categorical data and from a non-random sample, descriptive, not inferential, statistics were used to present general patterns on the data results. In addition to the five hierarchical coding trees used for qualitative analysis, the following non-hierarchical coding trees were used for quantitative analysis:

- Received media messages? (yes/no)
- Received messages upon entry to the U.S.? (yes/no)
- Was message upon entry instrumental? (yes/no)

Only the frequency counts for the top-level categories (Level 1) were used for quantitative analysis. Lower level categories were useful in analyzing the data qualitatively because they allowed me to describe in detail the nature of the top-level categories, but they were too specific to be useful for descriptive statistics. The percentages reported reflect "number of participant's answers" that were coded as the top category (e.g., Academic). Because the categories emerged from the children's answers, multiple codes might have been assigned to each child's responses. For example, a child may have given an answer that reflected academic and teacher categories. Therefore, the response sample size may be larger than the original sample size (Chinese n=74 and Mexican n=78). In the discussion, both percentages and frequencies are reported. In the text, the frequency count is reported in parentheses, next to the percentage figure—for example, 45% (13). Descriptive data were also used to portray the description of the sample in terms of student and school characteristics, including:

- Country of origin
- Gender
- Entry age
- Current age
- Years of residence in the U.S.
- Province of origin
- Father's educational level
- Mother's educational level
- Ethnic composition of school

- Free/reduced lunch program student participation
- Proportion of English language learners in the school

When generating proportions of answers by each of these variables, sometimes these proportions did not deviate significantly from the distribution of the overall sample defined by country of origin. This result may have been influenced by the fact that the sample profile for both Mexican and Chinese were heavily concentrated in certain variables (e.g., entry age, parent educational level). This resulted in very low frequency cell count once the sample was distributed along country of origin and another variable (e.g., Mexican children who came to the country between ages 4–7). Therefore, these variables were mostly used for a qualitative purpose.

When analyzing responses from students, I used these variables to create a context that described the experiences of the children who gave the responses. For some specific questions, there were some significant characteristics (in terms of student and school variables) that were dominant in the student profile. I used these variables to describe the kind of students (and their schools) that gave specific types of answers. However, I only reported these profiles when the sub-sample size was large enough to indicate patterns (e.g., 10 or higher) and when there was a distinctive characteristic (e.g., predominately female) that was important to discuss. When the profile is not discussed it is because the distributions of the student and school profiles by answer do not deviate from the general distribution of the whole sample by country of origin.

CHAPTER 4

Chinese and Mexican Transnational Migration

In this chapter, I present a brief overview of the immigration patterns and experiences as captured in the literature of Chinese and Mexican immigration and relate this information to the characteristics of the sample. Because this investigation focuses on schooling and education, a brief description of the education systems in these two countries is also included. Since most of the participant children have attended elementary schools in their country of origin, the discussion emphasizes elementary education. Some characteristics of the sending and receiving communities of the participants in this study are also presented.

STUDENT CHARACTERISTICS

The sample for this study is comprised of 152 students—74 Chinese and 78 Mexican students. Thirty-nine percent (29) of the Chinese sample were male and 61% (45) were female. For the Mexican sample, the gender distribution was 56% (44) male and 44% (34) female. The age range of the respondents was 11–17 years. Participants included from sixth graders to seniors in high school, but most of the participants were enrolled in middle and high schools. Most of the Chinese participants were ages 15–16 (43%, 32) and most of the Mexican participants were ages 13–15 (39%, 31).

In this sample, most Chinese participants immigrated at slightly older ages than the Mexican participants did. In terms of entry age, most the Chinese children came to the U.S. at ages 11–13 (41%, 30), while in the Mexican group, most children immigrated at ages 8–11

(57%, 45). Appendix B includes graphical representations of the major characteristics of both samples, including both student and school characteristics.

The sample profile reflects some important patterns and characteristics of immigrants from China and Mexico captured by the immigration literature. The following discussion is not intended to be exhaustive or even comprehensive, but rather, it aims to provide some context to the experiences of the sample under investigation in this study.

Chinese Immigration: A Brief Overview

Historical records document the first wave of Chinese immigration to the United States as beginning in the 1850s, and peaking by 1890 (Wong, 1998). The early Chinese settlers of the 1800s established themselves in the West, predominately in California, working mostly as railroad workers, miners, farmers, and domestics (Wong, 1998). However, Chinese have also had a considerable presence in the East Coast, especially in New York and the New England area (Sagara & Kiang, 1992).

History of Chinese Immigration

The history of Chinese immigration to the United States has been marked by abuse, discrimination, and struggle, as evidenced by the imposition of discriminatory immigration laws against Chinese. Among these, the Chinese Exclusion Act of 1882, the Anti-Chinese Scott Act of 1888, and the Geary Act of 1892 prohibited the entry and reentry of Chinese nationals, contributing to the decline of Chinese immigration to the U.S. during the first part of the 20th century (Wong, 1998). The elimination of these laws, the establishment of the socialist government in China in 1949, and the economic growth of Chinatowns across the country contributed to the increase of new Chinese immigrants after World War II (Wong, 1998; Sagara & Kiang, 1992l; Olsen, 1988). However, it was the establishment of the Immigration Reform Act of 1965 that allowed a new wave of Chinese immigrants (Wong, 1998). Most of the immigrants of this new wave were relatives of Chinese American citizens who sponsored them, bringing whole families (including children) to the U.S. (Wong, 1998). In the late 1980s, in anticipation to the return of Hong Kong from the British government to China in 1997, another wave of Chinese immigrants, who feared the uncertain political and economic repercussions of the transfer, emerged from Hong Kong (Olsen, 1988).

It is estimated that the United States admit about 40,000 Chinese immigrants every year (Wong, 1998). The Chinese government usually grants permission to leave the country for family reunification purposes, if the individual proves he or she has obtained the corresponding visa from the receiving country (Wong, 1998). However, it is important to note that while many Chinese immigrants come to the U.S. by obtaining family reunification visas, some economic incentives are also considered. Further, not all Chinese immigrants are documented.

According to the INS 1998 data, China is not among the top twenty sending countries of undocumented immigration. However, the literature documents that Chinese immigrants, especially from Fujian province, often seek clandestine ways to immigrate to the United States through the assistance of a Snakehead (human smuggler; Chin, 1999). The Snakeheads often have networks of people who seek recruits in specific Chinese provinces to embark in long and risky journeys to the United States. The immigrants often sell their valuables and properties to cover the down payment for the trip (usually $1,000–$5,000) out of a total payment that often reaches $20,000–$35,000 (Chin, 1999; Smolowe, 1993). Families pool their capital in order to be able to secure the down payment for just one relative to go to the United States (Smolowe, 1993). The Snakeheads arrange these journeys via air, land, and sea, usually stopping in intermediate points in Mexico, the Dominican Republic, and Central America (Chin, 1999).

The Chinatown: The Rise of the Ethnic Community

One important element that has sustained immigration from China has been the emergence of Chinatowns in the United States. Wong (1998) suggests that it was the fear of competition by Chinese against White enterprises that motivated the establishment of discriminatory laws against Chinese immigrants. The Chinese immigrants' response to these discriminatory measures was to become involved in industries that were not in competition with mainstream businesses, such as Chinese restaurants, laundries, and garment factories (Wong, 1998).

The emergence of these ethnic industries led to the formation of Chinatowns in major metropolitan areas of the United States (Zhou, 1997). Chinese entrepreneurs were looking for large markets for their ethnic businesses and they established themselves in Los Angeles, New York, Boston, San Francisco, and other metropolitan areas (Wong, 1998). By 1940, there were 28 Chinatowns in the United States (Wong, 1998).

Chinatown as an ethnic community provided a protective niche for the Chinese to survive economically in an era of discrimination. It also provided them with a web of social networks in which social capital was transferred among co-nationals based on kinship, friendship, regional solidarity, language, and trade (Zhou, 1997). As discrimination laws were abolished, the Chinese became more accepted and integrated into mainstream America, and many Chinese were able to assimilate outside the Chinatowns (Wong, 1998). However, many of these Chinese established in suburbia still continued to organize communities based on kinship, regional origin, and family names. One example is the community of Monterrey Park, outside Los Angeles, which has been considered the first "suburban Chinatown" established in the United States (Horton, 1996). By 1955, only 16 Chinatowns remained in the United States (Wong, 1998). But Chinatowns (urban or suburban) have remained as symbolic cultural centers and as significant points of entry for many new Chinese immigrants.

Chinese Immigrant Profile

The early Chinese immigrants were a rather homogeneous group, compared to the Chinese coming to America after 1965 (Wong, 1998). According to Bernard Wong (1998), the Chinese settlers of the 1800s came from the rural areas of the Guangdong province in southern China. These early settlers brought with them traditional ways to organize communities around kinship, regional, and dialectic solidarity (Wong, 1998). That is, they started to organize ethnic enclaves based on these characteristics. Most of these early settlers were male, and the imposition of restrictions on female immigration made Chinese immigration predominantly male until the 1940s, creating the image of Chinese communities as "Bachelors Societies" (Chin, 1994). However, after 1965, Chinese American citizens were able to sponsor their relatives in China and bring them to the United States (Wong, 1998).

This sponsorship brought a transformation in the Chinese immigrant profile, making a more balanced group across gender and age factors. Most Chinese immigrants after 1965 came as a family unit, including children. This trend of the new Chinese immigration is reflected in this sample, where 41% (30) of the Chinese participants came together as a family unit and 38% (28) had stayed in China with one parent, while the other parent already resided in the United States.

Reasons for Immigration

The literature on Chinese immigration cites family reunification and economic considerations as major reasons for immigration (Chin, 1999; Wong, 1998). Most of the Chinese parents in this sample came to the United States for family reunification purposes (42%, 31), while 33% (24) came for economic opportunities, and 14% (10) came for educational opportunities. Family unification as a major reason for immigration is explained by the long history of immigration and the already-established sponsor connections that Chinese families have in the U.S.

The literature on Chinese immigration also describes that these new immigrants view America as a permanent destination, having no intention of returning to China (Chin, 1999; Wong, 1998). As Wong (1998) states, "these new immigrants wish to establish roots and commit themselves to their new country and they come relatively prepared to do so" (p. 15). The economically advantaged and disadvantaged immigrants, those with family sponsors, or those seeking better economic opportunities, usually admire the freedom and democracy in the United States and plan on staying in this country permanently (Wong, 1998).

Education

The organization of the Chinese education system is similar to the U.S., including pre-school education (3–6 year-olds), primary school education (extended to six years), high school, and higher education (http://www.sh.com/china/edu/chedu.htm). However, secondary education is more varied, including different types of schools such as senior and junior middle schools, agricultural and vocational schools, regular secondary schools, secondary teachers' schools, secondary technical schools, and secondary professional schools (http://www-chaos.umd.edu/history/part3). Higher education is also comprised of a variety of schools, including regular colleges and universities, professional colleges, and short-term vocational universities (http://www-chaos.umd.edu/history/part3). While, since 1949, major improvements have been made in the country to provide primary education to most of the population, secondary and higher education is still not widely available (http://www-chaos.umd.edu/history/part3).

Education in China has been compulsory up to the 9th grade since 1986 (http://www.sh.com/china/edu/chedu.htm). The compulsory law of 1986 sought to bring junior middle school education to some major under-serviced areas within urban and developed areas in coastal provinces (major centers of migration to the U.S.) and in towns of medium development in rural areas (http://www-chaos.umd.edu/history/part3). However, rural areas have had limited resources, and standardized, universal primary education has not been institutionalized in the countryside. This has produced "generations of illiterates, only 60 percent of rural primary school graduates had met established standards" (http://www-chaos.umd.edu/history/part3). In the Chinese sample, most families came from major urban areas in China. Only 27% (20) came from rural locations. This overrepresentation of Chinese immigrants from urban localities may indicate that the majority of the children in the sample (73%, 54) and their parents had access to educational facilities in their country of origin.

Chinese enrollment in primary education has increased considerably over the years—from 20% in 1949, to 96% in 1985 (http://www.sh.com/china/edu/chedu.htm). Since the "Nine Year Compulsory Law" has been in place, primary education is tuition-free if the child attends the neighborhood school. However, parents are expected to pay fees for textbooks, materials, and school overhead expenses (e.g., heating). Low-income families could qualify for stipends to help alleviate the expense burden. The expansion of primary education, however, has increased the demand for qualified teachers (http://www.sh.com/china/edu/chedu.htm). Chinese primary curriculum focuses on the Chinese language, mathematics, basic science, Chinese history and geography, and moral education (http://www.sh.com/china/edu/chedu.htm). Children are also expected to participate in extracurricular activities (e.g., music and drawing), sports, and practical work experiences in the campus vicinity (http://www-chaos.umd.edu/history/part3). Foreign languages are usually taught in 3rd–6th grades, with English as the language of choice in most cases.

Moral and political awareness is also part of the curriculum, including "a general knowledge of politics and moral training, which stressed love of the motherland, love of the party, and love of the people" (http://www-chaos.umd.edu/history/part3). Despite the curriculum diversity, it is estimated that 60% of the class time is devoted to mathematics instruction, indicating a heavy emphasis on academic content—especially math—over the moral or political education (http://www-chaos.umd.edu/history/part3). The schedules are organized in six-day weeks for 9.5 months per year. Urban schools usually go for a full school day, while rural schools usually provide half-day schools. Most primary schools offer five-year programs, but a six-year program has been introduced in cities such as Beijing and Shanghai. However, as mentioned above, there is a disparity in educational services between urban and rural areas, favoring the urban schools (http://www-chaos.umd.edu/history/part3).

Another interesting fact of the Chinese education system is the presence of "Key Schools," at least in the past. In a government effort to revitalize education with limited resources, Key Schools—schools with demonstrated high academic performance—were given preference for funding, teacher placement, and equipment. These schools were identified as "Key Schools" based on the test scores on students' entrance examinations (http://www.sh.com/china/edu/chedu.htm). The concept of Key School was eliminated during the Cultural Revolution (1960s) but reappeared in the 1980s. The Key School concept reveals that there is a system of accountability and that Chinese parents are used to categorizing schools in terms of academic performance. The Key School system has created a consciousness in parents and students to "know" the right school to get into. Key Schools (usually middle schools) are identified as the "feeder" schools for the best secondary schools, which in turn are perceived to increase the students' chances for college admission. In the Key School system, the main goal of elementary and secondary education is to prepare students for college admittance, by tracking them into "quality feeder schools," since adequate academic preparation is required for the successful passing of the entrance exam. The Key School concept resembles the Exam Schools (selected public high schools with high academic standards and credentials) in Boston, where children are expected to pass an entrance examination for admission and these schools are perceived to have an excellent academic record. Nine children (12%) in this sample attend Exam Schools in Boston. Because of concerns that the Key School system favored urban children of economically and educationally advantaged parents, the system has been eliminated in some areas in Changchun, Shenyang, Shenzhen, Xiamen, and other cities (http://www .sh.com/china/edu/chedu.htm).

Over the years, the goals of Chinese education have been changed. During the 1950s and 1960s, Chinese education adopted a universal education system (education for all) to end the highly elitist nature of the education that created great social and cultural gaps between academic and non-academic populations. Since the late 1970s, the purpose of education in China has focused on economic modernization—especially in terms of scientific and technological advances. The ideological goals of education regarding political indoctrination and moral education have also been the focus of the Chinese education. Further, the highly competitive environment of Chinese schools, along with the tradition of academic elitism, seems to contribute to the high appreciation of academic excellence in Chinese society (http://www.sh.com/china/edu/chedu.htm).

Educational backgrounds of recent immigrants from China are characterized by higher levels of education than immigrants from other major sending countries (e.g., Mexico), but the levels of education are different across provinces. For example, in 1998 the national rate of illiteracy in China was 15.78%. However, provinces such as Beijing (6.51%) and Guangdong (9.25%) had illiteracy rates lower than the national rate. On the other hand, provinces such as Fujian (18.70%) and Shandong (22.5%) had higher levels of illiteracy than the national average (http://www.stats.gov.cn). These statistics reflect the urban/rural inequalities in terms of educational opportunities in China.

Hong Kong presents an interesting picture regarding education. According to the 1980 census, 80% of immigrants from Hong Kong had a high school education (Wu, 1997). Until the 1970s, higher education in Hong Kong was highly elitist, with only 2% of the population attending institutions of higher education (Wu, 1997). By 1990, higher education was greatly expanded to 18% of the population (Wu, 1997). Part of these highly educated people in Hong Kong is due to the high level of expenditures that the government spends in education, almost 40% of the government's budget in 1995–1996 (Wu, 1997).

The population in Mainland China has similar levels of education to Hong Kong—60% have completed a high school education (Wong, 1998). Gross enrollment ratios in 1997 showed that 100% of school age children attended elementary school, 70% attended secondary school, but only 6% attended institutions of higher education (http://www .software-engineering.ch).

In the Chinese sample, about 49% (36) of the fathers and 53% (39) of the mothers had some post-elementary education (9th grade). That is, about half of the sample had parents with less than high school education. The other half was comprised of parents that graduated from high school or trade school, or pursued some kind of higher education. About 15% (11) of the Chinese fathers and 14% (10) of the mothers had graduate and professional degrees, mostly in the medical, technical, and financial fields. More than half of these parents were professional couples (both mother and father holding professional degrees). Many highly educated Chinese immigrants have received third preference visas, which are reserved for highly skilled individuals seeking employment in the United States (Wong, 1998). According to LISA research assistants, many of these highly educated parents came as international graduate students and were able to stay on third preference visa.

Employment Trends

Employment among the Chinese immigrants seems to be concentrated in specific labor sectors. For this sample, LISA data on occupation were collected by occupational sectors, not as specific occupations. Therefore, it is unclear what kinds of jobs within a particular sector each parent had. For example, parents indicated working in the restaurant sector, however, it is unclear from the data the type of job within the sector that the individual held (e.g., restaurant owner/manager vs. cook or waiter). Because of this, occupational data were not used as a factor to determine socioeconomic status. However, these data reveal some of the trends in the immigrant-dependent sectors where Chinese immigrants are employed.

A major pattern is that most fathers and mothers were employed in a larger range of occupational sectors in their country of origin, compared to the limited number of occupational sectors in which they were employed in the United States. For example, the distribution of fathers' occupation in China shows a variety of sectors. The four top occupational sectors in which fathers were employed in China were restaurant, construction, production, and agricultural, accounting for 55% (41) of all fathers in the Chinese sample. About 50% (37) of the Chinese mothers were employed in agricultural, education, and production sectors in China. About 19% (14) of the Chinese mothers were unemployed in China. This distribution accounts for 64% of the Chinese mothers' sample.

However, once in the United States, 54% (40) of the Chinese fathers and 22% (16) of the mothers worked in the restaurant sector in the U.S., indicating that the restaurant job market is a significant sector that employs Chinese immigrants, especially males. Further, about 95% (70) of the fathers and 69% (51) of the mothers employed in the restaurant sector in the U.S. came from the Guangdong province, indicating some regional patterns between immigrants from Guangdong and the restaurant sector. Twenty percent (15) of Chinese mothers were unemployed in the U.S.

These trends reflect patterns documented in the literature, especially in relation to Chinese immigrants in Boston. Traditionally, the restaurant sector has been a major employment source for Chinese males in Boston, while the garment industry has provided occupational opportunities for Chinese females (Smolowe, 1993). These sectors often do not require employees to be English proficient and are accessible to new immigrants. Further, these sectors also provide employment for undocumented Chinese immigrants who usually get paid as little as $2 per hour in restaurants, garment factories, and dry-cleaning shops (Smolowe, 1993). The garment and restaurant sectors offer relatively low-paying jobs, and the restaurant jobs often require long hours of work and no benefits (Sagara & Kiang, 1992). Since the 1980s the garment industry has been affected by economic recessions, and Chinese females have been forced to find other alternatives, including jobs in food service, clerical, or medical technology, or remain unemployed (Sagara & Kiang, 1992). In the Chinese sample, only 9% (7) of mothers worked in the garment sector. All of these mothers came from Guangdong.

For more educated immigrants from Hong Kong, Taiwan, and urban areas in Mainland China, employment as educators, engineers, and entrepreneurs, or professional jobs in the banking, real estate, hotel, and international trading sectors, have been typical (Wong, 1998). Fathers who are doctors, lawyers, and college professors represent this segment in the sample. It is important to note that among those mothers and fathers with professional or graduate degrees, the occupational sectors in China and the U.S. remained the same. That is, parents with professional credentials were able to maintain employment within the same sector—usually higher education, medicine, and finance. The path for these professional immigrants was to come to the United States to enroll in graduate studies and then stay after graduation. However, some educated Chinese immigrants are still relegated to menial jobs, like the case of political dissidents who often take menial jobs in the United States, despite their "lofty credentials" (Power, 1998).

Sending Communities in China

There are some differences between immigrants from Mainland China and those from Hong Kong and their motivation to immigrate. Immigrants from Hong Kong, mostly from middle-class backgrounds, seek better educational opportunities for their children or escape from economic and political instability (Wong, 1998). However, undocumented Chinese immigrants and immigrants sponsored by relatives in the U.S. come mostly from Mainland China, especially the southern provinces (Chin, 1999; Wong, 1998). In this sample, however, the children from Hong Kong do not seem to be representing the "highly educated" immigrants that the literature usually mentions. Most of the children from Hong Kong had parents with some post-elementary education. In fact, the majority of children who had fathers (9 out of 11) and mothers (7 out of 10) with professional/graduate degrees came from provinces in Mainland China, not from Hong Kong.

In general, economic and political factors play a role in immigration from Mainland China. While many provinces such as Guangdong and Fujian have enjoyed tremendous economic growth, the benefits have not been distributed equally to all Chinese, especially to those lacking political connections or prestigious family name, and to those in the rural areas (Wong, 1998). Many immigrants, especially those from low-income family backgrounds or with low educational levels, also seek clandestine ways to immigrate (e.g., Snakeheads; Chin, 1999).

About 73% (54) of the Chinese sample came from urban settings. More than half of the Chinese participants (41) came from the southeastern coastal province of Guandong, 20% (16) came from Hong Kong, and 9% (6) came from Fujian. That is, 85% of the Chinese participants came from these three major areas. Further, most of the participants in this study came from the largest provinces in China, including Sichuan (largest), Shangdong (3rd largest), Guangdong (5th largest), and Hubei (9th largest; Osborne, Fu, & Men, 2000). While only a minority of the sample (7%, 5) came from provinces with the highest population density (Shanghai, Beijing, and Shandong), the majority of the sample (58%, 43) came from provinces with the largest GDP rates in China (Guangdong, Shandong, and Sichuan) (http://www.stats.gov.cn).

While China has experienced in the last twenty years "economic revolutions" (Donald, 1998), there have been important disparities. For example, the majority of Chinese consumers (800 million) have an annual purchasing power of less than $5,000 and only 2 million have an annual purchasing power of greater than $20,000 (Osborne, Fu, & Men, 2000). Therefore, it is important to state that China is a diverse country, and major regional differences should be considered, including the presence of ethnic minorities in regions such as Inner Mongolia, Shandong, and Sichuan (http://www.umich.edu/~iinet/chinadata).

In the following section, I will address some significant information on selected provinces where most of my sample came from—Guangdong, Hong Kong, and Fujian.

Guangdong

Forty-one Chinese children in this sample (16 boys and 25 girls) came from Guangdong, representing 56% of the sample. Guangdong province was the point of departure for the majority of the early Chinese immigrants in the 1800s. Today, because of the long history of immigration and the established kinship ties between Chinese Americans whose ancestors came from Guangdong and the new immigrants, this province is still one of the major sources of Chinese immigration to the U.S. However, today's immigrants from Guangdong do not come necessarily from rural areas since Guangdong has become a major economic center, an experimental free enterprise economy in socialist China. Guangdong is ranked first in terms of GDP contribution to China, and fifth in terms of per capita GDP (http://www.surchina.com).

Guangdong's economic boom is in part due to the export economy. Since 1979, Guangdong has been "looked upon as a laboratory, a testing ground for various economic reform policies" (Cheng, 2000, p. 1). In 2000, over 38% of Guangdong's economy relied on export activities (http://www.chineseembassy-canada.org). Because of this, domestic migration to Guangdong has increased. Between 1985 and 1990, Guangdong was the province with the highest rate of migration between provinces, with an influx of 1.26 million into the province (http://www.liasa.ac.at). Therefore, it is possible that the participant families from Guangdong may actually have roots in other provinces in China.

Another source of economic growth in the region has been the investment of Chinese immigrants overseas whose community of origin is Guangdong—they have brought entrepreneurial expertise and capital to the province (http://www.friends-partners.org/china). However, like in many other provinces in China, the economic benefits of the economic growth in Guangdong have not been equally distributed among all the sectors of the population. Part of this has been the effects of corruption, the heavy reliance on political connections to gain access to the benefits of economic reform, and the reluctance of political leaders to allow a more equal distribution of power (Cheng, 2000). Some argue that Guangdong has been used by the Chinese communist government as a way to secure its legitimacy by demonstrating its ability to provide improvements in the people's standards of living, but the distribution of these improvements has not necessarily been equal (Cheng, 2000).

In terms of the profile of Chinese participants from Guangdong (41 children), most were female (61%, 25; compared to 39%, 16 male). Most children are now 15–16 years old (46%, 19), came to the U.S. between 10–12 years of age, and have lived in the U.S. for 4–5 years. In terms of parent education, the sample shows a variation in backgrounds, but most had some post-elementary and high school education. About 15% of parents had some higher education (6 fathers and 5 mothers). Guangdong fathers often worked in construction, agricultural and restaurant sectors while they were in China. Mothers usually either worked in agriculture or were unemployed in China. However, once in the U.S. most Guangdong fathers (71%, 29) and mothers (29%, 12) were employed in the restaurant sector. More than half of the participants from Guangdong lived in the cities of Taishan and Guangzhou.

Hong Kong

Hong Kong was another important community of origin represented in this sample. Sixteen children (5 boys and 11 girls) came from Hong Kong (23). With a population of 6 million, Hong Kong has pursued an export-oriented economic strategy (Wu, 1997). Prior to 1997, Hong Kong was under the British rule, but the economy was built by the Chinese, mainly from the massive immigration from mainland China to Hong Kong after the establishment of the socialist government in 1949 (Wu, 1997). After the succession of Hong Kong back to the Chinese government, Hong Kong has continued with the export-oriented economy. (Wu, 1997).

Unlike immigrants from mainland China, the majority of Chinese immigrants from Hong Kong come from a middle-class background and arrive with significant economic capital (Wong, 1998). Immigrants from Hong Kong usually immigrated to the United States motivated by the political instability in their country of origin or in the search of educational opportunities for their children, rather than by escaping poverty (Wong, 1998). However, based on parental educational backgrounds, it seems like the children in the Chinese sample come from more modest backgrounds—since about 50% of the children had parents with less than post-elementary education.

Education in Hong Kong has been compulsory in primary education since 1971, and expanded to junior secondary education in 1978 (Wu, 1997). However, the restrictions on higher education (elitist system) often pushed young people to seek educational opportunities in the United States. In fact, in the mid–1980s, Hong Kong students were among the ten largest groups of overseas students in the United States (Wu, 1997). Note that because of the high cost of education for international students, only families with means are able to send children to universities in the United States (Wu, 1997).

In terms of the profile of Chinese participants from Hong Kong, again most were female. Children showed a diverse distribution in terms of age and entry age, but most (9) were recent immigrants (2–3 years). About half of the subjects had fathers and mothers with either elementary or some post-elementary education. However, more mothers had higher education than fathers did. An interesting finding is that for the Hong Kong fathers and mothers, there was much more variation in terms of occupational sectors in the U.S. and in China. While the samples from Guangdong and Fujian were heavily concentrated in the restaurant sector in the U.S., only 38% (6) of the fathers from Hong Kong worked in restaurants in the U.S. Only one mother stated she worked in the restaurant sector. The rest of the fathers and mothers presented a wide range of occupational sectors including sales, production, management, delivery, etc. There was also variation in terms of occupational sectors in which these people were employed in China, with no specific occupational group dominating the distribution. Some of the occupational sectors in China were education, construction, sales, and production.

Fujian

Six children in this sample came from Fujian (4 girls and 2 boys), accounting for 9% of the sample. Along with Guangdong, the Fujian province was another important source of immigration in the 1800s (Wong, 1998). The province has a history of 2000 years and it was opened to foreign trade in 1842 (http://www.friends-partners.org/china). According to the Immigration and Naturalization Service, the Fuzhou area in Fujian is the area where most undocumented Chinese immigrants come from (as cited in Chin, 1999).

During the 1970s, the "open-door policy" selected Fujian, along with the Guangdong province, as an experimental site with a market-oriented economy (Chin, 1999). Fujian's economy depends heavily on foreign trade—30% of economic activity in 2000 (http://www.chineseembassy-canada.org). The cities of Fuzhou and Xiamen have become important urban economic centers in China (http://www.chineseembassy-canada.org). However, it is the city of Changle that has been the major center of undocumented immigration and human smuggling in the province (Chin, 1999). In fact, very few young males remain in Changle because of the high level of migration to the U.S. from the area (Smolowe, 1993). Residents of Changle City are often characterized as aggressive, hard working, and motivated to earn money (Chin, 1999). Also, Changle males often do not consider it necessary to achieve higher education as a way to advance economically (Chin, 1999). Residents of Changle City often are less educated and have low paying jobs in the area. These factors often push these residents to seek clandestine ways to immigrate to the U.S. (Smolowe, 1993).

In terms of the profile of Chinese participants from Fujian, most were female (6 girls and 3 boys). Most of the children (7) were recent immigrants (2–3 years in the U.S.). Most Fujian parents (6) had elementary education. All of the parents with elementary education backgrounds were from Changle City, which reflects what the literature has documented. Further, all of the parents from Changle City worked in the restaurant sector in both the U.S. and in China.

Receiving Communities: Chinese in Boston

The Chinese community in Boston has had a growing and significant presence in the city. Between 1980 and 1990, the Asian population in Boston grew by 95.6%, reaching over 30,000 people (Sagara & Kiang, 1992). During the same period, 1980–1990, the Chinese were the fastest growing immigrant group in Massachusetts, accounting for 55% of the Asian population in Boston (Sagara & Kiang, 1992). Also, in 1990, about 70% of the Asian population in Boston was comprised of foreign-born individuals (Sagara & Kiang, 1992).

Chinese immigration to the Boston area started in 1870, when a shoe factory in North Adams recruited 75 Chinese males as workers (Sagara & Kiang, 1992). Ten years later, the Boston Chinatown was established with a population of 200. However, the Chinese Exclusion Act of 1882 successfully stopped Chinese immigration to the area for the next 85 years (Sagara & Kiang, 1992). Chinese immigration to Boston resumed after World War II, when the growing restaurant and garment industries in Chinatown provided job opportunities for new immigrants. In 1965, the Immigration Reform Act promoted an increase in the number of Chinese immigrants to Boston, mostly from immigrants who reunited with their families already established in the United States (Sagara & Kiang, 1992). In the 1980s, the garment industry declined, and since then many Chinese women have been finding jobs in Boston in other sectors including food service, medical technology, and clerical work (Lowe, 1992). The restaurant sector in Boston has been a major source of employment for Chinese males, which is reflected in the distribution of this sample. In general, Chinese immigrants who live outside Chinatown reflect higher levels of education and income.

Boston's Chinatown has been an entry point for many new Chinese immigrants. This community offers accessible markets and services, as well as cultural and social affirmation. However, because of the limitations imposed by zoning policies and the lack of adequate housing, very few new immigrants are able to stay in the area, and are forced to find housing outside the Boston Chinatown (Leong, 1996; Sagara & Kiang, 1992). According to the Chinatown Coalition (1994), some of the popular areas of settlement for the new Chinese immigrants include:

- Allston and Brighton: 57% of Asians in Boston live in this area. Most of the residents are males who have not graduated from high school, a lower median family income than other immigrant groups.
- Quincy: An emerging settlement, mostly blue and white collar White community, close to Chinatown, but with better housing and schools than Chinatown.
- Lexington: A Boston suburb where Asians represent the largest minority group of the town's population. A growing number of Chinese businesses, including restaurants, Chinese schools, and a bilingual library reflect the presence of Chinese immigrants.

While not a major concentration in some communities, affluent Chinese immigrants can be found in suburban towns around Cambridge such as Newton, Burlington, and Braintree.

Mexican Immigration: A Brief Overview

Connected by history and a strategic geographical position, the U.S.-Mexico relation has evolved through time, since the establishment of both nations as independent countries. One of the areas of tension, conflict, and occasional cooperation between Mexico and the United States has been the immigration flow of Mexican nationals to the United States—both documented and undocumented (Cornelius, 1998). While Mexican populations in the U.S. were the result of the acquisition of Mexican territory by the United States in the 19th century, Mexican immigration to the U.S. has contributed to the increase of the Mexican-origin population in the U.S. At several points in time, the U.S. has established policies to control and promote Mexican immigration.

Mexican immigration has passed through major waves from the early 1900s to 1970s (Burma, 1970). Prior to 1918, a few Mexicans crossed the border and settled in border areas. Between 1918 and 1930, the demand for cheap labor in the United States brought a wave of Mexican immigration after World War I. From 1930 to 1942, the economic recession during the Great Depression discouraged Mexican immigration, and many Mexican immigrants returned to Mexico (Valdez, 1996). The period of 1942–1964, with the emergence of the Bracero program, allowed Mexican farm workers to temporarily reside and work in the U.S. (Durand, Massey, & Parrado, 2000). However, the largest wave of Mexican immigration has been continuously increasing since the 1960s (Olsen, 1988). In 1986, the Immigration Reform and Control Act (IRCA) stimulated the growth of immigration, allowing 1.5 million long-term undocumented Mexican immigrants to regularize their immigration status and become legal residents (Cornelius, 1995). Once these immigrants became documented, they sought to bring their spouses and children to the United States (Cornelius, 1995), increasing the influx of Mexican immigrants, especially in California, from 1988 to the 1990s. During the last five years, Mexico has held first place as a source of both legal and undocumented immigration to the United States (http://www.ins.usdoj.gov).

Mexican Immigrant Profile

Research on immigration has categorized Mexican immigrants as having their roots in rural areas or small towns in Mexico (Cornelius, Chavez, & Castro, 1982). They have been characterized as leaving their country for economic reasons, finding jobs in the U.S. in factories and the service industries in urban areas, or in the agricultural sector in farming towns (Olsen, 1988; Cornelius, Chavez, & Castro, 1982). Another common characteristic of the Mexican immigrant profile is that men commonly arrive alone and send for their families later (Olsen, 1988). According to Mexico's National Council on Population (CONAPO) most Mexicans migrate to the U.S. either at early ages (as children) or shortly after age 25 (http://www.conapo.gob.mx).

My sample reflects some of the characteristics of the general Mexican immigrant profile as documented in the literature. Only 25% (20) of the Mexican participants came together as a family unit (compared to 44% in the Chinese group). Thirty-eight percent (30) of the participants stayed in Mexico while one parent immigrated to the United States and 25% (20) of participants stayed in Mexico with other relatives while the parents immigrated.

Mexican immigration has also been categorized in five major subgroups depending upon the nature of their migration and documentation status (Cornelius, Chavez, & Castro, 1986):

1. temporary/undocumented from deep in Mexico
2. temporary/documented from deep in Mexico
3. borderland commuter immigrants
4. long-term undocumented immigrants
5. permanent documented immigrants

Guadalupe Valdez (1996) offers a similar typology of the Mexican immigrants: permanent immigrants, short-term immigrants, and cyclical immigrants. Because of confidentiality reasons, data on documented status of participants were not collected. However, the vast majority of the sample (91%, 71) came from regions deep in Mexico (central and southern) rather than border towns. This may reflect the permanency of the participants in the U.S. In fact, one of the selection criteria for the LISA project was that the participants' families were planning on staying in the U.S. for the next five years from recruitment date.

Reasons for Immigration

Portes and Zhou (1992) have identified that for the Mexican immigrants, the most important reason for immigration often involve economic factors. In terms of reason for immigration, 60% (47) of the parents stated that they came to the U.S. for the economic opportunities, better jobs, and a better standard of living. Twenty-two percent (17) came for family reunification purposes, and only 8% (6) came for educational opportunities.

Education

In Mexico, the education system is divided into basic (1st–9th grade), upper secondary (10th–12th grade), and higher education. Basic education includes both elementary (1st–6th grade) and lower secondary (7th–9th grade). After the establishment of compulsory education to the 9th grade in 1993, the Secretariat of Education had included both levels into "basic education" (1993) (http://www.sep.gob.mx). The total enrollment for the 1998–1999 academic year shows that 81% of school age children were enrolled in elementary and lower secondary education (1st–9t^{h}), 10% in upper secondary (10th–12th), 6% in higher education, and 3% in job training programs.

Elementary education in Mexico is compulsory for children aged 6–14 (http://www.sep.gob.mx). There are diverse elementary education programs including general education, bilingual-bicultural (for indigenous populations), community education, and adult basic education. While Mexican enrollment in elementary education (1st–6th grade) has been consistently high over the last ten years (80–88%), enrollment in lower secondary schools (7th–9th grade) has increased dramatically in the last 30 years—from 30% in 1970, to 69% in 1990, and 79% in 1999.

Mexican education is free of tuition in elementary schools—1st–6th grades. Also, there is a national free textbooks program for the elementary grades that provides children with texts in Reading, Language Arts, Mathematics, Social Sciences, and Natural Sciences. However, parents are expected to buy school supplies, and pay for uniforms and other services. The Mexican school calendar comprises 200 days of instruction—starting in late August and ending in the first week of July. School days include 4 to 4.5 hours of actual class time.

The elementary curriculum includes the following courses: Spanish, Mathematics, Comprehensive Knowledge of the Environment, Natural Sciences, History, Geography, Civil Education, Artistic Education, and Physical Education. Most of the class time (30–45%) is devoted to reading, writing, and oral expression. Twenty-five percent of class time is devoted to the instruction of mathematics and science. According to the Secretariat of Public Education (http://www.sep.gob .mx) the goals of elementary education in Mexico are four:

1. Develop intellectual skills and habits for children to engage in independent learning as well as effectively carry on tasks in everyday life—reading, writing, oral expression, search for information, and basic mathematics.
2. Acquire a basic understanding of natural science regarding health and environmental conservation, as well as of Mexican geography and history.
3. Learn civil responsibility in terms of ethical values, understanding of rights and obligations in interpersonal relations and as members of a national community.
4. Develop appreciation for the arts, sports, and physical activities.

Compared to the Chinese education system, Mexican education places more emphasis on reading than mathematics. It also places civic education as a top priority, including nationalism, but the emphasis is mostly on personal relations, values, and ethics. Because of the realization that a small sector of the population actually pursues higher education (6%), or even upper secondary—10th–12th grade—(10%), the Mexican curricula seem to emphasize the acquisition of skills for everyday life and independent intellectual development.

In Mexico, the constitution grants the right to an education to Mexican nationals, stipulates compulsory attendance until 9th grade, and identifies the State as the provider of free, secular K–12 education (independent from any religious doctrine). Ideologically, Mexican education today emphasizes the principles of human development, love of country, awareness of international solidarity, and the promotion of Mexican culture (http://www.sep.gob.mx). Mexican education has taken the responsibility to promote modernization by supporting scientific and technological research. Mexican education is also guided by democratic principles that promote an egalitarian view of education, to promote the economic, social, and cultural growth of the Mexican people (http://www.sep.gob.mx).

An interesting contrast between the ideologies and principles behind Mexican and Chinese education is that Mexican education seems to emphasize more socio-political aspects of human development—interpersonal relations, civic duties, international solidarity. While the Mexican Secretariat of Public Education lists scientific and technological research as goals of education, the emphasis on mathematics and science curricula comprise only 25% of class time, compared to the Chinese curricula which devotes 60% of class time to mathematics alone. Also, most of the class time in Mexican elementary classrooms is devoted to language development—reading, writing, and oral expression.

Generally speaking, the majority of Mexican immigrants have been categorized as having lower levels of education compared to other immigrant groups, mostly at the elementary level (Portes & Zhou, 1992). In 1990, only 3.5% of adult Mexican immigrants had some college education—the lowest percentage of all ethnic groups in the U.S. (Rumbaut, 1995). The data on parents' educational level and occupational sector reveal that in fact these participants come from low educational backgrounds. For the Mexican participants, most fathers (67%, 52) and mothers (77%, 60) had less than high school education. In fact, most fathers and mothers had elementary education only. Only ten fathers and one mother had some higher education, but only one mother actually completed a degree.

Today, the average educational level of the Mexican population is 7.7 years, which is an impressive improvement from the average of 2.6 years in 1960 (http://www.embamexcan.com). Even though compulsory education until 9th grade has been in effect since 1993, the reality is that there is a disparity between urban and rural areas. For example, 75% of students in urban areas in Mexico complete a 6th grade education, compared to only 15% of students in rural areas completing 6th grade (Olsen, 1988). Also, while the national illiteracy rate is about 11.2%, some of regions of Mexico such as Tarimoro, Guanajuato experience an illiteracy rate of 21.2%. The states of Guerrero (23%), Oaxaca (19.7%) and Veracruz (16.6%) have higher illiteracy rates than the national average. However, decreases in illiteracy rates have been reported in the last ten years. In the 1970s, many states (e.g., Veracruz) had illiteracy rates as high as 35% (http://www.veracruz.gob.mx.). Also, there are regions such as Baja California Norte (4.6%) in which illiteracy rates fall below the national average.

Another source of disparities in educational levels among different Mexican communities is in availability of school facilities. For example, while major urban centers have K–12 school facilities and centers of higher education, small communities in the interior such as Tarimoro, Guanajuato lack institutions of higher education, or even lack high schools (http://www.guanjuato.gob.mx). This is an important factor in explaining the disparities among states in terms of college graduates. For example, while in 1995, Mexico City produced over 33,000 graduates from public universities; states such as Campeche only produced 99 graduates (http://www.anuies.mx). Appendix C includes a chart of the number of college graduates in the states where the Mexican sample came from. Note that about half of the Mexican children in this sample came from urban and semi-urban areas (49%, 38). Only 12% (9) came from rural areas. This may indicate that most of the children in this sample had access to educational opportunities in Mexico because they came from urban settings. In fact, 27% (21) of the Mexican sample came from major urban areas in Mexico.

Employment Trends

Some argue that because of the limited educational and occupational backgrounds of many Mexican immigrants, this group has been concentrated in the bottom segments of the U.S. labor market (Portes & Zhou, 1992). Mexican immigrants have contributed to several economic sectors in the U.S., including the construction of the railroad system, and have had significant participation in the agricultural, manufacturing, and urban service economies (Roberts, Frank, & Lozano-Ascencia, 1999).

As with the Chinese, the Mexican immigrants in this sample followed the same pattern of slightly more diversified employment in the country of origin compared to the U.S. job sectors. Father occupation data in Mexico shows that about half of the fathers were employed in agricultural and construction sectors while mothers were unemployed in Mexico. Some mothers worked in office work, restaurant, and janitorial jobs. Here in the United States, Mexican fathers worked in the construction sector while mothers worked in janitorial and restaurant sectors. Nineteen percent (15) of Mexican mothers were still unemployed in the United States. However, unlike in the Chinese sample where there was clearly a concentration of fathers and mothers working in the restaurant sector, the Mexican sample did not reveal any major concentration in any particular occupational sector. That is, there was more variety in the occupational sectors in the U.S. for Mexican participants than for the Chinese participants.

Sending Communities in Mexico

Traditionally, research on immigration has characterized Mexican immigration as mostly from rural areas (Adler, 2000). However, this sample shows a higher concentration of participants from urban and semi-urban areas of Mexico. This may reflect the fact that most of the participant families were recruited in urban centers around the San Francisco Bay Area, which may attract more immigrants from urban than rural areas. In the Mexican sample, 33% (26) came from the state of Jalisco (half of this proportion came from the city of Guadalajara—the capital of the state) and 14% (11) from Mexico City. Areas in Central Mexico and Baja California Norte accounted for 16% (12) of the sample.

Jalisco

The province of Jalisco represented the most dominant community of origin in this sample. Twenty-six children came from Jalisco. Interestingly, most of the children from Jalisco were male (18). Only eight were females.

Jalisco is a state that has enjoyed great economic development. Jalisco has the first place in employment generation and is the greatest contributor to the GNP in the Western region of Mexico (http://www.jalisco.gob.mx). Because of major urban centers such as Guadalajara, the most important economic sectors in the state include the service industry (31%), trade (23.4%), manufacturing (21.7%), and transportation (10.3%), while agriculture accounts for 8.5% of the economic activity of the state. Guadalajara, the capital of the state, faces the typical problems of urbanization. For example, one of the major education goals of the state department of education was to promote the "Drug-Free Schools" programs (http://www.jalisco.gob .mx).

In terms of the profile of participants from Jalisco, there was an overwhelming concentration of males (69%, 18) compared to females (31%, 8). Most children are now 15–16 years old. In terms of fathers' education, the majority (16) had elementary education. Only two fathers from Guadalajara had some college education. Most mothers had either elementary (11) or some post-elementary (12). Only two mothers had graduated from high school and one had some college education. These mothers with higher levels of education (high school and college) also came from Guadalajara.

In regards to father occupation in Mexico, fathers worked in agricultural and construction sectors. Six fathers were unemployed in Mexico. These unemployed fathers included the two fathers with college education from Guadalajara. The majority of the Jalisco mothers were unemployed in Mexico (56%, 15), but some mothers worked either in office work, janitorial, or garment industry sectors. Occupations in the U.S. for the Jalisco fathers were varied. For mothers, while some were still unemployed in the U.S. (33%, 9), others found jobs in restaurant and janitorial sectors.

Mexico City

Eleven children came from Mexico City (5 boys and 6 girls), representing 14% of the sample. As the capital of the country, Mexico City has one of the highest levels of economic activity in the nation. However, as a major urban center, it does suffer from major problems such as pollution, traffic, unemployment, crime, and poverty. In general, the migration from Mexico City to the U.S. has been characterized by temporary migration during periods of economic recession rather than more permanent settlements (Roberts, Frank, & Lozano-Ascencio, 1999). Approximately 10% of the population of Mexico City is non-native and has migrated from other states of the interior (http://www.ddf.gob.mx). Because of this, it is possible that many immigrants to the U.S. from Mexico City migrate through contacts with relatives from the interior, rather than through contacts of immigrants from Mexico City.

Most of the children from Mexico City were 15–16 year-olds who came to the U.S. at ages 10–12, and had lived in the U.S. 4–5 years. Their fathers and mothers had some post-elementary or elementary education. In terms of occupational backgrounds, the parents of children from Mexico City showed a great variation of occupational sectors, but mostly service oriented jobs—sales, beautician, restaurant. Occupation in the U.S also showed concentration on the service sector in the U.S.—construction, restaurants, and janitorial.

Central Mexico: The State of Mexico, Hidalgo, Puebla, and Zacatecas.

Combined, provinces in Central Mexico accounted for 14% of the sample, or 11 children (5 boys and 6 girls). Most of the immigrants from Central Mexico seem to have rural backgrounds, since agriculture is a major economic sector in these states. In Puebla, 86.7% of the state's land is used for agricultural purposes. In Zacatecas, 43.3% of the state population is employed in agriculture. Rural areas in Mexico are often characterized by high illiteracy rates and low school attendance in children populations (Adler, 2000).

Over 50% of these children were 13–14, came to the U.S. at ages 10–11, and had been in the U.S. for less than three years. The children from Central Mexico were more recent immigrants than the children from Jalisco or Mexico City. Nine fathers and 11 mothers had less than some post-elementary education. Two fathers—one from Hidalgo and the other from Zacatecas—indicated they had some college education but no degree. Most fathers worked in construction in Mexico and continued working in this sector in the U.S. For mothers from Central Mexico, there was variation in occupational backgrounds in Mexico—including sales, production, and restaurant. However, in the U.S., most mothers worked in the janitorial sector.

Baja California Norte

Children from Baja California Norte accounted for 8% of the sample (1 boy and 5 girls). Baja California Norte is one of the states in Mexico that has enjoyed rapid economic growth, in part due to the *maquiladora* industry (http://www.baja.gob.mx). With a population of 2 million, Baja California Norte has one of lowest unemployment rates in the region (1.1%). This is in part due to the fact that 80% of the population resides in the two major border cities in the state, Tijuana and Mexicali, which have enjoyed a rapid economic growth in the last decade. Most people in the state (91%) live in urban areas. Baja California Norte has one of the lowest illiteracy rates in the country (4.6% in 1992, down from 12.7% in 1970). Cities such as Mexicali and Tijuana have educational facilities for K–12 and also important higher education centers (http://www.baja.gob.mx). This has contributed to the higher levels of education among the population of Baja California Norte compared to other Mexican provinces. For example, about 55% of people aged 15 and older in Baja California Norte have completed a high school education.

Most of the children who came from Baja California Norte were females, ages 11–12, who came to the U.S. at 7–9 years of age, and have lived in the U.S. 4–5 years. All of these children came from urban areas, including Ensenada, Tijuana, and Mexicali. Their parents had elementary education or some post-elementary. Most fathers worked in construction or car repair. An interesting fact in the mothers' background is that six out of eight mothers were employed in Mexico (unlike the general pattern for other provinces where most mothers were unemployed). These mothers were employed in service sectors—including restaurants and technology (*maquiladoras*). Here in the U.S., fathers from Baja California Norte are employed either in construction or janitorial sectors. Mothers also work in the janitorial sector, but some work in the restaurant sector, and others are unemployed.

Receiving Communities: Mexicans in the Bay Area

In 1990, over 57% of all the Mexican immigrant population resided in California (Rumbaut, 1995). While Mexican immigration has traditionally been concentrated in Southern California (Cornelius, Chavez, & Castro, 1992), the San Francisco Bay Area and other areas of Northern California have also been popular destinations for Mexican immigrants who find jobs as agricultural workers (Menjivar, 1997; Peshkin, 1991).

The San Francisco Bay Area in Northern California is an immigrant area. In 1991, the Immigration and Naturalization Service reported that 30,000 new immigrants came to San Francisco; 13% of these were from Mexico (as cited in Hamel, 1993). In California, the San Francisco and Imperial counties have the greatest concentrations of immigrant students enrolled in public schools (Olsen, 1988). The San Francisco Unified School District ranks second (after Los Angeles Unified) in terms of number of immigrant students (Olsen, 1988). However, it is important to note than when comparing the average annual immigration rates of 1980–1989 with the rates of 1990–1997, the San Francisco area shows a 28% decline (Aurbach, 1999).

Unlike the Chinese in Boston, Mexicans usually do not have a formal community infrastructure of reception in Northern California

(Menjivar, 1997). However, the long history of immigration often leads to the formation of informal human collectivities that can serve as transnational social spaces and sources of social capital. The literature on transnational social spaces supports the notion of community organizations of Mexican immigrants in major urban centers such as Los Angeles and New York (Smith, 1998). The benefits of these community organizations are often enjoyed by a transnational elite of immigrants who have the economic capital and political connections to take advantage of these organized, formal transnational networks (Guarnizo, 1998; Smith, 1998b). Therefore, it is likely that most Mexican immigrants from more modest backgrounds rely on kinship groups, rather than more formal transnational networks or communities.

SCHOOL CHARACTERISTICS

Following Portes' idea of the importance of the receiving community, I chose to analyze not only student characteristics, but also characteristics of the schools that students attended. My rationale was based on Portes' typology of resources and vulnerabilities. Portes identified color, location, and lack of mobility ladders as vulnerabilities, while government programs for immigrants, absence of prejudice, and established ethnic communities as resources. As mentioned in my introduction, I was interested in isolating two factors from Portes' typology—location and ethnic community resources—and exploring the idea of placing these in a transnational context. Since most immigrant children live their lives in the context of the school for a considerable part of the day, I thought it would be important to contextualize the notion of location and ethnic community resources in terms of the school context.

In order to assess the existence of an ethnic community in the school and the potential vulnerabilities of the school location, I explored three variables: school ethnic composition, school participation in free/reduced lunch programs, and proportion of students who are English language learners. A strong presence of ethnic minority students and English language learners would indicate that the school may be serving an immigrant ethnic community. The fact that a high proportion of students participated in free/reduced lunch programs could indicate some socioeconomic vulnerabilities of the receiving location. The data for school characteristics were organized in terms of percentage ranges: 80–100%, 60–79%, 40–59%, 20–39%, and 0–19%.

Information on ethnic composition of the school was gathered for all of the schools that children in this study attended at the time of the interview in 2000. This information was recorded and organized by the percentage ranges explained above. Schools were then classified according to the predominant group present in the school, usually 40% or more (in some schools over 60%). The predominant group had the highest percentages of any ethnic group in that particular school. Schools that did not have a predominant ethnic group present were classified as "diverse" schools. The data on ethnic composition of the schools were collected via the Internet on the California Department of Education and the Massachusetts Department of Education web sites. The ethnic categories were taken from the official school designations, which often were described as follows:

- Asian: Children of Chinese, Japanese, Korean, and other southern Asian countries.
- African American: Children of Black racial backgrounds, excluding Latinos
- Latinos: Children of Latin American background, including Mexican, South and Central American, Puerto Rican, and other Spanish speaking Caribbean countries.
- White: Children of Anglo Saxon or European backgrounds, excluding Latino

Table 4.1 presents a brief profile of the modal characteristics by ethnicity, English language learners and children in free/reduced lunch programs.

In the samples for this study, the Chinese and Mexican samples had more or less similar student characteristics; however, they were not really comparable in terms of school characteristics (see Table 4.1). Most Chinese and Mexican children in the sample came more or less at the same age (Chinese a bit older), had lived here for the same number of years, and had both mothers and fathers with similar educational levels (Mexican a bit less educated). However, it was in the school characteristics where differences appeared. For example, Chinese children attended schools that were predominantly White, with low concentrations of English learners (0–19%). Mexican students attended schools where Latinos were the majority group, with an important presence of second language learners (40–59%). Also, children in the Mexican sample attended schools where more children participated in school-wide free lunch programs. In fact, 84% of the Mexican sample attended schools where the free/reduced participation was over 40%, compared to 62% of the Chinese sample.

Table 4.1.
Profile of Modal Characteristics of Immigrant Children in Sample

Profile Characteristic	Chinese	Mexican
Student current age	15	14
Student age at time of immigration	11	9
Student years of residence in U.S.	4–5 years	4–5 years
Student gender	Females	Males
Province of origin	Guangdong	Jalisco
Type of community of origin	Urban	Semi-urban
Father educational level	Some post elementary	Elementary
Mother educational level	Some post elementary	Elementary
Predominant ethnic group in school	White	Latino
% Free/reduced lunch program	40% and higher	60% and higher
% of English Language Learners	0–19%	40–59%

The profile of the Chinese and Mexican sample may indicate some vulnerabilities and resources in terms of student and school characteristics. Mexican children in this sample seemed to have at least slightly more disadvantaged circumstances than the Chinese children did. Also, there was a group of Chinese participants (11–15%) whose parents had very high educational backgrounds and no such counterpart existed for the Mexican sample. I will refer to the students and school characteristics to frame how the students' responses may reflect some of the vulnerabilities and resources established by the school and student characteristics in the children's profiles.

CHAPTER 5

Prior Messages
Voices across Borders

As noted in chapter 2, empirical research on transnational activities has established that everyday actions of transnational migrants that cross and overlap boundaries constitute a transnational social space. Research has defined these activities around the economic, social, cultural and political involvement of transnational people across borders. One of the goals of this investigation was to assess if immigrant children participate in activities–specifically the diffusion of information–that can be transnational in nature and may influence their participation in U.S. schools. The focus of this and the next two chapters (5–7) is on the messages across borders that these children received from co-nationals about schools in the United States.

When analyzing transnational messages, it is necessary to contextualize these messages around a number of variables that are likely to influence both the nature and the source of messages. The variables were grouped into student characteristics and school characteristics (chapter 4). While in general terms, the distribution of these characteristics followed the general pattern of the overall sample, sometimes certain elements in the school or student profiles were worthy of mention and discussion. Unless otherwise indicated, the profile of the student and school characteristics followed the general distribution of the overall sample (Appendix B and Table 4.1).

From the open-ended interview data, eight major categories emerged to qualify the nature of transnational messages:

- *Academic*: Messages about curriculum, instruction, and educational opportunities.

"The subjects are more diverse and the study in the U.S. is much easier than in China."

—13 year-old Chinese boy from Guangdong

▪ *English*: Messages about English learning and need for proficiency.

"[I was told] that I was not going to understand because they speak English."

—13 year-old Mexican boy from Guerrero

▪ *General:* Broad qualitative messages (e.g., good, bad).

"Schools are not so good. The education and students are not so good."

—13 year-old Chinese girl from Hong Kong

▪ *Peers:* Messages about peer relations and perceptions of peers.

"Most people said that the kids [in schools] here are better, even those in China [said that]"

—13 year-old Chinese girl from Fujian

▪ *School:* Messages about the school infrastructure, organization, and services.

"School was pretty here. Schools were very pretty. They had swimming pools."

—13 year-old Mexican girl from Jalisco

▪ *Social:* Messages about social issues (e.g., discrimination) within the school context that do not specifically address peer or teacher interactions (if they do, they are classified as Peer or Teacher Messages)

"[I heard] that the schools were better. That there wasn't any racism."

—Mexican girl from Puebla (no age data)

- *Teachers*: Messages about students' perceptions of teachers' abilities, personality, and student-teacher relationships.

"Education in the United States is very good. Teachers are very nice. They know a lot."
—15 year-old Chinese boy from Hong Kong

- *No answer*: Students did not receive messages or did not remember.

These eight major categories were used to analyze messages prior to immigration, upon entry to the U.S. school system, and for messages they currently construct. These messages were identified as Prior Messages, Welcoming Messages, and Current Messages respectively. These are discussed in detail in chapters 5 through 7. Because children often articulated more than one message in their responses to one question (e.g., children talking about teachers and peers prior to immigration), there is no one question-one answer correspondence. The percentages and frequency counts reported in the discussion refer to number/proportion of children's responses. Therefore, the response sample size does not necessarily correspond to the student sample size (e.g., Chinese = 74, Mexican = 78) because the same child's response may include multiple categories of themes (e.g., academic, peers, and teachers), increasing the response sample size compared to the students' sample size. The response sample sizes are noted in appropriate frequency tables. Frequency counts are noted in the text in parentheses or separated by commas after the percentages—45% (39) or (45%, 39).

Because of the constraints of a retrospective questionnaire to assess the existence of messages prior to immigration in these groups, data on participants' and parents' perceptions of the U.S. collected by the LISA study in the school year 1997–1998 prior to immigration were also analyzed. The LISA study asked both parents and children the following question: "How did you imagine the U.S. when you lived in your country of origin?" While this question did not specifically addressed issues of schools or education or information per se, I wanted to corroborate if school and educational issues were part of these perceptions about the U.S. prior to immigration. These data are identified in the text as LISA 1997–1998 Parent and Student data.

PRIOR MESSAGES: EXPECTATIONS OF U.S. SCHOOLS

The majority of the participant children in this study did receive some information about the U.S. that specifically addressed school issues. Sixty-one percent (60) of Chinese respondents and 68% (73) of the Mexican respondents indicated some kind of information received prior to immigration. Table 5.1 shows the breakdown of the Prior Messages for both groups.

Table 5.1.
Students' Messages about U.S. Schools Prior to Immigration

Types of Messages	Chinese		Mexican	
	N	%	N	%
Academic	24	23%	15	14%
English	3	3%	8	7%
General	9	9%	15	14%
Peers	5	5%	13	12%
School	13	12%	17	16%
Teachers	10	10%	5	5%
No School Message	39	38%	34	32%
Total	103	100%	107	100%

These categories–derived from the data–were also defined in terms of positive and negative messages within each category. Appendix D shows the distribution of negative and positive messages by gender.

The Chinese group shows that most messages prior to immigration were about academic, school, and teacher issues. For the Mexican group, the distribution of messages over categories was more equal. Mexican children received information about school, academic, and peer issues, as well as general statements (positive and negative) about U.S. schools (e.g., school is good, or bad). More Mexican children gave general statements than Chinese children did. It is also clear that Chinese children received more messages about classroom experiences (academic and teachers) 34% (34) than Mexican children did (19%, 20).

Academic Demands and the Definition of Educational Opportunity

Academic Messages were categorized under several major themes–curriculum, instruction, schoolwork, assessment, studying, and classroom behavior.

Chinese Academic Messages: Less Stressful School Life

While the range of Academic Messages was wide, most of the Chinese children indicated that they received more positive Academic Messages than negative (Appendix D). Negative Academic Messages included two main themes:

- Perceptions of specific academic subjects such as reading and language arts as being difficult because of student's limited English language proficiency.
- Low quality of education in the U.S.

The fact that only girls received negative messages about academic issues may indicate that some of these messages are genderized. However, this may also be just a reflection of the sample distribution. There are more girls than there are boys in the Chinese sample.

Positive Academic Messages in the Chinese group emphasize three main themes:

- The less demanding curriculum and schoolwork in American schools
- The attainability of academic excellence due to the less demanding nature of academic life in the U.S. school.
- Opportunity to attend institutions of higher education in the U.S.

Chinese children often emphasized how they were told that American schools were "easy."

"[I heard that] the subjects are more diverse and the study in the U.S. is much easier than China."

　　　　　　　　　　　　　—13 year-old boy from Guangdong

"[I heard that] the schools and homework are easy and that in the U.S. kids don't have to do homework."

　　　　　　　　　　　　　—12 year-old girl from Hong Kong

The nature of the positive perception of the lower academic demands in the U.S. among Chinese participants is constructed around what children perceived to be a less stressful academic environment. This less stressful perception of academic demands in the U.S. is linked to perceptions of a less demanding assessment.

"I heard students don't need to take final exams every year. There is not as much tension or worry."

　　　　　　　　　　　　　—15 year-old girl from Guangdong

A girl shared that prior to immigration she heard that the academic environment was less stressful in the U.S. in terms of lack of accountability and supervision:

"Even if you fail a test, you don't need to get parent's signature. No need to wear school uniform. American schools are easier. It is easier to adapt to American schools. American schools have fewer pressures than Hong Kong schools."

　　　　　　　　　　　　　—16 year-old girl from Hong Kong

This girl's message presented an expectation of a less stressful academic environment in the U.S. where children were less controlled. The research assistant who interviewed this child explained the following:

"In Hong Kong, if a student fails a test, the teacher may ask the parent to sign to make sure the parent knows how the student is doing in school, to make sure the parent is aware of the poor academic performance."

Advancement in education in China has usually been determined by rigorous examinations that eliminate less qualified applicants from access to higher levels of education. A description of the educational system in China depicts this:

> [In order to access] higher education, students must pass examinations of all levels. First, one should pass the entrance examination for senior middle schools or middle-level technical schools. Then after two, three or four years, one may sit in for the national college entrance examination, which usually takes place on July 7 to 9. Due the grueling weather and the stress one bears all those days, the month of July is widely nicknamed the "black July." (http://www.sh.com)

The fact that the U.S. schools do not use entrance examinations in most public schools may signify a relief for the potential Chinese immigrant who is presented with the opportunity of a less stressful academic environment. Furthermore, Chinese children perceive the less rigorous academic demands in the U.S. school as an opportunity to reach academic excellence (e.g., good grades) without too much stress or effort:

> "My aunt and uncle were in the U.S. first and they told me school was easy, relaxed. You don't need to study hard to get good grades."
>
> —12 year-old girl from Hong Kong

This perception of schools being less stressful was confirmed by a number of Chinese research assistants who commented that some Chinese children are enthusiastic about the fact that in the U.S. they do not have the pressure of the rigorous and competitive academic environment of Chinese schools. The message prior to immigration that co-nationals give to Chinese immigrants is that academic excellence is attainable in the U.S. school because schools are less demanding.

Prior to immigration, most children (over 60% of children who received Academic Messages) were from Hong Kong and Guangdong. This may reflect some regional differences on the emphasis of academic issues among immigrants. Hong Kong has one of the highest literacy rates in Southeast Asia. It is estimated that more than 90% of

Hong Kong youth complete high school or technical education (http://www.hkta.org/superlatives/well.html). Because of the emphasis on Academic Messages Prior to Immigration in the Hong Kong sample, it would be important to investigate in future studies if regional differences reveal how immigrants from Hong Kong value and emphasize education as part of their immigration goals, compared to immigrants from other Chinese provinces.

For Chinese parents, Academic Messages referred to the educational opportunities in the U.S., especially in the Boston area. For some parents, Boston became a key place to immigrate because of the availability of educational opportunities:

> "Boston is a cultural and educational center, provides a good favorable conditions for children to study."
> —College-graduate-parent from Guangdong

> "I don't know. I came here only for my child [so he could] have more choice in studies and places. Boston is an academic area. It is better for children. To me, I sacrificed a lot because I came here in my old age"
> —High School-graduate-parent from Hong Kong

While there was variation among the mothers, all of the fathers that indicated Academic Messages Prior to Immigration had more than high school education.

Responses from the LISA 1997–1998 data from students also reflected that children heard about school in the U.S. as being "easy" (especially regarding math curriculum and less homework) as compared to China. But, some students also articulated that they intended to pursue higher education.

> "American school system offers a lot of opportunities to go into high school and college"
> —11 year-old girl from Macau

Mexican Academic Messages: The Easy American School

Academic Messages were the second most popular kind of messages among the Mexican participants, along with General Messages.

However, in the Mexican group, the proportions of positive and negative messages were more equally distributed than in the Chinese group (Appendix D).

Negative messages in the Mexican group referred to three main issues:

- Low quality of instruction in the U.S.
- The difficulty of curriculum due to student's lack of English proficiency
- The perception of a less advanced curriculum compared to Mexican schools

Mexican children stated that they were warned about schools being boring because they could not understand the language and about U.S. schools not providing adequate instruction.

> "[I heard] that they [American schools] were boring because they were in English and one cannot understand."
> —16 year-old girl from Guanajuato

> "[In American schools] they didn't teach right and very little [few things]"
> —14 year-old girl from Baja California Norte

> "[In American schools] they treat students wrong and [I heard] that they [teachers] didn't teach the right way."
> —13 year-old girl from Colima

Some children received negative messages not only regarding quality of instruction, but also about the content of curriculum, indicating that the scope and sequence of U.S. curricula were less advanced than the curricula in Mexican schools. Mexican children indicated that U.S. schools were "behind" compared to Mexican schools. That is, that subject matter that is taught in earlier grades in Mexico (e.g., 2nd or 3rd grade) is being taught in advanced grades in the U.S. (e.g., 5th or 6th grade).

"That they [schools] are behind as compared to Mexican schools' [curriculum] but that they have more advantages in getting a career."

—14 year-old boy from Jalisco

This answer provides a distinction between basic education and higher education in the U.S. This boy's answer implies that while the perception is that people can get higher education opportunities in the U.S., there is a realization about the content of the curriculum being "behind" as compared to Mexican curriculum.

Academic Messages were mostly positive among the Mexican group and referred to the following issues:

- The anticipation of lower academic demands and less demanding school workloads as compared to Mexico.
- Opportunities to continue pursuing basic education due to the free tuition and materials that U.S. schools provide for students

Like the Chinese students, Mexican participants also reported hearing about the "easy" American school.

"[That] the schools were easy. They didn't give you work like in Mexico."

—13 year-old girl from Mexico City

Analyzing the parents' responses to the messages about the U.S. prior to immigration (LISA data 1997–1998), positive Academic Messages related how parents heard about educational opportunities in the U.S. for their children. However, they were not very specific in delineating what an educational opportunity meant.

"[I heard the United States were] very beautiful. I believed one could live better in the U.S. The economic and educational situation would be better for my children"

—Elementary-educated parent from Veracruz

"[I heard that] it was a better way of life here [in the United States] and better education for the kids"
    —Trade-school-educated parent from Baja California Norte

"[I thought] that maybe my son would have more opportunity to study, to learn other language, live more comfortably. In Mexico you have to pay for the materials to go to school."
    —Elementary-educated parent from the State of Mexico

This parent was referring to K–12 education, not higher education. Mexico has a free textbook program from first to sixth grades (http://www.sep.gob.mx). However, beginning in 7th grade, parents are responsible for textbooks and materials. While compulsory education is mandatory up to ninth grade, the high cost of education in terms of textbooks and school supplies may prevent some parents from sending their children beyond 6th grade.

LISA 1997–1998 responses indicate that children also had positive expectations regarding better educational opportunities in the U.S.

"[I heard that the United States were] better than in Mexico. That there was better education."
    —13 year-old boy from Mexico City

The Academic Messages in the Mexican sample do not depict a specific perception of the meaning of lower academic demands (e.g., attaining academic excellence), as in the Chinese sample. However, in my ethnographic work in a middle school in California, I have documented how some Mexican children in this sample learn to become less academically engaged due to the less rigorous academic demands and expectations. In 1998, a 14 year-old Mexican boy from Guadalajara, Jalisco explained to me the reason why he did not bring homework on a regular basis:

"I remember the first time I forgot my homework. I was very scared that the teacher would scold me or would give me a bad grade. But not, she did nothing. She told me to bring it later. From that day on, I realized that it is not a big deal if I don't bring my homework. So, I don't worry much about it.

Sometimes, I don't pay attention in class because I already know what they are teaching."

This response indicates that some Mexican children may actually disengage from classroom activities due to the perception that they "already" know what it is taught in American schools. Also, lack of rigorous classroom routines (e.g., negative consequences for not bringing homework) may promote academic disengagement in these children who are used to stricter classroom environments.

Chinese-Mexican Comparison of Academic Messages

Academic Messages Prior to Immigration are prevalent among immigrant children, and they include perceptions of educational opportunities and low academic demands in the U.S. Both Chinese and Mexican children heard about the low academic demands in U.S. schools in terms of how "behind" the curriculum was in the U.S. compared to their country of origin. Both groups also referred to messages regarding less schoolwork in American schools, less homework. However, Chinese children had a very unique reaction to this–educational life could be less stressful in the U.S. and this is perceived as providing the opportunity of achieving academic excellence.

Education in China is characterized as "strict in discipline, with tightly structured long school days, and relying a great deal on lecturing and rote memorization" (Olsen, 1988, p. 21). In a sense, for Chinese participants, the "easy" American school meant that academic excellence in the U.S. could become more attainable and less stressful than it was in China. For the Mexican group, there is a potential danger that the low academic demands and the less advanced curriculum in the U.S. school may actually promote the academic disengagement among immigrant children.

Another distinction between Chinese and Mexican participants was the construction of educational opportunities. Within the Chinese sample, parents and children retold messages about educational opportunities related mostly to higher education opportunities–the opportunity to go to college and the importance of assimilating into a city (e.g., Boston as an educational center) that could provide such opportunities. Because of the highly competitive nature of Chinese education, opportunities for higher education are reserved for a few. According to Dr. Min Zhou from the Department of Sociology at UCLA, Chinese parents stress higher education as a given, as something that must be achieved in this country (personal communication, 12/06/2000). Therefore, education is highly valued not only as a means of social mobility but also as a source of prestige within the community in China as well as in the U.S. In a sense, higher education in the Chinese community becomes a status marker within the community.

For the Mexican parents and children, educational opportunities are valued and important. However, these are constructed in a more vague manner–"children have better opportunities." While for the Chinese, some messages about educational opportunities are articulated in terms of higher education opportunities, this is not really clear among the Mexican messages. For example, the LISA 1997–1998 data show that about seven Chinese parents articulated messages about educational opportunities in the U.S., four of these related to higher education. On the other hand, 12 Mexican parents indicated in the same year issues of educational opportunities in the U.S. However, none of these related to higher education. Most of these messages were very general–(e.g., "there are more opportunities to study"). Further, it seems that when Mexican immigrants heard messages about "educational opportunities" in the U.S. for their children, they referred mostly to K–12 education, the opportunity to send their children to school because of the advantages that schools in the U.S. offer in terms of free tuition, textbooks, and materials. While Chinese do talk about issues related to the fewer "out-of-pocket" expenses in American schools (School Messages section), these messages do not seem to be constructed necessarily as an "opportunity," but rather as a characteristic of American schools. While it is an advantage that American schools provide free tuition, the emphasis that Chinese parents give to educational opportunity is more focused on higher education.

English Only: An Opportunity and a Challenge

English Messages referred to ideas regarding the English language and the process of English language learning. Messages regarding English language learning and proficiency were not dominant in Prior Messages for either group. However, they reveal important issues regarding the perception of English as both an opportunity and a challenge.

Chinese English Messages–A Minority Perspective

Transnational messages regarding the English language were much less prevalent among the Chinese participants than in the Mexican group. Chinese English Messages Prior to Immigration reflected two main themes:

- Lack of English proficiency as a block to academic participation (negative)
- Opportunity to learn English (positive).

Interestingly, while some Chinese children were aware of the difficulties that not knowing enough English would impose on their academic life, they were also alerted of how their academic experiences in China could be an asset in the U.S.

> "[Co-nationals told me that] language arts would be hard for me because you have to learn English, but Math would be easier for me."
> —14 year-old girl from Guangdong

The only positive English Message in the Chinese sample came from a child whose father had a high school education and worked in the restaurant industry:

> [Co-nationals said] "You can learn English. You can earn money and send money to China."
> —13 year-old boy from Guangdong

The LISA 1997–1998 data show that no Chinese parents heard or articulated English Messages Prior to Immigration. Only two female students from Guangdong stated that they heard messages about English language according to LISA 1997–1998 data. These messages were about lack of English proficiency and the fact that English is spoken in this country.

Mexican English Messages: Getting Lost in School

English Messages were a bit more prevalent in the Mexican group than in the Chinese group (Table 5.1). Most of the English Prior Messages in the Mexican sample were negative (Appendix D). English Messages in the Mexican sample were similar to the Chinese responses.

- English is the only language spoken in school
- Lack of English proficiency making children feel "lost" in school.
- Opportunity to learn English

Negative English Messages emphasized how Mexican children heard that they would be "lost" or they would "not understand anything" in school.

> "[Co-nationals told me] that I was not going to understand because they speak English."
> —13 year-old boy from Guerrero

> "[Co-nationals told me] that it was all in English and that almost nobody in school spoke Spanish."
> —13 year-old boy from Zacatecas

Two boys recalled positive messages about English, in terms of the opportunity to learn English.

> "[I heard that] schools were fine. That's why I wanted to come here because I was going to learn and study here, that they teach you well. That I could learn English."
> —13 year-old boy from Guerrero

LISA 1997–1998 data support that some Mexican children received ideas about language barriers prior to immigration:

> "Nobody spoke Spanish, that it [the U.S.] was prettier than in Mexico."
> —15 year-old girl from Jalisco

Mexican parents also reported ideas about the English language–both as an opportunity and as a barrier.

"More education here. There is so much education here. My children are already talking to me in English."
                                                            —Elementary educated parent from Jalisco

"Hard, because of the new language."
                                                            —Elementary educated parent from Jalisco

Chinese–Mexican Comparison of English Messages

In general, transnational messages about English focused on alerting the children to the fact that a different language was spoken in this country. Both groups received messages about English language as both a barrier and an opportunity. For the Chinese children, the emphasis was on the barrier that lack of English proficiency presented for academic participation (e.g., not doing well in language arts classes).

Mexican children were told about the frustrations of the language barrier–feeling lost and not able to understand. However, unlike the Chinese group, these messages did not specifically address the negative effects of limited English proficiency in the ability to understand academic content (e.g., reading). Further, the idea of the English language spoken in the U.S. was also constructed as an opportunity to learn a second language for both groups. However, more children in both groups received more negative messages.

The fact that messages about English are not predominant prior to immigration for either group raises important questions about why English language issues may not necessarily be exchanged among co-nationals. In the Chinese group, the open-economy has opened doors to use English as the major language of business transactions, especially in Hong Kong. In fact, English as a foreign language is often taught in public schools in China from third grade. Therefore, some Chinese students may indeed come with a level of English proficiency. Further, the lack of emphasis on English Messages may indicate that Chinese students take the English language as a given, therefore, there is no need to talk about it. That is, it is understood English is spoken in the

U.S. Therefore, it becomes an obvious fact that may not need to be discussed in the transnational conversations.

For the Mexican group, Mexican children may have fewer opportunities to develop a second language in Mexico. Public schools usually do not offer foreign language courses, especially in elementary grades and rural areas. Therefore, this may prompt the children to construct learning a second language as an opportunity, especially if they articulate this opportunity as not having to pay for it. It is the general perception in Mexico that foreign language learning is available to the economically affluent because it is usually offered in private schools. Foreign language curricula are usually offered in Mexico in the secondary, not elementary grades (http://www.sep.gob.mx). It is also possible that the absence of English Messages in the Mexican sample may be attributed to the fact that most Mexican children assimilate into mostly Latino schools where co-nationals are present. Therefore, the issue of English may not be very salient to this group to socializing within the peer group in school, or within the community. Also, some of these children may be receiving bilingual instruction, enhancing the opportunities to interact in the first language. However, most of the Mexican negative English Messages presented perceptions of feeling lost and this may predispose children to be intimidated about the new school experience.

Peers: Bullies and Gangsters

Another transnational message that is shared across borders prior to immigration is the issue of peers. Peer Messages referred to perceptions of peers (specific student groups) and peer relations.

Chinese Peer Messages: "Ghosts" Disturbing the Classroom

While just a minority of Chinese students heard messages about peers, most of these messages were negative and addressed the following issues:

- Negative peer behaviors that obstruct academic participation (e.g., disturbing the teacher).

- Negative perceptions towards Anglo-American and African American students that characterized these peer groups as bullies.

The interesting fact about negative Peer Messages is that these not only refer to negative peer behaviors toward the Chinese student, but also towards the teacher, making it very hard for the students to follow the content of the class.

"American students are very noisy in class, making the teachers unable to teach."
—17 year-old girl from Guangdong

Some Chinese students also heard negative perceptions about specific student groups, especially White students.

"[I heard that] those little devils are annoying. They are disruptive all the time. They fight all the time. I am talking about White ghosts. I am not talking about Black ghosts."
—13 year-old boy from Hong Kong

Note that Chinese students often used the word "ghost" as a negative adjective for non-Chinese peers.

LISA 1997–1998 data indicate that prior to immigration, Chinese children heard mostly negative messages about peers. Some Chinese children seemed to be exposed to negative perceptions of certain groups in the United States from both interpersonal relations and media messages:

"Black people give others a sense of fear. I learned this from TV in China."
—13 year-old girl from Guangdong

This message is a very powerful testimony of the negative impact of stereotypes projected in American media about African Americans and other minority groups. This girl observed that her negative perceptions of African Americans originated from television images (most likely from American shows and movies) she observed in her country of origin.

It is interesting to note that these children eventually attended diverse schools where these "ghosts" (White and others) would be present. Therefore, it is likely that when children attended these schools, they were already expecting bad behaviors from non-Chinese peers.

Only one child reported positive Peer Messages regarding general positive perceptions about American children as "good kids." No parents reported Peer Messages in LISA 1997–1998 data. A few children reported Peer Messages in 1997–1998 regarding the opportunity to make friends in the U.S.

> "[I would] get to know many foreign friends and play with them."
>
> —17 year-old girl from Guangdong

Mexican Peer Messages: Gangs and Violence

Peer Messages were more prevalent in the Mexican sample. All of the Mexican children heard messages prior to immigration that promoted the following negative perceptions:

- Peers as fighters and bullies
- Peers as gang members
- Peers as racists
- Negative perceptions towards African Americans

The ideas about negative peer behaviors that Mexican children received prior to immigration were not necessarily about playground bullies or classroom disturbance, but to major violent incidents and gang activity.

> "On movies I saw gangs and how they beat others in schools. My dad told me on the phone when I was younger that here in the U.S. schools there were many teachers and many classes. He also told me there were gangs. There are also gangs in Mexico but not so many. Where I lived, there were no gangs."
>
> —13 year-old girl from Sinaloa

This girl's response also emphasizes the role of media in disseminating negative images about diverse student groups in U.S. schools (e.g., there are gangs in U.S. schools).

Another disturbing finding in the Mexican group is that many of these negative images of violence were attributed to African American peers, creating the perpetuation of negative perceptions towards minority groups in the U.S., even before these children have the opportunity to interact with these groups.

> "[I heard] that they [schools] were dangerous when the Blacks fight"
>
> —16 year-old girl from Veracruz

> "[I heard] that they [schools] were bad and that students were racists."
>
> —13 year-old girl from Puebla

Most children who heard messages about gangs were female (8 out of 11 children). LISA 1997–1998 data also support that these negative perceptions toward peer groups were present in parents' responses regarding perceptions of the U.S. For example, one father who actually has lived in the U.S. since he was a teenager expressed:

> "As a teenager, I didn't want to come here and my fears were confirmed. There were fights between Blacks and Latinos."
>
> —Post-elementary-educated parent from San Luis Potosi

This response raises issues regarding the socialization of immigrant children via these transnational messages that promote specific behaviors and expectations regarding inter-racial interactions.

Children's responses in the LISA 1997–1998 data also show some concerns about making friends and socializing with peers, again because of the limited English proficiency.

> "The only things I imagined were that it would be difficult [to live here] because we weren't going to know the language and [I would not] have friends."
>
> —13 year-old girl from Mexico City

Chinese-Mexican Comparison of Peer Messages

One of the striking findings about Peer Messages Prior to Immigration is that the majority of them were negative. In fact, in the Mexican sample, all of them were negative. In the Chinese sample, negative Peer Messages were constructed around classroom behavior and the interference that negative peer behavior causes in the classroom. In the Mexican group, most of these messages were messages regarding the involvement of peers in gang behaviors, rather than classroom disruptions.

Messages about gangs were not even mentioned in the Chinese sample. One of the possible explanations for this is the school context the Chinese children in this sample assimilated in. It is likely that people who shared these messages about school prior to immigration were familiar with the schools that Chinese participants would eventually attend. These schools are predominantly White, with low percentages of English Language Learners, in suburban communities in Boston, where gang involvement may be less predominant than in inner-city schools.

Another possible explanation is what Dr. Min Zhou offered in a personal communication on December 6, 2000. She stated that while Chinese communities may be exposed to gang activity, it is likely that children view this as a community or street problem, not a school problem. Therefore, even if peers are involved in gangs in the school, it is likely that Chinese participants did not construct the issue of gangs as something that "belongs" to the school. Since the question was framed around "school," gang activity may not be included in the cognitive map of "schools" in the Chinese children. This also brings some explanation about the emphasis on academic issues in the transnational messages. That is, it is possible that Chinese children emphasize academic issues when asked questions about school because in their socially constructed cognitive map of school issues, they may include academic messages only, even if they are exposed to non-academic factors in the school context.

Peer Messages also project negative perceptions of inter-racial relations and specific student groups–in this case African American for the Mexican and Whites for the Chinese. These messages may also have a negative effect on children's sense of safety in the school, creating frustration and intimidation in the newcomers. Further, these messages may promote stereotypical views of diverse groups in the U.S., reproducing negative racial attitudes among newcomers.

Finally, both groups referred to media sources of negative perceptions about other minority groups in the U.S. Peer Messages evidenced how the negative effect of stereotypical images about minorities in the U.S. also reach global audiences who eventually construct negative attitudes towards certain minority groups when they immigrate to the United States. It is important to reflect on the "exportation of prejudice" that the U.S. media may be promoting once their productions reach international audiences.

School Messages: The American "Giving" School

School Messages refer to messages regarding issues that pertain to the physical and organizational elements of school life. For example, School Messages included references to the physical look of the school, to the school culture as it is established by institutional measurements such as school rules (not informal interactions), and to services provided by the school including facilities and school programs. They also include organizational characteristics of the schools such as schedules, school routines, and administrative measures.

Chinese School Messages: Better Schedules and Free Tuition

In the Chinese sample, School Messages were the second largest category of messages Prior to Immigration. All of the School Messages were positive. Among these positive messages, the following were salient themes:

- Free services–especially free tuition and school buses
- Less demanding school schedules—shorter days (as compared to China)
- Less restrictive school culture (lack of supervision)
- Perceptions of quality learning activities (e.g., field trips, diverse classes)

The most prevalent message prior to immigration that Chinese children heard was that schools in the U.S. had free tuition:

"Yes, people said schools in the U.S. are free. Tuition in China for primary school is at least $350 each semester. Tuition includes books and materials. No school is free, different schools have different charges."

—13 year-old girl from Guangdong

Another aspect that children heard about schools was in regards to free facilities and services, specifically school buses. Interestingly, no children stated they heard about free meals in schools.

"[Co-nationals] said that in the U.S. you didn't have to go home after school. You don't have to go home for lunch then go back to school again. There are school buses to take you home."

—15 year-old boy from Guangdong

Chinese children also heard positive messages about the organization of schools, especially regarding less rigid schedules and less restrictive supervision from school officials.

"[There is] A lot of freedom. Nobody supervise you. Nobody say you must go to school."

—16 year-old girl from Hong Kong

Again, among Chinese children, the possibility of a less restrictive school environment was perceived as a positive characteristic of American schools. Some children shared that teachers in China talked positively about American schools, including the perception of quality learning activities in the schools in the U.S.:

"Teachers in China told me that schools are very good in the U.S. Students got to school at 8:30 and take off at 2:00 p.m. Not much homework to do. A lot of field trips, clean classrooms."

—16 year-old girl from Guanxi

However, the research assistant that interviewed this girl noted that after her response, the "informant said that all these are lies, she said the school that she goes to is like a haunted house, old and broken."

This notation indicates that for this girl, a level of disappointment regarding the disparity between the reality of the U.S. school and what she heard prior to immigration is present. This girl attends a school that is predominantly African American (57%), with more than 50% of students in free/reduced lunch programs, and about 20% of English language learners. This is a school that has been classified by the Massachusetts Department of Education as having an academic performance that is "critically low" based on the 1999–2000 results on the MCAS (Massachusetts Comprehensive Assessment System), reflecting some vulnerabilities in the school context (e.g., low income community).

Mexican School Messages: Nice Facilities and Free Resources

School Messages were the predominant theme among Mexican participants. Most of the School Messages were positive (Appendix D). The only two negative School Messages received prior to immigration involved two major themes:

- Concerns about documented status to be able to attend school in the U.S.
- Concerns about school staff treating children in a bad manner

Both children had parents who had high school or some college education.

Positive School Messages Prior to Immigration included a variety of topics including:

- High quality of facilities in the U.S. schools
- Free services provided in the U.S. (e.g., lunch)
- Positive perceptions of the U.S. educational system, especially regarding the wide range of classes available in the U.S. (not necessarily extra curricular activities, but standard non-academic classes such as Music and Art).

Most children expressed that they heard that schools in the U.S. were pretty, big, with clean classrooms, nice playgrounds, and so forth, and that they provided free services to students:

"That it was better, it was easier to get books and other resources."

—16 year-old boy from Veracruz

Some children said that they were told of the many classes that were available in American schools.

"Nothing, we didn't talk about school. Oh yeah, that they had computers and different separate classes."

—16 year-old boy from Jalisco

"That middle schools had programs like the private schools in Mexico."

—14 year-old girl from Hidalgo

This last response indicates that there is a perception that the regular curricula in U.S. public schools provide the immigrant children with an education that could be equivalent to a private school in Mexico. As in the case of English as a foreign language, Mexican public schools may not offer some of the classes that are available in the U.S. such as computer labs, music training, or art. Even if they do, many times parents have to provide the materials, instruments, and supplies for their children to participate. Again, the idea that schools in the U.S. can provide services, materials, and classes that can only be available in private schools, can be an important incentive for parents to send their children to U.S. schools. That is, schools in the U.S. provide an opportunity for obtaining a better education without as many out-of-pocket expenses as could be the case in Mexico.

Looking at the LISA 1997–1998 data, School Messages referred to messages about the physical characteristics of the schools–either big or nice. Parents stated they heard about the free tuition and materials U.S. schools provide for children. Some parents spoke of these "free services" in terms of schools "caring for their children." In fact the LISA data from 1997–1998 show that some Mexican parents spoke of how American schools "take care of children in the U.S."

"I do like it [school]. [Schools] care about feeding our children. They know if we don't have resources, then they provide for the children. They have transportation."
                                    —Elementary-educated parent from Jalisco

In other words, some Mexican parents perceive the positive contribution of American schools in terms of the services and materials that they provide for their children, alleviating the parents' burden of the cost of their children's education.

Chinese-Mexican Comparison of School Messages

School Messages were predominant in both groups. Both groups emphasized the free services and materials offered in U.S. schools and the availability of diverse school activities and classes. This translates into the consideration of lower cost of education in the U.S. as compared to China or Mexico. However, while the Chinese messages emphasized tuition and buses, the Mexican messages emphasized free meals and school materials (e.g., books).

Another difference is that the Chinese attention focused mostly on organizational elements of the school (e.g., schedules) and still emphasized the less restrictive and demanding nature of the American school, especially regarding less demanding schedules. This indicates the consistent view of U.S. schools as much less restrictive and demanding than Chinese schools, not only in terms of academic demands, but also school climate (less supervision and more individual freedom).

School Messages are an important consideration in terms of understanding the construction of school influence in the lives of immigrants. For both Chinese and Mexican students, the services provided by the school represent a considerable help for some parents who may not afford tuition, materials, nor even meals. In my ethnographic experience with some of the Mexican children, it is clear that for some of these families, especially those with a large number of family members, school provides many services (e.g., meals, materials) that represent a considerable assistance to the limited budget that many immigrants live on.

If we look at the parent educational data for both groups, all of the children who received School Messages regarding free services and materials had parents with less than some post-elementary education. Only one Chinese girl whose parents have professional degrees mentioned she heard that tuition was free. But this girl did not mention other "free" services and materials that the American school provided. If we make the connection between level of education and socioeconomic status, we may infer that the children who received School Messages about school resources may come from families with limited resources. Therefore, the school becomes an institution that not only provides academic opportunities, but in a sense, that also provides economic support for these immigrant families. This leads us to reconsider how immigrant parents view schools, not only in terms of academic performance, but also in terms of social services that schools may provide, which in turn may translate into the alleviation of some economic burdens on families. That is, for some immigrant parents who have limited income, school quality may be constructed not necessarily in terms of "academic quality," but in terms of how parents perceive school as "taking care of their children" beyond academic needs. This "taking care" may take the form of providing lunch or medical services (e.g., having a school nurse), clothes (clothes banks). Given the immediate economic needs of some families, parents may have a positive perception of American schools, even those that are academically weak, if the parents perceive that the school is "taking care of their children" in other capacities (e.g., providing free lunch).

Teacher Messages: Not Much to Talk About

Teacher Messages Prior to Immigration represented a minority for both samples (Table 5.1). Teacher Messages referred to perceptions of teacher's quality, personality, and student-teacher relationships.

Chinese Teacher Messages: Nice and Less Restrictive Teachers

Prior to immigration, Chinese children received some messages about teacher behaviors and performance. All of these messages were positive and referred to the following:

- Teachers in the U.S. having less strict discipline styles, including no corporal punishment
- Teachers in the U.S. having nicer personalities.

The issue of having a less restrictive and disciplinary classroom atmosphere was the focus of Teacher Messages Prior to Immigration among the Chinese children, echoing the general perceptions that U.S. schools are less demanding and restrictive:

> "Yes. I heard about things related to learning in the class. For example, they told me that in the class, it was not as restrained as it was in Hong Kong. Here you had more freedom. In other words, you could do whatever you wanted to do and the teachers would not mind about it."
>
> —16 year-old girl from Hong Kong

> "Nothing, they just said it was very comfortable here. That is, you have no homework to do, teachers won't scold you and won't beat you up."
>
> —16 year-old girl from Fujian

> "Teachers here in the U.S. don't scold students. They don't beat students up."
>
> —17 year-old girl from Fujian

In accord with the Academic Messages about an easier, less demanding curriculum, Chinese students seem to have a hopeful and optimistic view of coming to American schools and finding a nicer, less demanding, and less strict teacher. These children appreciate the fact that corporal punishment is not allowed in American schools.

Mexican Teacher Messages: Mixed Perceptions of Teachers

Unlike the Chinese children, Mexican children received both positive and negative messages about teachers in the U.S. Teacher Messages revealed the following views:

- Teachers are mean and strict (negative)
- Supportive teachers (positive)
- Lack of corporal punishment (positive)

The children who received negative messages about U.S. teachers referred to teachers as "mean" and "stricter" than in Mexico.

"That teachers were mean."
—12 year-old girl from the State of Mexico

But other Mexican children heard messages about how teachers in the U.S. help students:

"That [schools] were very good that teachers helped students."
—13 year-old boy from Michoacan

The lack of corporal punishment in U.S. schools was mentioned in these transnational messages about teachers:

"My dad also told me that unlike in Mexico where sometimes teachers hit you, here they don't hit you because here in the U.S. if the teacher hits you it is a crime."
—13 year-old girl from Sinaloa

Chinese–Mexican comparison of Teacher Messages

Teacher Messages in the Mexican and Chinese group accounted for just a minority of the messages. Transnational messages Prior to Immigration about teachers reflect mostly a positive perception of the teacher in the U.S., especially in relation to discipline. This is more emphasized in the Chinese sample, where children recalled hearing messages about no corporal punishment, and about teachers creating a more relaxing atmosphere due to a less restrictive disciplinary style. Chinese children used words such as "more relaxed" and "comfortable" when referring to the classroom atmosphere. Again, this reflects some difference in the educational systems in the U.S. and in China. While Teacher Messages were less prevalent in the Mexican example, these also reflected issues of no corporal punishment, but some children stated they heard messages regarding negative perceptions of American teachers' personality (e.g., teachers are mean).

It is also interesting that in both groups, most of the children who received Teacher Messages Prior to Immigration were females. This may raise questions regarding the differences between gender groups in the relationships with teachers and the children's socialization within schools. For example, do girls tend to focus on affective aspects in school?

SOURCES OF MESSAGES

Besides the content of the transnational messages, I was also interested in identifying the sources of these messages. The data on sources of messages clearly reveal the transnational interaction of immigrant children in kinship and other interpersonal groups that establish social links between their respective countries of origin and the U.S. The distribution of sources of messages for those students who received transnational messages prior to immigration is presented in Table 5.2.

Table 5.2.
Sources of Messages about U.S. Schools Prior to Immigration

Sources of Messages	Chinese		Mexican	
	N	%	N	%
Interpersonal	36	90%	45	94%
Media	4	10%	3	6%
Total	40	100%	48	100%

For both groups, the interpersonal connections in the country of origin and the U.S. as well as the interaction with transnational migrants (people who come back and forth between the country of origin and the U.S.) are the major source of information about U.S. schools. Over 90% of the children (both Chinese and Mexican) who heard information about the U.S. schools prior to immigration received these messages from interpersonal communications. Most of these interpersonal communications came from relatives and acquaintances that lived either in the U.S. or in their country of origin, but had family or business connections in the U.S.

LISA 1997–1998 data show responses from parents and their children about their images of the U.S. when they lived in their country of origin. Tables 5.3 and 5.4 depict the distribution of these sources of messages about the U.S. for parents and children who reported transnational messages prior to immigration

Table 5.3.
Parents' Sources of Messages about U.S. Prior to Immigration

Source of Messages	Chinese		Mexican	
	N	%	N	%
Interpersonal	40	48%	60	70%
Imagination	0	0%	1	1%
Media	38	46%	18	21%
Visits to U.S.	5	6%	7	8%
Total	83	100%	86	100%

Table 5.4.
Students' Sources of Messages about U.S. Prior to Immigration

Source of Messages	Chinese		Mexican	
	N	%	N	%
Interpersonal	49	51%	53	58%
Imagination	4	4%	6	7%
Media	39	41%	32	35%
Visits to U.S.	4	4%	0	0%
Total	96	100%	91	100%

The LISA 1997–1998 data show that a majority of parents and children did hear things about the U.S. prior to immigration. Interpersonal relations were also the main source of transnational messages for children and parents according to LISA 1997–1998 data. However, while media were hardly the source of messages about American schools, this was not so regarding messages about the U.S. in general, especially for the Chinese participants (Tables 5.3. and 5.4).

Interpersonal Sources

Interpersonal relations are the main source of messages about U.S. schools for the Chinese children in this study. By interpersonal relations I refer to any contact, either personal or via remote communication (e.g., phone, letter) with people. More than half of the students who reported interpersonal sources stated they heard these messages from their relatives. However most of these relatives were either transnational migrants(coming back and forth from the U.S. to China) or permanent residents in the U.S.

> "When my relatives in the U.S. returned to China and talked about schools in the U.S."
>
> —17 year-old girl from Fujian

The relatives mentioned as sources of messages were mostly uncles, aunts, and cousins who already lived in the U.S. or have visited the U.S. An interesting source of messages about U.S. schools for Chinese children was their teachers and their peers in the Chinese school. Chinese children stated that many peers in Chinese schools talked about what their parents (who had lived in the U.S.) had told them about the U.S.

The LISA 1997–1998 data show that interpersonal relations were also the main source of messages about the U.S. prior to immigration. However, for the Chinese parents, most messages came from acquaintances and relatives living in the U.S. For students, the main sources of messages about U.S. prior to immigration were both relatives and parents.

The Mexican group showed a very similar distribution to the Chinese sources of messages. Again, interpersonal relations were the main sources of messages, mostly from relatives. The relatives included aunts, uncles, cousins, and grandparents. These relatives were either transnational migrants or U.S. residents. An interesting source of messages was friends. Unlike the Chinese, whose friends were mostly students in China whose parents were in the U.S., most of the Mexican friends who shared messages about U.S. schools were transnational. They lived in the U.S. and came back to Mexico to visit. This must be related to the physical proximity of Mexico to the U.S. in comparison to China. As with the Chinese sample, parents were not a significant source of messages about school.

Media Sources

In general, a minority of children learned about the U.S. school via media messages. Chinese students learned about the U.S. schools from television, mostly news shows. Mexican students learned about U.S. schools from films and news.

While media were not a significant source of messages about U.S. schools, they were a significant source of General Messages about the U.S. Most Chinese parents received messages about the U.S. from print media (newspapers and magazine) and from television. For the Chinese students, most of the media images about the U.S. came from television. Most media messages for the Mexican parents came from television and movies, not print media. For the Mexican children, most messages about the U.S. also came from television.

One of the interesting distinctions about the media messages across the two groups is that an important source for the Chinese parents was print media, suggesting a higher rate of literacy and higher levels of education (high school education and college educated).

REACTION TO PRIOR MESSAGES

In this study, I was interested not only in investigating whether a flow of information about U.S. schools in transnational spaces existed, but also in the reaction of the children to these transnational messages. Participant children were asked about their reaction to the information they had about U.S. schools prior to immigration. They were asked about their thoughts and feelings after they heard the transnational messages and they knew that they would probably attend an American school once they immigrated to the U.S. Table 5.5 depicts the distribution of the reaction to the Prior Messages.

Most children, both Mexican and Chinese, stated some kind of reaction to the message, 58% for the Chinese group (40), and 62% for the Mexican group (48). While the percentages are similar from group to group, looking a bit deeper into the natures of the reactions can uncover some interesting findings.

Table 5.5.
Reaction to Messages Prior to Immigration

Source of Messages	Chinese		Mexican	
	N	**%**	**N**	**%**
Mixed	1	1%	3	3%
Negative	17	20%	20	23%
Neutral	8	10%	7	8%
Positive	18	22%	22	26%
Strategic	4	5%	2	2%
No reaction	35	42%	32	38%
Total	83	100%	86	100%

Chinese Reactions

Chinese reactions to messages prior to immigration were almost equally distributed between negative and positive reactions (Table 5.5). Overall, more Chinese girls stated some kind of reaction to the message than boys did (32 girls and 15 boys). Some children had mixed or neutral reactions. Negative Chinese reactions refer to the following issues:

- Concerns about limited English proficiency
- Concerns about cultural differences in the U.S.

Both issues were constructed in terms of limitations to participation in academic and social contexts in the U.S.

"A little bit scared. Because I don't know English and I don't know people here"
                                         —13 year-old girl from Guangdong

"I was afraid that my English was not good enough."
                                         —15 year-old boy from Hong Kong

This is a surprising finding because while only a few children actually heard messages about English (3), more children (7) stated negative reactions about English proficiency. This indicates that while English Messages were not articulated, Chinese children were indeed concerned about English proficiency. These concerns were about the English proficient in relation to socialization and academic participation issues. For example, a Chinese girl stated that while she was not concerned prior to immigration, she became concerned about the English language barrier and her ability to communicate in social and academic contexts:

> "I felt nothing. I worried about it after I moved here because I was afraid my English was not good enough to talk to teachers and to fit in and make friends with White boys and girls."
>
> —12 year-old girl from Hong Kong

An interesting note is that this girl from Hong Kong constructs the need for English proficiency as an element to socialize with Anglo-Americans, not other English-speaking groups. Other children echoed their concern about their limited English language proficiency.

> "I was afraid that my English was not good enough."
>
> —15 year-old boy from Hong Kong

> "I wanted to come to school here but I was scared because I was afraid I would not speak English."
>
> —15 year-old girl from Guangdong

It is interesting that the children from Hong Kong stated concerns about their "English [proficiency] not being good enough," indicating some level of prior knowledge of the English language. The other children, who stated being concerned about "not knowing English," came from Guangdong.

Chinese children also reported some feelings about assimilation and adaptation to the United States. Some children expressed some concern about inter-cultural interactions and adaptation to a new life:

"Very different. I didn't know how to get adjusted to life here. I didn't know how to treat people who are [of] different ethnicity and physically [different]."

—16 year-old girl from Guangdong

These findings suggest awareness in the Chinese immigrant children about cross-cultural differences and how these may interfere with their participation in the new locality in the United States. However, for some students, these cultural differences and the opportunity to experience different educational systems were constructed as positive:

"I felt it is a good thing because I can experience other educational systems. I felt that I had to polish my English in order to succeed"

—13 year-old boy from Guangdong

Note how this child positions English language proficiency as a "requirement" for success.

Positive reactions were also more present in girls than in boys. Chinese children who reported positive reactions to messages about school prior to immigration referred to optimistic view towards:

- The less demanding work in the U.S. school
- The academic opportunities available to ensure participation in higher education

These reactions carried an important notion about the opportunity to succeed in school without the stress and the hard work that was required in China to succeed in school.

"Pretty happy because everybody said it was easy to get good grades."

—16 year-old boy from Beijing

"I felt that I was going to succeed very easily."

—15 year-old girl from Hubei

In order words, Chinese children in this sample shared that they thought that academic success in the U.S. was more attainable than in China.

Mexican Reactions

Mexican reactions were balanced in terms of gender–29 boys and 25 girls stated some kind of reaction to Prior Messages. The Mexican participants had an almost equal proportion of positive (26%, 22) and negative reactions (23%, 20) to messages prior to immigration. Mexican children who had negative reactions to the Prior Messages stated concerns about:

- Limited English proficiency
- Specific ethnic groups in the U.S. who have been negatively perceived within the co-national group
- Gangs and violence in the school

Lack of English proficiency created a sense of concern for the Mexican children. A boy expressed that the lack of English proficiency would motivate him to hang out with co-nationals:

"[I felt] that I was not going to understand and that I thought that those who would not understand me, they would have to manage to understand me. I would hang out with those that speak Spanish."

—14 year-old boy from Jalisco

Some students expressed concern with specific ethnic groups:

"I felt afraid, concerned about the Blacks."

—14 year-old boy from Jalisco

However, most girls, especially younger girls, had reactions about gangs and violence:

"Scared, knowing that my school would have gangs"

—12 year-old girl from Baja California Norte

"Fear, if a gang was going to get me, I wouldn't like to become like them."

—12 y ear old girl from Guanajuato

"I was afraid of coming here. Because the schools were violent, I was told"

—13 year-old girl from Colima

One interesting finding is that more Mexican than Chinese children stated disappointment upon arrival:

"Excited. I felt deceived when I arrived."

—16 year-old boy from Jalisco

"Real excited. But when I got here, I realized it is a piece of junk."

—17 year-old boy from Colima

It is important to contextualize this disappointment in terms of the specific school context these children assimilate into. For example, these two boys attended a school that had been categorized as having several incidents of violence. During the past year, some acts of violence such as rapes and gang-related stabbing incidents were reported in this school. Both boys came from families that have been involved in their children's education, and their teachers have regarded both boys as high achievers. It seems that these children had higher expectations about their life in American schools and were disappointed when they entered the system. The 1997–1998, LISA data show that the boy from Jalisco stated that he heard that "everything was perfect" in American schools. The boy from Colima, in his answer to the question "what did you hear about American schools?" expressed a level of disappointment:

"[I heard that] they [schools] were the best. Nothing to compare them to. But you can compare it to a jail."

Positive reactions to transnational messages prior to immigration included optimistic views about:

- The academic quality of U.S. schools
- Expectations of obtaining a better education in the U.S.
- The opportunity of learning English.

The following quote evidenced the optimistic view of Mexican children about a better life in the U.S.

"Very good. That I was going to learn English, to make something of my future."
— 12 year-old boy from Jalisco

Mexican positive reactions show an optimistic outlook to a new life in the United States. Most children expressed enthusiasm about being able to go to school and use education as a means to "make it in life." However, most of the responses in the Mexican sample were very general, just expressing excitement, happiness, or motivation to go to the United States.

More Mexican males than females stated positive reactions to messages prior to immigration. These boys had parents with low educational backgrounds (less than high school). Most came from a region (Jalisco) that has been documented as a major source of Mexican immigration to the U.S. (Cornelius & Bustamante, 1989). This profile raises issues about the socialization of youth who live in transnational social spaces. It would be interesting to research further the role of gender in the socialization of immigrants. Do Mexican boys tend to be socialized in a way that promotes positive expectations about life in the United States? Are these young males being socialized to aspire to immigration as a potential way of succeeding in life? My question emerges from the fact that some of these boys who articulated these messages spoke of "making a life" in the U.S., as if success was not a possibility in their country of origin. Further, another interesting fact is that all of these children felt motivated to go to the United States as a result of the Message Prior to Immigration. All of these boys gave answers like "I wanted to come" as a reaction to the message.

In conclusion, it is important to reflect on the kinds of messages the children receive prior to immigration, the sources of these messages, and the reaction that these messages provoke in children, especially what the immigrant children viewed as salient themes about American schools. First, it is important to investigate the role of non-parental sources of messages, since these seem to be the primary source of messages about the U.S. schools. Who are these people? What kind of educational experiences do they have? Can they provide models of educational paths for the newcomers?

Second, it is important to evaluate the match between the message and the reaction to the message. Prior Messages to the Chinese often spoke of a less stressful academic environment and this elicited optimism in this group about their academic success in the U.S. However, while not articulated in the Prior Messages, more Chinese children reported negative reactions that revealed concerns about their English proficiency. Likewise, Mexican children received more messages about the school in general; however, they reacted mostly to the English and violence messages.

Third, the analysis revealed some interesting gender issues regarding the socialization of "immigrants" along gender lines. For Mexican girls, issues regarding their safety in school were more salient. For boys, a positive reaction to a so-called "immigrant's dream" of success and a better life was present. However, this reaction was very general, without any specific reference to how this success would be attained—other than via education and learning English.

CHAPTER 6

Welcoming Messages
Advice and Information for the Newcomer

Before addressing the different types of messages that immigrant children received upon arrival to the U.S. school, from their co-nationals in the school, I will address the issue of the presence of the co-national in the school. For the purpose of this study, I define a co-national as an individual who is an immigrant from the same country of origin as the student.

CO-NATIONALS IN SCHOOLS: A SOURCE OF MESSAGES

As noted in chapter 3, immigrant students socialize with their co-nationals in the U.S. school as a source of support and familiarity in the unfamiliar school context (Olson, 1997). Before I could establish any influence from the co-nationals in the school experiences of the children in this study, I wanted to establish the extent of the presence of the co-nationals in the school and the extent to which the participants choose to interact with co-nationals. The school ethnicity profiles (Appendix B) show that most of the Mexican children in the sample (59%, 46) attended schools that have a strong Latino presence, but this does not necessarily mean that these Latinos are co-nationals (immigrant children from Mexico). However, this indicates that the Mexican children in this sample have more exposure to co-ethnic peers (children of Latino background) than Chinese children do. Most of the Chinese children (53%, 39) in this sample attended predominantly White schools, indicating that the presence of co-nationals was more limited for these children.

In order to assess if children socialized with the co-nationals in the school (regardless of whether they were the predominant group in school), I used LISA 1998–2000 data regarding children's choice of peers. On an annual basis, children were asked where would they say most of their friends were from and what ethnic group would they say most of their friends belong to. Because children identified several friends, the sample sizes of the responses to these questions do not correspond to the overall Chinese (n=74) and Mexican (n=78) sample sizes. The categories for peer choice (generated from the data) included the following:

- Americans—student did not specify ethnic or racial background of their "American" peers
- Co-ethnics—individuals who shared the ethnic or racial background of the student (e.g., Asian, Latinos, Hispanics) but students did not indicate these peers were from their country of origin
- Co-nationals—individuals born in the participant's country of origin
- U.S.-Born Co-nationals—individuals born in the U.S., whose parents were born in the participant's country of origin
- Non–co-ethnic immigrants: Students born outside the U.S. but who did not share the ethnic or racial background of the participant (e.g., Russian immigrants)
- U.S. racial/ethnic groups: Asian, African American, Latinos, White (Asian and Latino groups' responses were incorporated into the co-ethnic counts for the Chinese and Mexican group respectively).

The LISA 1998–2000 data indicate that through time, most Chinese and Mexican participants socialized with other co-nationals (over 60%), indicating the potential creation of a transnational social space. Table 6.1 shows longitudinal data on the choice of peers of the participants from 1998–2000. For the sake of ease, only percentages are reported in Peer Tables.

While for both groups of students the co-national group represented the majority of their friends, Chinese students showed higher percentages of interaction with groups other than co-nationals and co-ethnics than Mexican students did. Further, most of the Mexican participants had friends from the same ethnic background—co-nationals, co-ethnic peers, and U.S. co-nationals. Chinese participants had higher percentages of American friends than of co-ethnic or U.S.-born co-national groups.

Table 6.1
Longitudinal LISA Data on Students' Peer Choice

Peer Choice	Chinese			Mexican		
	1998 N=91	1999 N=85	2000 N=97	1998 N=103	1999 N=96	2000 N=100
Americans not specified	14%	4%	13%	7%	2%	3%
Co-ethnic peers	1%	7%	5%	11%	16%	23%
Co-nationals	63%	60%	58%	60%	63%	59%
No answer	3%	5%	12%	3%	3%	4%
Asian	0%	0%	0%	1%	1%	4%
African-Americans	2%	7%	1%	0%	2%	1%
Latino	3%	2%	1%	0%	0%	0%
U.S.-born co-national	9%	9%	4%	16%	10%	6%
White	4%	5%	4%	1%	2%	0%
Non–co-ethnic immigrant	1%	1%	2%	1%	1%	0%

Of course, peer choice is influenced by the ethnic composition of schools the children attend. Table 6.2 shows the relationship between peer choice and school ethnic composition in 1999–2000 school year, the year when the interview for this study took place. The table shows the predominant ethnic group in the schools where children attended according to the peer choice group. For example, it indicates that most children that had American friends attended schools where the predominant group was Whites.

Table 6.2 shows that Chinese children do make friends with co-nationals even if they are not the predominant group. In fact, for those Chinese children who stated they made friends with co-nationals in

1999–2000, only 9% (5) attend schools where the predominant group is Asian.

Table 6.2.
Predominant Ethnic Group in Schools in Relation to Peer Choice

Peer Choice	Chinese	Mexican
	Predominant Ethnic Group in School	Predominant Ethnic Group in School
Americans not specified	White	Latino and White
Co-ethnic peers	Asian, African American, White, or Diverse	Latino and White
Co-nationals	White	Latino
Asian	(See co-ethnic)	Latino and White
African-Americans	White	Latino
Latino	White	(See co-ethnic)
U.S.-born co-national	Asian	Latino
White	White	N/A
Non–co-ethnic immigrant	White	N/A

In general, regardless of the predominant ethnic group, most Mexican children also make friends with co-nationals, co-ethnic peers, or U.S.-born co-nationals. However, we need to keep in mind that 59% (46) of Mexican students attend schools where Latinos are the predominant group. In the Mexican sample, when the predominant group in the school is other than Latino, Mexican children still tend to socialize with co-nationals. However, the opposite is also found—most children who socialize outside the Latino group attend mostly Latino schools.

Changes over time can be triggered by changes in schools (e.g., students leaving the elementary school and entering middle school). However, the descriptive statistics overall indicate that the co-national group is by far the most important group that provides peer interactions and friendship to the immigrant children in this study. I wanted to look closer at the profile of the children who associated with different kinds of groups. One of the most interesting patterns was in gender differences across groups. Table 6.3 shows the distribution of peer choice in 1999–2000 by gender groups.

Table 6.3.
Peer Choice by Gender Groups

Peer Group	Chinese Girls N=56	Chinese Boys N=49	Mexican Girls N=40	Mexican Boys N=56
Americans not specified	7%	21%	4%	2%
Co-ethnics	7%	5%	20%	26%
Co-nationals	57%	51%	59%	58%
Asian	0%	0%	4%	4%
Blacks	0%	2%	2%	0%
Latino	4%	0%	0%	0%
Not specified	7%	0%	0%	0%
U.S.-born co-nationals	7%	2%	9%	5%
White	2%	7%	0%	0%
Non-co-ethnic immigrants	2%	2%	0%	0%
No answer	7%	10%	2%	5%
Total	100%	100%	100%	100%

The distribution by gender shows that more Chinese boys tended to socialize outside the co-national, co-ethnic, and U.S.-born co-national groups. Also, girls showed higher percentages of co-national, co-ethnic, and U.S.-born co-national peer choices than the boys did. In the Mexican sample, the opposite pattern occurs. While very small percentages of boys and girls socialized outside the Latino group, more Mexican girls than boys socialized with Americans and African Americans. A deep analysis of gender issues is beyond the scope of this book. However, these findings raise important issues about gender roles and perhaps differences regarding the instrumentality of the association with people outside the ethnic groups across these two immigrant groups—Mexican and Chinese.

Age factors also seemed to influence peer choice. Table 6.4 shows the distribution of peer choice among different age groups.

Table 6.4.
Peer Choice Distribution by Age Groups

Peer Choice	11–12 year-olds		13–14 year-olds		15–16 year-olds		17–18 year-olds	
	Chinese N=16	Mexican N=23	Chinese N=31	Mexican N=41	Chinese N=41	Mexican N=26	Chinese N=13	Mexican N=3
Americans(n/s)	7%	4%	19%	2%	0%	4%	0%	0%
Co-ethnics	7%	20%	7%	26%	5%	24%	9%	25%
Co-nationals	58%	52%	52%	58%	56%	64%	73%	50%
Asian	0%	4%	0%	5%	0%	4%	0%	0%
Blacks	0%	0%	0%	2%	7%	0%	0%	0%
Latino	0%	0%	0%	0%	2%	0%	0%	0%
Not specified	0%	0%	7%	0%	0%	0%	9%	0%
U.S.-born (c/n)	21%	12%	0%	5%	5%	0%	0%	25%
White	0%	0%	4%	0%	15%	0%	0%	0%
Non–co-ethnic	7%	0%	0%	0%	5%	0%	0%	0%
No answer	0%	8%	11%	2%	5%	4%	9%	0%
TOTAL	100%	100%	100%	100%	100%	100%	100%	100%

n/s: not specified; c/n: co-nationals

The distribution shows that across all age groups, Chinese students socialize with co-nationals, but this is especially true for older children (17 and older). In terms of socialization patterns outside the co-national group, younger Chinese children (11–12) socialize with U.S.-born co-nationals, while older children branch out to American peers, specifically White. The Mexican socialization patterns show that across all age groups, the co-national peers are a significant peer group. For those children who socialize outside the co-national group, the percentages are more or less constant across all age groups for children who socialized with co-ethnic and American groups. Older children (17 and older) tend to socialize more with U.S.-born co-nationals.

In terms of parent education, some interesting patterns emerged that reflect the relationships between parent education, type of school, and peer choice. For example, more than half of the Chinese children who socialized with Americans had fathers and mothers with college or graduate degrees. This pattern of high parent education level was also found in the Chinese children who made friends with White children. All of the children that socialized with Whites had fathers with graduate/professional degrees and 50% had mothers with graduate/professional degrees. For other categories of peer choice, the distribution of parent education was similar to the overall pattern in the general Chinese sample (mostly some-post elementary). A reason for this concentration of highly educated parents among children who socialize with White Americans may be related to the fact that predominantly White schools are located in more privileged areas of Boston. For example, the schools in this sample with a White population of 90% and higher have a less than 3% student population in free/reduced programs.

Another pattern regarding peer choice among Chinese students and their preference to make friends with Americans seems to be linked to the preoccupation of assimilation among the Chinese group, and some prejudice issues against minority groups. A Chinese boy explained his preference to make friends with White Americans:

"Because the whites, anyway, they are better than the blacks. And the Americans are very polite and they are quite nice. You should know some Whites and you have to adjust yourself to the Whites. You have to learn more English."
—15 year-old from Hong Kong

Discussing this phenomenon with the Chinese research assistants in the LISA project, several research assistants indicated that it is the parents, especially those parents that are highly educated who encourage their children to socialize with White Americans as a way to acculturate and learn the "American ways." A Chinese father expressed the importance of getting exposure to society as a way to advance in the United States:

"Then they [children] also should pay attention to activities in
the society. They can't know things of American society by
staying home alone. They [children] need to come out to
communicate with others. This will help them a lot."
                                    —High School graduate parent from Hong Kong

This raises interesting questions about the construction of America
as a White country, not a diverse country in the minds of the Chinese
immigrants. Do Chinese immigrant have preconceived notions about
the White population in the United States in terms of the distribution of
power? Is it the White, middle-class, mainstream model that they try to
assimilate into? On the other hand, it would be interesting to investigate
the perceptions of White American peers towards Chinese students.
That is, Chinese seek to socialize with White Americans, but are White
Americans more likely to accept Chinese as friends than peers from
other groups?

Another interesting distinction among groups is the perception of
parents about who their children's friends are. Table 6.5 shows the
distribution of parents' responses regarding their children's friends.

Table 6.5.
Parents' Perception of Students' Peers

Peer Choice	Chinese (N=97)	Mexican (N=100)
Americans	3%	1%
Co-ethnic peers	1%	13%
Co-nationals	59%	60%
Asian	0%	3%
Blacks	6%	0%
Latino	2%	2%
U.S.-born co-national	· 13%	17%
White	11%	1%
Non–co-ethnic immigrant	2%	1%
No answer	3%	2%
Total	100%	100%

In 1997–1998, the LISA study asked parents where they thought most of their children's friends were from. Parents were also asked to which ethnic background their children's friends belonged. Again, the co-national group represents the majority.

Most Mexican and Chinese parents thought that their children socialized with co-nationals in the school. Mexican parents, like their children, indicated that their children socialized mostly with co-ethnic peers or U.S.-born co-nationals. On the other hand, the two other major groups (other than co-national) that Chinese parents indicated that they believed their children socialized with were U.S.-born co-nationals and White Americans.

Peer choice is often not only a factor of student preference, but also of school placement, parent influence, and choices made by their peers. Because the majority of the immigrant children in this sample (approximately 60% of children in each group) do socialize with their co-nationals in the school, I think it is important to inquire about what messages of reception the co-national in the school can provide to the newcomer.

WELCOMING MESSAGES: LEARNING ABOUT SCHOOLS

The co-national group is a significant peer group to which the immigrant children come to contact in the school, and many of them socialize with co-nationals as they establish friendships. Children in the study were asked if these co-nationals in the school shared information about U.S. schools with them when they first arrived to an American school and found co-nationals in the school. I call these messages Welcoming Messages. Table 6.6 shows the distribution of Welcoming Messages.

Table 6.6 shows that in fact, the co-national in the school was not a significant source of messages for the Chinese children upon entry, only 38% (37) received Welcoming Messages from co-nationals in the school. However, it was more significant for the Mexican children—78% (87) received messages from co-nationals in the school. Note that in Welcoming Messages, a new category emerged—Social. Social Messages refer to ideas regarding social conditions for immigrants in the U.S. (e.g., discrimination and racism) that did not specifically address social interactions between teachers and peers.

Table 6.6. Welcoming Messages about U.S. Schools from Co-nationals at the School (Upon entry to U.S. schools)

Types of Messages	Chinese		Mexican	
	N	%	N	%
Academic	11	12%	24	21%
English	1	1%	4	4%
General	3	3%	14	12%
Peers	4	4%	17	15%
School	8	9%	16	14%
Social	4	4%	4	4%
Teachers	6	6%	9	8%
No co-nationals in school	8	8%	0	0%
No School Message	50	53%	26	22%
Total	95	100%	114	100%

For the Chinese group, Academic Messages continued being the most dominant topic of transnational messages upon entry to the U.S. (as they were prior to immigration). No other category was dominant in Welcoming Messages for the Chinese students. In the Mexican group, Academic Messages became the dominant category (School Messages were the dominant category for Mexican Messages prior to immigration). However, School Messages and Peer Messages were also important categories in Welcoming Messages.

An interesting pattern is that the concentration of messages from co-nationals indeed reflects the distribution of messages prior to immigration—predominantly Academic Messages for the Chinese group and predominantly School Messages for the Mexican group, indicating some consistency over time. However, as I discuss later, even though the top categories remained the same (comparing Prior and Welcoming Messages), the nature of these messages changed. Let us explore some of these issues.

Academic Messages: Advice on Classroom Behaviors

As in Prior Messages, Welcoming Messages emphasized the lower academic demands that American schools place on students compared to the schools in the country of origin (e.g., China and Mexico). However, the perceptions of these lower academic demands were somehow different between the two groups.

Chinese Academic Messages: Learning to Succeed in the U.S. School

Academic Messages received from co-national peers represented only 12% (11) of the messages. While not a large proportion, it still places Academic Messages as the top category among the Chinese sample. This may be explained by the fact that Prior Messages were mostly received from adult relatives, who may place academic issues as more relevant to communicate to the immigrant children than the co-national peers place them.

Negative messages usually referred to:

- Apathy towards school issues
- Academic difficulty in U.S. schools.

For example, Chinese children were told by their co-nationals that school was "hard" or "not worthy of be talked about." However, most Academic Messages were indeed positive. Positive Academic Messages were given in the form of academic advice—what to do to achieve academically. This advice included information about:

- How to behave in the classroom and classroom routines
- Importance of following teacher's instructions
- Pursuing higher education (college).

Chinese students were told specific ways to navigate the classroom setting for academic participation. Many of these Academic Messages consisted of behavioral advice regarding how to behave in class and how to follow teacher's instructions. These messages were constructed around "classroom behavior," not general behavior in the school context:

"[Co-nationals told me] that you have to write your name and date on homework, otherwise you will be punished by the teacher. You have to raise your hand and ask for permission before leaving your seat. Otherwise, you will be punished, writing lines. Fail to do your homework you get punished too."

—11 year-old girl from Guangdong

While these messages may sound like somehow exaggerated perceptions of classroom routines (consider the age of the child), the importance of the message is in the degree of detail that the peers used to share with their peers.

Some children expressed that they shared information about college.

"Yes, about going to college. Nothing else, particularly about American schools."

—15 year-old boy from Hong Kong

One interesting distinction of the Welcoming Message is that the "less demanding schoolwork" perception is not emphasized as much as it was in the Prior to Immigration Messages. However, the theme continues to be part of the transnational messages.

"It is easy to study in the U.S. You will be fine if you pay attention in class."

—15 year-old boy from Hong Kong

The Chinese children who received positive Academic Messages upon arrival were older children ages 15–16, who immigrated to the U.S. a little older than most of the children (10–12 years of age). This may reflect that as children are older, academic participation is more salient, revealing an important source of information to help the newcomers to assimilate in the U.S. school.

School Academic Reputation: The Exam Schools Case

One important aspect of Chinese immigrant children in Boston is the participation of these children in schools that are identified as promoting high academic performance. According to Dr. Min Zhou (personal communication 12/6/00), Chinese parents often rely on community information to learn about which are the best schools in a particular town. In Boston, there are three academically prestigious public high schools that require entrance examinations to be admitted, known as "Exam Schools." Table 6.7 provides a profile of these Exam Schools in Boston. Nine of the participants in this study (12% of the sample) attend these "Exam Schools."

Table 6.7.
Boston Exam Schools Profile

Boston Exam Schools	Blacks	Asian	Latino	White	Other	Free Lunch	ELL
Exam School 1	18.5%	22.7%	8.4%	50.1%	0.3%	29.3%	0.6%
Exam School 2	27.4%	20.5%	8.0%	43.9%	0.2%	39.2%	2.8%
Exam School 3	45.1%	31.8%	13.4%	9.4%	0.3%	N/A	18.3%

ELL: English Language Learners

The profile of the children attending these Exam Schools shows interesting variations. Most of these children are female (6), compared to male children (3). Most of these children came to the U.S. as 10–12 year-olds. Over half of them came from Guangdong. Most of the parents from Guangdong had a less than high school education. The profile of the Chinese children in Exam Schools shows that there is a representation across parental educational level groups in all these schools—six children had parents with less than high school education and three children had parents with higher education. This may be linked to what Dr. Zhou refers to as Chinese communities being a source of valuable information about the prestigious schools within a specific city or town, regardless of parental educational background.

I analyzed the responses of this group of children in the Exam Schools about messages received from co-nationals upon entry to American schools. Of course, when these children came to the U.S., they were not in the Exam Schools, but in elementary and a few in middle schools. However, according to the LISA research assistants, Chinese parents tend to identify "feeder schools" for the Exam Schools. Therefore, peers in the "feeder schools" could eventually join these children in the Exam Schools.

More than half of the Exam School group did not hear anything from co-nationals in the school. Four students heard messages about schools being "easy." However, some of the children in the Exam Schools reflected on the "easy" School Message, establishing that the co-national in the school made them aware of the fallacy in the Prior to Immigration Messages about U.S. schools being "easy."

> "They [co-national peers] would tell me how reality is different from what they heard in China. New immigrants also have to work very hard in this country. Schools here are just very different than what I heard in China"
>
> —17 year-old girl from Guangdong

This message reveals that prior to immigration, Chinese children are presented with the picture of an "easy" school. However, upon entry to the U.S., co-national peers state that these Prior Messages do not accurately describe the reality in the U.S. school. This girl entered the U.S. when she was 14 and attended 8th grade in an urban middle school that is very diverse. This school has a bilingual Chinese program, taught by Chinese teachers, who are usually regarded as supportive, yet demanding. The fact that this girl attended the bilingual Chinese program with teachers that are immigrant Chinese, may actually mean that she was not presented a very different picture from what she experienced in China upon entry to U.S. school. This situation raises an important question about the different effects of hiring co-national teachers who may "import" the educational styles and expectations of the country of origin into the U.S. school. In the case of this Chinese girl, the fact that she found the American school as hard as it was in China allowed her to continue meeting rigorous academic demands that could have contributed to her acceptance to an Exam School. Further, the importation of teachers may imply that co-national teachers may also be part of the transnational social space.

For Chinese children who now attend Exam Schools, most of the positive Academic Messages were given in the form of instrumental advice—the know-how of American schools. One girl from Hong Kong who attends Exam School 2 expresses:

> "The majority of them [co-nationals] were here longer than I was. They knew more and they understood American schools better and deeper. They told me about the school situations. For example, what it was like during class, what tests were like, and the interpersonal relationships between each other."
>
> —15 year-old girl from Hong Kong

This answer reflects a clearly instrumental message that aims to help the newcomer student to assimilate into the school life. This child was 12 years old when she first entered school in the U.S., yet she articulated very specific issues about school life that the co-national peers provided for her upon arrival to the school. The co-national becomes an experienced source of information about interacting within American schools.

Mexican Messages: Academic Demands and The Guiding Co-national

In the Mexican sample, more children received Academic Messages from their co-national peers at school than in the Chinese group. The messages were more positive than negative. More boys than girls received negative Academic Messages from co-nationals in the school (Appendix D). The negative Academic Messages received upon entry to the U.S. schools were concentrated on curriculum and schoolwork:

- More classes in the U.S. increase the amount of schoolwork as compared to Mexico
- Lack of English proficiency limits the academic participation of children
- Curriculum in the U.S. is less advanced than in Mexico

Contrary to what the Mexican children learned prior to immigration about the U.S. school being easy, some children heard messages that expressed the contrary, especially in terms of the amount of homework assigned.

"[Co-nationals told me] that here there are more classes periods in a school. Over there in Mexico there is only one. That the bad thing is having homework in all of them."
—12 year-old boy from Guadalajara

In my ethnographic work, I recognized this is a common view of Mexican children who attend middle schools in the U.S. The curious thing is that even though secondary schools in Mexico (7–9 grade) are organized similarly to the U.S. middle school system (one teacher per subject area), many Mexican children did not seem to recognize this similarity. They seem to construct that one of the differences between the Mexican and the U.S. schools is the fact that you have more classes in the U.S. and therefore more work in the U.S. school. This may indicate a lack of familiarity among some Mexican immigrant students with the secondary education system in their own country, perhaps reflecting a lack of experience with secondary schools in Mexico.

Another element in the "difficulty" of the American school was related to the language of instruction being English. However, another salient message was about the perception of a less advanced curriculum, as compared to their country of origin. Mexican children said that co-nationals advised them that the school curriculum was "behind" and it covered content that is taught in Mexico in earlier grades, similar views to those expressed in Prior Messages.

"[I heard] that [schools] were less advanced, more behind here than in Mexico."
—11 year-old boy from the State of Mexico

While for some children the "easy" American schools elicited a positive reaction, for others it indicated fewer learning opportunities. Negative messages about academic issues in the Mexican group presented a rather discouraging picture—more homework, more classes, language barriers, and limited opportunities for new learning because academic content include things already learned in Mexico. While these messages were given to a minority of students, they encapsulate ideas that can become discouraging for the new arrivals.

Most Academic Messages among the Mexican sample were positive. More boys than girls received these Academic Messages (Appendix D). Positive Academic Messages included:

- Behavioral advice that promoted academic engagement
- Academic content in the U.S. is easier
- Opportunity to learn more in the U.S.

As in the Chinese group, one category of Academic Messages was advice. The Mexican children reported that their co-nationals provided three kinds of advice—good behavior, learning English, and study hard, applying oneself to study.

"They taught me, told me to pay attention."
—15 year-old boy from Guerrero

"That I should work very hard because I didn't know English."
—Mexican girl from Colima (no age data)

Welcoming Messages also referred to the U.S. curriculum as being easier than in Mexico, not only less demanding but also "behind" in terms of academic content as compared to Mexican curricula.

"[Co-nationals told me] that everything was easy. That [schools] were lower [in what they teach], more behind here than in Mexico."
—11 year-old boy from the State of Mexico

Interestingly, while for some Mexican children the less advanced curricula in U.S. schools were perceived as something negative (fewer opportunities to learn), for others, it was perceived as something positive because school would be less demanding than in Mexico.

Other messages provided positive perceptions about instruction and the possibility to learn. Statements such as "you will learn a lot" were common among Mexican students.

"That I should go to school because you learn many things here such as English."
—12 year-old boy from Jalisco

Because the responses from the Mexican students are not very elaborated, it is hard to identify any specific reaction or quality of the positive Academic Messages, other than "positive" in relation to the ideas of less demanding or less advanced curriculum in the U.S. school. Do these children view this as an opportunity to get ahead and attain academic excellence? Or do these children view this as an opportunity to pay less attention to school and invest less in their school participation, given that they "already know" what it is being taught? In chapter 5, I discussed how for some Mexican children, the "easy" school often promotes academic disengagement. Is this less demanding curriculum not challenging these Mexican students to their full academic potential? These are questions that require more research linked to outcome measures that are outside the scope of this paper.

Chinese–Mexican Comparison of Academic Messages

Both Chinese and Mexican immigrant children received messages from their co-nationals in the school regarding behaviors that could help the newcomers to understand classroom interactions and participation. Interestingly, in both groups, more boys than girls received Academic Messages. In general, both groups received positive messages that were very similar in content—orientation to classroom behaviors and teacher expectations. However, some interesting differences can be identified between the groups.

First, Chinese messages revealed more specific classroom behaviors than Mexican messages. The Chinese emphasize specific behaviors about what to do in classroom situations. Mexican children received more general messages about paying attention or applying oneself to study, but not many messages revealed specific behaviors as the Chinese messages did. Second, while both groups received negative messages regarding the academic demands in school, Mexican children received more negative messages about this issue. Expectations of demanding schoolwork, along with the difficulty of understanding content in the second language, were more prevalent in the Mexican group. Third, Chinese children received messages from co-nationals in a way that indicated some instrumental value in the suggested behavior—getting good grades or avoiding trouble with the teacher. Mexican messages were more general in content and emphasized "being good" without linking this behavior to a particular academic goal. Finally, while Chinese children received messages about pursuing higher education, Mexican children did not. The Mexican perception of learning opportunities seemed to be localized in the public school context—the opportunity to learn more.

English Messages: The Proficiency Issue

One interesting finding is that in the Chinese sample, only one student stated that he heard messages regarding the English language.

> "There were ESL programs here. I was in ESL."
> —14 year-old girl from Guangdong

In the Mexican sample, English Messages accounted for more of the responses than in the Chinese sample. All of these messages were negative. Unlike the messages Prior to Immigration, which included the "opportunity to learn English." Welcoming Messages about English emphasized the difficulty and the frustration that low English proficiency presents for the newcomers.

> "That the schools were boring and difficult because they [co-national peers] didn't know how to speak English."
> —14 year-old boy from the State of Mexico

> "[Co-national peers] told me learning English would be difficult because I didn't know anything of English."
> —15 year-old boy from Guerrero

Chinese–Mexican Comparison of English Messages

While it is not clear from the data on these students—both Mexican and Chinese—if they had already had a level of English proficiency upon arrival to the U.S., I tend to assume that most children did not. In the Chinese sample, the Welcoming Messages did not emphasize issues of English proficiency at all (only one English Message). Even the only girl who stated such a message had a perception is that there is a way to learning English—the ESL class. In the Mexican sample, the few children who received English Messages received a less enthusiastic picture—lack of English proficiency will make things harder and learning English in itself is difficult. This response, while a minority, may indicate the potential for Mexican children to adopt negative perceptions towards the process of learning English from what they hear from the co-nationals in the schools.

Annoying Peers and Careful Choices

In the Chinese sample, Peer Messages still represented only 4% of the transnational messages (in close proportion to Prior Messages). However, for the Mexican sample, Peer Messages upon entry to the U.S. became a more dominant category of transnational messages than they were in Prior Messages. This may be the result of the source of messages for Welcoming Messages being peers in the school, while the source of messages in Prior Messages was family members, both minors and adults.

Chinese Peer Messages: Friendly/Unfriendly

As in Prior Messages, negative Peer Messages spoke of non-Chinese peers as being disruptive in the classroom. However, in Welcoming Messages ideas about more aggressive behaviors such as fighting also emerged. For example, a boy whose parents both have graduate degrees explained:

> "[Co-nationals] told me that people were mean. People beat other people up."
>
> —13 year-old boy from Inner Mongolia

Some Chinese children expressed that co-nationals told them positive things about their peers:

> "They told me teachers are nice and kids are easy to get along with and kids are very friendly."
>
> —13 year-old boy from Guangdong

While Chinese children who received negative messages about their peers attend mostly White schools, children who received positive Peer Messages actually attend mostly Asian or diverse schools. This may indicate that the "positive" perception of messages towards peers is in reference to co-nationals or co-ethnic students, not to non-Chinese students. However, in the Welcoming Messages, Chinese children did not report hearing about specific student groups (e.g., ethnic groups). Most of the negative messages made references to "children" or "students" in general.

Mexican Peer Messages: The Recurring Themes of Gangs and Violence

For the Mexican group, peers were a more recurrent theme in the Welcoming Messages. Most of the Peer Messages were about negative perception of peers and included messages about:

- Peers' aggressive behaviors (e.g., fighting)
- Peers' involvement in gangs
- Promoting the avoidance of specific student groups (e.g., African Americans and gang members).

Just like in the case of Prior Messages, gang involvement was an issue among the Mexican group. In Welcoming Messages, fights started to be more salient than in Prior Messages. This may be because as children socialize within the school, they become witnesses and perhaps participants in these physical conflicts, especially in the urban schools where the Mexican participants go. However, gangs are still the predominant theme regarding peer behaviors. Children received warning messages from their co-nationals about the existence of gangs in school and they were advised to avoid them because they posed a bad influence on children:

> "[Co-nationals] told me not to hang out with gang members. They said 'if you let them, they make you become like them, gangsters.'"
>
> —12 year-old girl from Guanajuato

> "[There are] a lot of gangs. Don't get involved with them."
> —17 year-old boy from Jalisco

As in the case of Prior Messages, females recalled most of the messages about gangs. On the other hand, most boys received messages about fighting. This may indicate also a perception on the girls' part that any fight or any act of violence is related to gangs, when it may not necessarily be that way. However, both messages still reflect some concerns about violence in schools.

Mexican children also received messages advising them to avoid specific groups by ethnicity, because their co-national peers perceived the members as bad people. The most targeted group was the African American group. These messages were shared mostly among boys.

"Don't hang out with Blacks because they fight."
—14 year-old boy from Jalisco

"[Co-nationals told me] that I should not hang out with the Blacks."
—13 year-old boy from Guerrero

"That they [co-nationals] told me I had to be careful with African Americans because they would rob me. That they [African American peers] would invite me to cut classes."
—17 year-old girl from Jalisco

"[Co-nationals] told me that there were a few problems. Some Blacks fought other Blacks. Many friends told me that some students were not very nice. That they were troublemakers."
—14 year-old boy from Jalisco

"There are gangs, don't get involved with Black students."
—14 year-old girl from Veracruz

One child reported negative perceptions of Chicanos (U.S.-born co-nationals).

"They [co-national peers] told me not to hang out with children from here, like Chicanos."
—13 year-old boy from Mexico City

All of the children who received negative Peer Messages attend schools in the same neighborhood in the Bay Area. This town, which I will call San Patricio, is the poorest community in the county with a high population density of about 10,000 per square mile (total population is about 27,000). The ethnic composition of the city based on Census 1990 is shown in Table 6.8.

Table 6.8.
Ethnic Composition of the City of San Patricio

Ethnic Group	Population	% of total
White	12,453	39%
African American	5,368	17%
Hispanic	6,434	20%
Asian	4,323	13%
Other	3,420	11%

The predominant Hispanic group is Mexican (73% of Hispanic group) and the predominant Asian groups are Filipino (36% of Asian group) and Laotian (25% of Asian group). The FBI has ranked this city among the top ten cities in California (No. 6) for indices of violent crimes. According to the principal of the local middle school, there are about 17 gangs operating in the city, which comprises only 2.6 square miles. Many of these gangs are organized along ethnic lines—African American, Asian, and Latino.

In such a dense city with limited resources (unemployment rate is 11.7%), high crime, and about 18% of households being overcrowded, it is likely that the tensions in the community are reflected in the school. About 58% (45) of the Mexican sample attend school in the district that serves San Patricio—71% (32) of these attend schools in San Patricio.

The fact that the children who received negative messages against African American students are going to highly segregated schools, where there is gang involvement within the community, speaks of the influence of the community and the vulnerabilities that some of these receiving communities present to the new immigrants. Negative perceptions of African American peers may be a reflection of the inter-cultural relations in the neighborhood and the presence of gangs organized by race. What is a concern is that immigrant students learn to stereotype certain groups and associate them with negative behaviors that reflect the violence and economic stress of the community at large.

Another potential implication of Mexican negative messages about peers is that they seem to be articulated in terms of peer choice. The co-national in the school presents negative pictures of some peer groups and advises avoidance of these groups. These messages carry out the potential danger of promoting segregation, inter-ethnic conflict, and the perpetuation of prejudice and isolation among immigrant students. Further, it is important for us to contextualize these messages around the community realities and to recognize the importance of fostering positive experiences with diversity–beyond what a distressed community such as San Patricio can provide for children, including immigrant children.

A few Mexican children expressed some positive perceptions toward their own friends, indicating that these co-national friends helped them or offered friendship once they entered the U.S. school.

Chinese–Mexican Comparison of Peer Messages

Peer Messages in the Welcoming category are distinctive in their qualities, between the Chinese and the Mexican samples. First, Peer Messages became less dominant in the Chinese sample in Welcoming Messages, while they became more dominant in the Mexican sample. This pattern elicits questions about how Chinese may perceive social behaviors in the context of school as compared to the Mexican children. Do Chinese children perceive social issues in the school to be less significant than academic issues?

Second, Chinese messages included both positive and negative perceptions of peers. That is, the co-nationals in the school presented the newcomers with both positive and negative views of peers. Further, Chinese messages did not specify a particular student group (e.g., by ethnicity). This is a different perspective from Prior Messages, where messages included negative perceptions toward specific groups. Mexican messages, on the other hand, emphasized negative perceptions of peers, especially towards African Americans. It is important to note that Mexican messages in the Welcoming category emphasized the same themes as in Prior Messages—gangs and negative perceptions of peers. This indicates that through time, Mexican co-nationals communicated messages that continued presenting negative perceptions of specific peer groups and awareness of gang involvement in school, a reproduction of these messages over time.

School Messages: Orientations and Expectations

School Messages were an important topic of transnational messages upon entry. Co-nationals in the school provided information and guidance to the newcomers about how to get acquainted with school life. For both groups, School Messages continued to be consistent messages from co-nationals.

Chinese School Messages: An Introduction to School Life

School Messages among the Chinese group were slightly less dominant in Welcoming Messages than they were in Prior Messages. All the School Messages were positive in the Chinese group. More girls than boys received School Messages.

School Messages in the Chinese group provided information and orientation about schools and usually referred to:

- Orientation to the school campus.
- Orientation to school routines and school rules.

The co-national in the school helped the newcomer to get acquainted with the physical environment of the school campus (e.g., classroom locations and schedules).

> "[Co-nationals] talked about schedule in the school."
> —16 year-old boy from Guangdong

The themes around School Messages were varied including school routines, rules, and resources available to students (e.g., ESL programs or counseling). For example, some children shared that their co-nationals told them to walk (not run) in the halls, or to write their names on their work at all times, or to talk to the counselor to report any problems.

Mexican School Messages: School as a Provider

In the Mexican group, the proportion of School Messages remained constant between Prior Messages and Welcoming Messages. All of the Welcoming School Messages among the Mexican peers were positive. More girls than boys received positive School Messages. There were a diverse number of themes about U.S. schools shared in Welcoming Messages. School Messages in the Mexican group included:

- Orientation to the school campus
- Orientation to school routines and rules
- Creating awareness of the free services and materials that school provided to students
- English language support from co-nationals (in the form of translations).

The main kind of messages were those that provided orientation to campus life.

> "They told me where everything was. When we changed reading classes, they would tell me where to go. They would take me where the cafeteria was and library."
> —11 year-old boy from Tijuana

> "[Co-nationals] showed me around school. My cousin went to the same school and he stayed with me. He showed me the school. He was in the same class."
> —14 year-old girl from Michoacan

One important distinction in this girl's answer is the fact that the co-national in the school that helped her around was a relative. This is something that is important to keep in mind given the close-knit patterns of certain immigrant groups. That is, it is likely that the co-nationals in the school may in fact be relatives of the children, indicating an expansion of the family circle into the school site. This may also indicate that resources as well as vulnerabilities in the family life could represent an influence in immigrant children's education where there are relatives in the school.

Some of the orientation messages about school also related to school rules and routines.

> "[Co-nationals] say school was very easy. That [school] gave us breakfast and lunch free. [Co-nationals] told me the school rules since I didn't speak any English. I just did what they had told me. I did not understand."
>
> —15 year-old girl from Jalisco

> "[Co-nationals] told me 'Don't go outside because the security guards are going to grab you, and they are going to give you a little paper, a referral.' When you are new, you feel afraid, but then you don't feel afraid anymore."
>
> —15 year-old girl from the State of Mexico

In terms of school as a provider, children shared themes that included the availability of free lunch in the school and more classes available in the U.S. Interestingly, all of the children who got messages about the free services offered in the American school referred to free meals.

> "[Co-nationals told me] That you got free food, that the lunches were free."
>
> —11 year-old boy from the State of Mexico

> "[Co-nationals told me] That it was all right, give us lunch, longer hours, [teachers] expect more from us and teach more."
>
> —13 year-old boy from Mexico City

Co-nationals were also offered English language support from other more established co-nationals.

> "[Co-nationals] helped me with English things. I didn't know much and they helped me. Or they told me where a class was, a class I didn't know where it was."
>
> —13 year-old girl from Jalisco

Support from co-national peers in terms of English language development is an interesting finding when contrasted with the Chinese sample. For the Chinese, English language development is attainable through the ESL class and they did not specify that the co-national could be a support for English language development. However, in the Mexican sample, while the co-national in the school presented the idea of the "difficulty" of learning English, the co-national in the school also provided some support with English. That is, Mexican children were invited to ask co-nationals for English language support.

> "[Co-nationals told me] that it was good. That if I didn't understand something to ask them. Like [if I didn't understand something] in English."
>
> —11 year-old boy from Jalisco

However, this support seems to be more of a survival device (e.g., translations to navigate in the classroom environment), rather than a support for English language learning.

Chinese–Mexican Comparison of School Messages

School Messages that immigrant children, both Chinese and Mexican, received from their co-national peers provided an orientation to the school environment—both in the physical sense (campus orientation) and the social sense (school rules and routines). However, there are two interesting distinctions between the Chinese and Mexican messages upon entry. First, the Mexican messages emphasized the free services and resources that the school in the U.S. provides to the students. Chinese messages did not. This reveals that some Mexican immigrants construct the benefits or positive aspects of "school" beyond academic preparation, to include services and infrastructures that may not be available in their country of origin. Second, while School Messages were still predominant among co-nationals upon entry to the U.S. in the Mexican sample, this category became much less dominant in the Chinese sample (compared with Prior Messages). This indicates that upon arrival the Mexican co-national in the school continued emphasizing school issues, but Chinese co-nationals emphasized more academic issues. This may be an indication of the different priorities or emphasis that Chinese and Mexican children have regarding school experiences. For example, this may indicate differences in the social construction of "schools" among different immigrant groups—such as

Chinese constructing schools predominantly around academic issues, even if they are aware and affected by non-academic factors.

Social Messages: Awareness of the Immigrant's Challenges

In Welcoming Messages, a distinctive category emerged that was not present in Prior Messages—Social Messages. By Social Messages, I refer to information about life in the U.S. for immigrants in general and awareness of social and political factors in the U.S. society (e.g., discrimination) that are not exclusively the product of social interactions in the school context. While still a minority of the Welcoming Messages, the fact that some immigrant children received these kinds of messages is worthy of mention because of all these messages (both Mexican and Chinese) refer to racial discrimination.

> "They [co-national peers] said that it was very mixed, a lot of racial discrimination."
>
> —16 year-old girl from Guangdong

Social Messages reveal an awareness of the social mirroring (Suarez-Orozco, 2000) that schools present to immigrant children in terms of perceptions of discrimination against immigrants in the context of the U.S. society, not only school.

Teacher Messages: Nice and Easy

Teacher Messages were a minority of the messages. As in Prior Messages, Teacher Messages were a predominantly female category. For both groups, it was mostly girls who received these messages, either positive or negative.

Chinese Teacher Messages: The Nice Teacher

Most of these messages among Chinese co-nationals talked positively about teachers. Most of the children who received positive Teacher Messages upon entry to the U.S. school were females. Only one Chinese child expressed receiving some mixed impressions about teachers from her co-nationals:

"[Co-nationals] didn't tell me anything. Talking about school
is boring. But sometimes we talk about the teachers, whether
they are nice or not. They are mostly nice except for two
teachers."

—14 year-old girl from Guangdong

All of these positive perceptions were about the teacher personality
(e.g., teachers are nice), rather than about teacher quality or
preparation.

"American schools are better. American teachers are nicer
than Chinese teacher."

—15 year-old girl from Guangdong

"In Squaw Peak School the kids told me that the school was so
cool. The teachers were nice."

—13 year-old girl from Hong Kong

Squaw Peak School is a mostly White school, with 0–19% of
English learners and 0–19% of children in free/reduced lunch
programs.

About half of the children who received Teacher Messages
attended White schools. The rest of the children attended
predominantly Asian or African American schools, and diverse
schools. However, these schools also show the same proportions (less
than 20%) of English learners and students on free/reduced lunch
programs as the White schools do.

Mexican Teacher Messages: More Negative than Positive

More Mexican girls than boys received Teacher Messages (Appendix
D). However, for Mexican students, most of these messages were
negative. These negative messages refer to:

- Negative perceptions of teachers' personality
- Lack of teachers' concern about their students
- Students' discontent with disciplinary actions.

For example, some students explained that co-nationals told them that teachers were mean or got mad at students constantly.

"Some teachers were mean and got mad at you."
—14 year-old girl from Jalisco

"[Co-nationals told me] that teachers didn't care about you."
—12 year-old boy from Mexico City

All of the Mexican children who received negative Teacher Messages from co-nationals attended schools in San Patricio or in the vicinity of this city. The negative perception of teacher's personality in schools in San Patricio seems to reflect the emphasis that teachers in these schools usually put on discipline. Note that children in San Patricio also received all of the negative Peer Messages in the Mexican sample.

In my ethnographic work in schools in San Patricio, I have learned that many teachers are deeply concerned with the incidence of violence on the school grounds, and discipline has become a major priority in their daily routines, in part as a precautionary measure to protect themselves. Therefore, Mexican children may perceive teachers in San Patricio as less tolerant and more strict.

The positive messages Mexican children received about teachers from their co-nationals in the school referred to positive perceptions towards:

- The teachers' personalities
- Teachers' instructional quality
- Teachers' bilingual ability
- Lack of corporal punishment as a form of discipline.

Unlike the Chinese students who made no reference to the quality of instruction that teachers in the U.S. provide, Mexican children seemed to have heard that some teachers taught "well."

"[Co-nationals told me] that teachers were very nice and that they knew how to explain things well. [Co-nationals told me] that they were very good teachers."
—14 year-old girl from Jalisco

This is a different view from Prior Messages, where co-nationals alerted Mexican children that in the U.S. schools teachers "did not teach right."

Chinese–Mexican Comparison of Teacher Messages

Welcoming Messages regarding teachers present somehow similar attitudes towards teachers in both groups. Both Chinese and Mexican children received messages from their co-nationals that reflected positive experiences with and attitudes towards teachers, especially regarding teacher personality and student-teacher relations. However, more Mexican children received negative messages about teacher's personalities from their co-nationals. It is interesting that all of the children who received negative Teacher Messages attended schools in the same community. This raises important issues regarding the attitudes of teachers in particular schools and how the community and school contexts may influence teacher expectations and student-teacher relations. The fact that Mexican children seem to perceive teachers as capable of delivering quality instruction raises issues about the academic and instructional standards that these children are used to from their countries of origin. It raises issues about how these standards are compared to U.S. academic, pedagogical, and instructional standards within the schools the immigrant children eventually attend.

The co-national, as the major reference group for immigrants in the school, was a source of transnational messages about U.S. schools. More than actual information, the co-national served as a guide into the school culture and environment, leading the newcomer to certain expectations and behaviors.

THE INSTRUMENTAL VALUE OF WELCOMING MESSAGES

As in the case of messages prior to immigration, I was also interested in investigating the reaction and instrumental value that these messages elicited in immigrant children. Participant students were asked if they have found these messages from co-nationals helpful. More Mexican children (36) found the Welcoming Message instrumental than did Chinese children (13). Table 6.9 presents the distribution of instrumental value by gender.

Table 6.9.
Instrumental Value of Welcoming Messages by Gender

Found Message Instrumental?	Chinese				Mexican			
	Males		Females		Males		Females	
	N	%	N	%	N	%	N	%
Yes	6	21%	7	16%	19	45%	17	47%
No	4	14%	7	16%	9	21%	12	33%
Not applicable	19	65%	31	68%	11	27%	6	17%
Missing data	0	0%	0	0%	2	5%	0	0%
No answer	0	0%	0	0%	0	0%	1	3%
Don't know	0	0%	0	0%	1	2%	0	0%
Total	29	100%	45	100%	42	100%	36	100%

Those children who found these messages useful were asked to elaborate on how the messages were useful, to establish any instrumental value of the message from the co-national in the school. The categories for the instrumental value of the messages were generated from the analysis of the data, no pre-conceived options were given to the children. These categories included:

- Behavioral change—message influenced student to change his behavior
- Comfortability—message provided a sense of comfort
- Support—co-national offered assistance or support to the student
- Information—message provided information or orientation to school life
- No support—student indicated that co-nationals in the school did not offer support or assistance.

The distribution of the instrumental value of these messages for the students who indicated that they found the message helpful is shown in Table 6.10.

Table 6.10.
Instrumental Value of Welcoming Messages

Types of Messages	Chinese		Mexican	
	N	%	N	%
Behavioral Change	7	9%	20	22%
Comfortability	2	3%	10	11%
Support	1	1%	14	16%
Information	7	9%	6	7%
No support	57	78%	40	44%
Total	74	100%	90	100%

Chinese Welcoming Messages: Knowing School Behaviors

Across gender groups, most of the Chinese students found that the advice and messages of the co-nationals helped them either in learning the appropriate behaviors to have in school or just to get information about school life. For the Chinese students, most of the behavioral changes took the form of avoiding trouble with the teacher. For example, some Chinese students said that students provided information about appropriate classroom behaviors, and having this information allowed them to behave in the classroom.

> "[The messages helped me to] know the rules. [In a way that I] won't break the rules"
>
> —15 year-old boy from Guangdong

The other kind of behavioral change was in relation to peers. Some Chinese children reported that after hearing the information about peers, this helped them to be prepared and learn how to avoid trouble:

> "The more I heard, the more I knew so I [could] prepare and protect myself."
>
> —17 year-old girl from Guangdong

"[The message] made me aware not to bother any bigger kids."

—16 year-old boy from Inner Mongolia

Other kinds of information that the Chinese children found valuable included information about teacher's expectations, study tips, and college information. However, most Chinese students stated that their co-nationals did not help them or they did not receive information from them.

Mexican Welcoming Messages: Providing Comfort and Support

For the Mexican children, one of the major values in the messages from co-nationals was the fact that the co-national in the school provided the students with a sense of comfort and security.

"[Messages helped me] not to be afraid of being into a new school."

—14 year-old girl from Guanajuato

In fact, information was not a dominant form of support for Mexicans. Behavioral change, support, and comfort represented the most dominant forms of instrumental value of the Welcoming Messages. For Mexican boys, behavioral change and support from co-nationals were the most frequent responses. While for Mexican girls behavioral change and support were also predominant, comfortability was also an important form of co-national support (e.g., feeling comfortable in the school).

In the Mexican group, the instrumental value of the messages was social rather than academic, specifically about how to change their social behaviors (not academic ones) regarding how to avoid trouble and how to choose peers.

"[Messages helped me] to get to know who were the troublemakers and who could be good friends. To get to know teachers who were good and those whom I don't understand, those teachers who only come to school to get money."

—13 year-old boy from Jalisco

"[Co-nationals] oriented me. They kept me away from trouble so I didn't get in trouble."

—15 year-old girl from the State of Mexico

"They [co-nationals] helped me to have friends, meet people."

—12 year-old boy from Jalisco

Further, some children stated that the co-nationals' messages about negative perceptions of peers motivated them to "avoid" certain student groups.

"I didn't hang out with them [African American students]. I had no more problems with them as a result. They [African American students] had taken my cap once. They gave me a black eye."

—14 year-old boy from Sonora

"I didn't hang out with the Chicanos. I only hanged out with others."

—13 year-old boy from Mexico City

This child from Mexico City is the one who received negative Peer Messages about Chicanos in the school. As a result of this message, he chose not to socialize with Chicanos. This illustrates the effect of negative Peer Messages in the peer selection of newcomers.

Mexican students also stated that the co-national in the school provided them with a sense of comfort and familiarity, especially regarding the fact that the co-national was another person who spoke their first language.

"Because they told me that there were kids that spoke Spanish. I felt better."

—13 year-old boy from Zacatecas

Linked to the availability of first language speakers, the co-national in the school also helped newcomers with English. Co-nationals in the school who were more proficient in English helped them with translation:

"To learn English. [Co-nationals] told me the words in English. Then I asked them and they translated for me."
— 13 year-old girl from Jalisco

For others, the information in the Welcoming Messages helped the newcomers to experience an easier transition into the school life and culture:

"[Messages helped me] to get to know how things it was going to be. To learn about how the school was to be ready, be alert."
— 13 year-old boy from Guerrero

Co-nationals in the school provided useful information that helped immigrant children to adopt behaviors that children reported helped them to make a transition into the school life. The main distinction between the two groups is that for the Chinese students, the instrumental value of the Welcoming Messages often emphasized classroom activities, while Mexicans emphasized social activities.

While the co-nationals in the school may not necessarily articulate specific "messages" to the newcomers, their behaviors and socialization patterns may influence the path of the newcomers. The data on the instrumentality of Welcoming Messages have shown that for some children the co-national in school can be a helping hand in the transition to a new environment, as children reported. But this "help" seems to be limited to campus orientation and social behaviors, not necessarily academic support. However, some of these social behaviors may in fact help children to become more academically engaged—like knowing the rules and understanding teacher expectations.

CHAPTER 7
Current Messages
Speaking from Experience

In the analysis of messages about U.S. schools in transnational social spaces, I was also interested in the children's perceptions about U.S. schools that could potentially become transnational messages when these children shared them with other co-nationals. In order to approach this inquiry, students were asked what they would tell a cousin, who lived in their country of origin, and who was about to immigrate to the U.S. in about a month, about American schools. These potential transnational messages that depicted the children's perceptions of American schools were identified as Current Messages. The distribution of Current Messages is presented in Table 7.1.

Table 7.1.
Current Messages about U.S. Schools

Types of Messages	Chinese		Mexican	
	N	%	N	%
Academic	53	24%	47	21%
English	13	5%	18	8%
General	20	9%	37	17%
Peers	33	15%	22	10%
School	44	20%	32	15%
Social	20	9%	22	10%
Teachers	38	17%	33	15%
No School Message	3	1%	8	4%
Total	224	100%	219	100%

Both groups clearly focused their messages about American schools on academic, peers, teachers, and school issues. While this indicates that both groups may construct perceptions of schools around the same themes, a closer look at the nature of these messages shows distinctions between the two groups.

ACADEMIC MESSAGES: THE "EASY AMERICAN SCHOOL"

Academic Messages were the top category for both groups, indicating that, over time, Academic Messages continue to be a major theme in the context of transnational messages. In terms of gender, Academic Messages were more or less equally distributed in both the Chinese and the Mexican group (Appendix D).

Chinese Academic Messages: Perspectives on Academic Demands

The Chinese students indicated more positive Academic Messages than negative (Appendix D). Negative messages emphasized disappointment with the less demanding and less advanced curricula in the U.S. because this represented two major drawbacks:

- Limited learning opportunities in the U.S. for Chinese children as compared to the learning they could have obtained in China.
- Evidence of low quality of instruction and education in the U.S.

In other words, some Chinese children articulated that the "easy" American school not only meant that they were not learning much in school, but also that the quality of education and instruction was poor.

Some Chinese students did not necessarily see perceptions of less demanding American curricula as positive. In Prior Messages, a less demanding curriculum was something to be excited about because Chinese children perceived this as less stressful schoolwork and better chances to excel academically. In Welcoming Messages, this theme was not very salient. However, in Current Messages, a few children expressed disappointment in relation to the less demanding curriculum as this fact evidenced low quality of schools in the U.S.

"If possible, do not come to this country. In terms of study, it is not very good here. The curriculum is easy here. The things I am learning now are like things Hong Kong people learn in Primary 5 or Primary 6. Those who study here in the U.S. could not catch up with the curriculum in Hong Kong. I used to take science classes in Hong Kong. Those were much harder. Students who attend elementary or middle schools here, they look like they have learned nothing in elementary [or in] middle schools."

— 16 year-old girl from Hong Kong

"They are so bad. Don't come here. The education is too easy."

— 13 year-old girl from Hong Kong

"[It would be] very boring. Slow teaching style. School has a lot of slow children. When you come here, math would be easy for you. [It would be] very easy for you. English may be hard, but if you try it may be easy"

— 16 year-old boy from Guangdong

While this boy seems to have a negative message about the academic standards of the American school, his answer reveals a positive aspect regarding a comparison between children educated in American schools and those educated in China. This student seems to construct that the children educated in China would have a competitive edge against the children educated in the U.S.

Most of the children who articulated the negative messages came from Hong Kong. These children have had time to experience the American educational system and compare it with what they perceive to be higher standards of Hong Kong education. Also, the majority of the children who expressed negative Academic Messages attend schools that have been categorized as "academically low" by the MCAS (Massachusetts Comprehensive Assessment System). This reflects that in fact, most of the children that expressed negative Academic Messages go to schools that are not necessarily academically strong. In general terms, it seems like the Chinese children who have negative perceptions towards the "easy" school perceive this "easiness" as an indicator of low educational quality.

Most Chinese children stated that they would offer positive advice regarding academic issues to potential newcomers—rather than stating positive perceptions of academic issues in the U.S. schools. This reflects the same issues of Welcoming Messages, where academic advice, rather than actual information seems to be the predominant theme. This advice was given around the following themes:

- Promoting behaviors that demonstrate academic engagement (e.g., study, following teacher's directions)
- Creating awareness of the less demanding academic nature of American schools and how this implies a less stressful academic life in American schools
- Promoting strategies to capitalize on the "less demanding" academic content in U.S. schools (e.g., emphasize English language development over mathematics)
- Promoting an awareness of the attainability of academic excellence due to the less demanding academic standards in American schools.

Half of the Chinese students who gave Academic Messages indicated that they would provide some advice to the newcomer regarding how to become academically engaged—studying hard. However, these answers presented very specific patterns of academic demands at different grade levels.

> "Homework. Don't expect too much homework between 1st and 5th grade. Expect a lot of homework from 6th grade on. Things to do, always finish your homework, try to get good grades."
>
> —13 year-old boy from Inner Mongolia

> "Just because when you come over here, you may think you are advanced over students here and you probably are. But the school years in the first years are easy, simple, like in 6th grade you are still doing [the] simplest observations. But then from sixth to seventh grade [there] are some of the most difficult things you will ever face because suddenly everything gets harder and everybody becomes more competitive and you have no time. You really have to manage your family, your

schoolwork, and your extracurricular activities. So, you have to be ready for new kinds of influences."

—16 year-old boy from Beijing

Most of these children attend schools that have been categorized from "moderate" to "high" in terms of academic performance based on the MCAS scores. This may indicate that these children are exposed to more rigorous academic standards than are the children who constructed negative messages about academic issues.

Advice to newcomers again reflects the idea of schools in the U.S. being less demanding than in China as a positive thing. The nature of this message speaks of how Chinese students feel about a less stressful academic routine and more opportunities to attain academic success in the U.S.:

"The teachers here don't punish you as hard as in Hong Kong. The stuff, the learning level, probably math, (but not the English level) is easier. [There is] not as much homework [as in China]. Try to have fun."

—12 year-old girl from Hong Kong

"American schools are easier. Teachers are less stern, strict. Homework is easier. School curriculum here is slower than that in Hong Kong."

—13 year-old girl from Hong Kong

"In China there is more homework and teachers are stricter, studying in China is more difficult. In here, you can learn more things."

—17 year-old girl from Fujian

A number of children expressed that schoolwork was less demanding in the U.S. also in terms of the workload.

"Schools are very good. Homework is more relaxed, less intense."

—15 year-old girl from Hong Kong

Some children gave specific academic strategies for newcomers to achieve academic excellence:

> "First, I will tell him that the U.S. offers more subjects than in China so he can see which subjects he is best in and try hard in that subject."
>
> —13 year-old boy from Guangdong

Current Academic Messages in the Chinese group reveal a reproduction of the idea about the less demanding academic standards of the U.S. school. For some children, "lower academic standards" becomes an impediment to learning new things and represents proof of the low quality of education in the U.S. For others it implies a less stressful academic life and a competitive edge in the U.S. educational system. Other children recognize that academic demands fluctuate from easy (elementary) to more rigorous (middle and high schools).

Mexican Messages: Views on the "Easy American School"

Academic issues were not the most frequent theme of messages prior to immigration or upon entry to the U.S. for the Mexican group. However, it is a major theme among the Current Messages that Mexican children articulate to their co-nationals. This may indicate a degree of familiarity that children acquire towards academic issues in school or an issue of maturity as children grow and become exposed to higher academic demands in high schools. Generally, most Mexican children articulated more positive Academic Messages (Appendix D). Negative Academic Messages in the Mexican group were in reference to curriculum and instruction:

- Difficult curricula in the U.S.
- Limited learning opportunities in the U.S. for Mexican children as compared to the learning they could have obtained in Mexico.

Interestingly, Mexican children viewed the fact that U.S. schools could be both hard and easy as negative. In reference to a more demanding nature of the U.S. curriculum, a child explained:

"Some classes are hard. The one who comes from Mexico is
not going to understand, it is going to be hard, and as time
goes by it is going to get harder."
— 13 year boy old from Jalisco

However, it is not clear in this child's answer if the source of
difficulty is the academic demands of the curriculum, the content of the
curriculum, or the English barrier. Some children just articulated that
the school or classes were "hard."

As some of the Chinese children who expressed negative
Academic Messages, some Mexican children viewed curricula in the
U.S. as "less advanced" than in Mexico. That is, these children said that
they would let co-nationals know that in the U.S. they would face a
curriculum that is "way behind" what they can learn in Mexico.

"I remember than in Mexico they told me that supposedly here
I had more possibilities to study, to learn more. The truth is
that you don't learn here. Here what you see in social sciences,
you already saw that in Mexico. The science stuff, you already
saw it in Mexico. Here everything you are seeing right now,
you already saw it in Mexico."
— 15 year-old girl from the State of Mexico

Her disappointment with the "easy" curriculum is based on her
belief that what she already learned in Mexico is being taught in the
U.S. This implies that the student feels she is not learning new content,
and is restricted in her opportunities for learning and acquiring a high
quality education. As the Chinese did, Mexican children also expressed
that a less advanced curriculum implied limited learning opportunities
for them in the U.S.

"The schools are not good. They take everything very
superficially. They don't have materials. Schools in Mexico
are better. They gave you seven books. Here we only use
one."
— 15 year-old boy from Jalisco

This child is referring to the free textbooks that children up to 6th
grade receive in Mexican schools.

For those children who consider a less advanced curriculum a drawback, it signifies the dissolution of the opportunity for learning or having a better life in the U.S. A less advanced curriculum is translated into the potential for fewer opportunities to advance in the U.S.

> "Here [U.S.] you learn in a week what you learn there [Mexico] in a day."
>
> —12 year-old from Jalisco

Most of these Mexican children (82% of those who stated negative Academic Messages) attend schools in San Patricio, mainly the local high school and middle school. According to the California Department of Education's Academic Performance Index, the local high school and middle school in San Patricio have been ranked 1 (from a scale of 1–10, where 1 is the lowest) based on the 2000 data of the STAR9 test. The STAR9 is a test that has been adopted by the California Department of Education for school accountability purposes. However, we must take into consideration that the test is given in English and these schools have populations of English Language Learners of 40% and higher. Nevertheless, this information indicates that based on standardized testing measures, the schools where the Mexican children provided negative Academic Messages are considered low performing schools. This may indicate that these children develop negative perceptions of schools that reflect the low academic performance of these schools (refer to Appendix B).

The majority of the Mexican children expressed positive Academic Messages that they would share with their co-nationals. Positive Academic Messages referred to the following themes:

- Displaying appropriate classroom behaviors (behave nicely)
- Becoming academically engaged (e.g., studying hard and applying oneself to learn in the school)
- Creating awareness of less demanding curriculum that provides a competitive edge for children educated in Mexico and a less demanding schoolwork load
- Creating awareness of the quality of instruction and educational opportunities in the U.S.

More than half of the positive Academic Messages were given in terms of advice. Most of the advice that Mexican children would give to co-nationals refers to behaving civilly, being a "good kid," and applying oneself to learn in school.

> "Pay attention, don't break the rules, behave, and get good grades."
>
> —12 year-old girl from Guanajuato

> "[In U.S. school] they teach you. Everything depends on her [co-national cousin]. If she does her part in class. Some classes are easy some are hard."
>
> —15 year-old girl from Mexico City

Another important theme about academic issues in the Mexican sample was in issues regarding curriculum. As in the Chinese group, Mexican students articulated that the low academic standards or the less advanced curriculum would give the newcomer a competitive advantage:

> "[I would tell my cousin] that she would find herself ahead in Math and World History but she would have to work hard in English."
>
> —14 year-old boy from Jalisco

Other students articulated a less demanding academic life in terms of coursework load.

> "[I would tell my cousin] that it is good [in U.S. schools]. They don't give a lot of homework."
>
> —14 year-old boy from the State of Mexico

Yet another form of positive Academic Messages related to the quality of instruction and learning opportunities the U.S. school provides because there were more classes available in the U.S.

> "I would tell him that [schools] are good because here they teach you better things. That they teach you all the subjects."
>
> —12 year-old from Jalisco

Chinese–Mexican Comparison of Academic Messages

One commonality between perceptions of academic issues among Chinese and Mexican students is that in both groups, Current Messages were given more in terms of advice than in terms of depictions of the academic life in the U.S. schools. However, while Chinese advice concentrated on academic behaviors, Mexican messages revealed not only academic engagement, but also the need to display good behaviors that Mexican children seem to link to the idea of being a good student (well-behaved child).

Academic Messages in both groups continue to reflect a realization that curriculum in the U.S. is less demanding. While some Chinese and Mexican children had negative perceptions of the less demanding nature of school in the U.S., most children in both groups have a positive perception of this. The Chinese group seemed to emphasize what this means in terms of attaining academic success. A few Mexican children also stated that their co-nationals would find themselves "ahead" of other students (due to educational experiences in Mexico).

Current Messages reveal that the reproduction of Academic Messages continues over the years, but we need to reflect more on what the diffusion of a "less demanding curriculum" may pre-dispose children to do. While most children feel more optimistic about their opportunities to excel in American schools, for both groups, a minority of children indeed feels disappointed about the low academic demands they are exposed to in American schools. Children in both groups expressed views about how education in the country of origin had more quality in curriculum and instruction than schools in the U.S. In a sense, these children feel their chances for a "quality education" in the U.S. may not be realistic.

ENGLISH MESSAGES: DIFFERENT DIMENSIONS OF ESL

English Messages among the immigrant children in the sample were not dominant; however, they became more salient than in Prior or Welcoming Messages. In the Chinese sample, English Messages were predominately female while in the Mexican group, the distribution by gender was equal (Appendix D). While both groups usually emphasized some preoccupation with English proficiency, there were some differences in the way children articulated these messages.

Chinese English Messages: Attaining English Proficiency

Most of the English Messages in the Chinese group regarded limited English proficiency as something negative, a source of problems not only in terms of academic ability, but also social competence. Chinese children warned their co-nationals that if they did not speak English they would face two major obstacles:

- Limited ability to academic participation
- Being the subject of teasing and discrimination from peers.

Most of the Chinese children who expressed negative messages were female. Some children expressed messages that refer to the need for having English proficiency:

"The homework is hard because [your] English is not so good."
                    —15 year-old girl from Guangdong

"It is best to learn English before you come here, to set a good foundation. My cousin is going to go to Canada. I tell her to study English well."
                    —14 year-old girl from Guangdong

Another interesting preoccupation among the Chinese children was how their lack of English proficiency would make them the target of abuse by peers.

"If your English is not good, you would be bullied by other students."
                    —17 year-old girl from Guangdong

A girl, whose parents are both professionals in the medical field, explains how not speaking English fluently becomes a social marker in the school context that isolates immigrant children. Her advice is to observe, seek support, and learn English:

"If your English is bad, don't talk much because if you speak with an accent, people are likely to laugh at you. And go to an

ESL class. And just ask what other people do because if you don't, people laugh at you too. You do really have to because I didn't. People will probably say you are a nerd, but well. ...Anyway, try to do good in school if you can, especially in math areas since your English is bad."

—15 year-old girl from Hubei

The positive English Messages among the Chinese referred to:

- The opportunity of learning a second language
- The availability of school programs for learning English (e.g., ESL)
- The perception of limited English proficiency as the "only problem", a problem that is possible to overcome.

Chinese messages about English issues also revealed a positive attitude towards English language acquisition—it is attainable. Therefore, the attitude towards English language proficiency is somehow mixed—negative because of the realization that at the beginning, lack of English proficiency will present an obstacle. Yet, it is also positive because English language acquisition will eventually be accomplished by participating in ESL programs in the American school. For example, a child whose parents have professional medical degrees, and who attends a predominantly White school, shared this positive message about the U.S. school:

"Your only real problem would be if you couldn't understand English, but they have ESL, so there is no real problem."

—15 year-old girl from Shanghai

While she recognized that limited English proficiency presents a problem for the newcomer, she does not view this as a permanent obstacle because proficiency is attainable through ESL classes.

"At the very first, [in the] beginning, you may not know English. But there are ESL classes and teachers will help you."

—11 year-old girl from Macau

Chinese children are not overly concerned about their performance in English, in part because they perceive academic standards to be less rigorous in the U.S. than in China. Therefore, Chinese children still feel they will be doing well while they take the time to learn English. For example, a boy whose mother has some college education (no father data available) explained his message to a potential co-national:

> "To learn English is enough. To have good command of English is enough, because if your English is not good, you can [still] catch up here with things and rules. You [the co-national cousin] also studied in China, so your standards will not be particularly low compared to other students in the U.S."
> —17 year-old boy from Guangdong

In fact, some children expressed negative perceptions about the bilingual programs because of the linguistic isolation they promote, according to some children. These Chinese children seem to perceive the bilingual program as a block to learning English because of the limited opportunities that expose these children to English. A Chinese girl advises potential newcomers against bilingual programs and their impact on English acquisition:

> "Nevertheless, don't go to bilingual programs because in the bilingual programs you speak Chinese all the time and you can't learn English."
> —15 year-old girl from Guangdong

This girl's response reflects her perception about learning English and how this cannot be accomplished in a bilingual classroom that is not "bilingual" if it does not include an English language development component. This girl observed, "you speak Chinese all the time." Note that all the children who articulated positive English Messages were girls.

One thing revealing about this perception is that Chinese children were less preoccupied with learning English, considering it more of a skill that eventually will be mastered. Even for those children who perceived some negative issues about limited English proficiency, this condition was not seen as a permanent one—all these children rationalized that eventually they would acquire English (e.g., by attending ESL classes).

The profiles of the students who talked about English Messages indicate two important factors. First, they come from more educated family backgrounds (high school and higher, including college-educated parents), which may indicate that these students are more academically inclined, and they may also feel that they have the aptitude to learn English. Second, they attend schools that are predominately White with English speakers, which may present more pressure to assimilate into the mainstream culture of the school and learn English. Further, children in the Chinese sample who had less educated parents or attended more diverse schools did not emphasize English proficiency in the messages.

Mexican English Messages: English is Hard but Necessary

For the Mexican group, English Messages accounted for a slightly larger proportion of the Current Messages than for the Chinese group. However, in the Mexican case, there was a more diverse pattern in the responses–negative, positive, and neutral. Some Mexican children stated more neutral positions about the English language–neither positive or negative, just that English was the language spoken in school.

> "They [schools] are almost the same. The only difference is the language."
>
> —14 year-old boy from Jalisco

This is a very interesting pattern, in which Mexican children articulate that the only difference in schools is the language of instruction, but otherwise Mexican and American schools are the same.

However, negative English Messages prevailed in the Mexican sample. Unlike the Chinese children who saw the acquisition of English as something that eventually will be accomplished, more Mexican children reported that English was a language that it was difficult to learn.

"[I would tell my cousin] that when he comes here it is going to be difficult because he doesn't speak English."
—14 year-old boy from Jalisco

"Teachers speak English only but they are nice. Learning English is difficult to learn."
—13 year-old boy from Mexico City

"It [school] is very different. English is hard when you don't know it."
—14 year-old girl from Jalisco

"Also that learning English is hard. They [co-nationals] should learn English in Mexico."
—14 year-old girl from Jalisco

Negative messages about English language acquisition present a rather frustrating picture for the newcomer—regarding the difficulty of learning the English language. Only three children stated some kind of positive English Messages. These included:

- The opportunity to learn English
- English language support from teachers and friends.

It is interesting that Mexican children construct English language support from friends who often are also English language learners with slightly higher English language proficiency than the newcomers.

"[I would tell my cousin] that here all your friends help you learn English."
—11 year-old from the State of Mexico

"Teachers will help her [my cousin] and she will learn English soon."
—15 year-old from Jalisco

Chinese–Mexican Comparison of English Messages

The perception towards the English language is a little different for Mexican children. First, Chinese children constructed the idea of English support in terms of ESL programs, not just teachers or friends, as Mexican did. Also, while Chinese children articulated feelings of being left out or discriminated against because they were not English proficient, Mexican children did not. This may reflect the presence of first language speakers in the schools that Mexican children attend—with high proportions of Latino English learners—and the majority of these children socializing with co-nationals in the school.

Another dimension not present in the Chinese sample is the neutral position towards English as the language of instruction. In the Mexican sample, some children included the fact that English was spoken in schools but without specifying if these was a negative or positive thing. These messages usually refer to "they speak English here."

The low proportion of English Messages among co-nationals in both groups raises questions about the role of the English language in the education of immigrant children from the child's point of view—is it a major consideration for immigrant children? Do they perceive it as a pre-requisite for academic or social participation? Further, it is also important to understand the way these children are being served in terms of language programs and how these programs may be creating more frustration in the learning process, which in turn may negatively influence the academic achievement of these children. Why may Mexican children perceive learning English as a difficult task and Chinese children perceive this as an attainable task?

Part of the answer lies in the types of school these children attend and the quality of ESL programs available in these schools. Let us remember that most of the Chinese children who articulated English Messages attended predominately White, middle-class schools, with low percentages of English learners. Given that these schools are located in middle-class suburbs around Boston, it is expected that these schools may have higher quality programs than the inner-city schools that the Mexican children attend in California. How do English language development programs available to English language learners influence the children's perceptions of their possibilities to acquire English fluency?

PEER MESSAGES: MORE CAREFUL CHOICES

Peer Messages constitute the third top category of themes for Current Messages in both groups. For both groups, Peer Messages became a more dominant category in Current Messages than in Prior or Welcoming Messages. The distribution by gender was balanced in both samples, a little bit more dominant among boys (Appendix D).

Chinese Peer Messages: Co-nationals vs. Non–Co-national Peers

One of the surprising changes in the Chinese group is that, contrary to Prior and Welcoming Messages where most of the reaction towards peers was negative, Current Messages reflect more positive attitudes towards peers than negative perceptions. In the Chinese sample, negative messages towards peers were more dominant among females than among males. Negative messages about peers focused on:

- Negative peer behaviors against Chinese students (e.g., bullying, teasing)
- Strategic advice for Chinese students regarding peer interactions based on stereotypes (how to interact and gain acceptance with peers)
- Awareness of the importance of peer choice (avoiding negative peer influences)
- Negative perceptions towards specific student groups.

Chinese students mostly warned potential newcomers of "bullies" in the school. Some of the Chinese students attributed being "bullied" by non-Chinese students as evidence of discrimination towards Chinese.

> "They [peers] discriminate Chinese. Be psychologically prepared for that. The U.S. is not that good. It is easier for me to make friends in Hong Kong."
> —16 year-old girl from Hong Kong

Some children expressed concern about being bullied because of how differently they looked or dressed. This prompted some children to advise the potential newcomer about "changing" their look to fit in:

"Change the fashion style. If you dress too backwardly or unfashionably, the Black students will tease you or bully you. Don't speak too directly or honestly. For example, if somebody looks ugly, you can't say he or she is ugly."

—16 year-old girl from Guanxi

A boy gave an interesting piece of advice to a newcomer about not acting too academically oriented (getting good grades) to avoid teasing from American children and being perceived as a "nerd."

"Things to do: Finish always your homework, try to get good grades, but try not to act like a nerd too much. Otherwise American kids would make fun of you. Avoid fights because you get in a lot of trouble. I have a friend who threw a chair."

—13 year-old from Inner Mongolia

Chinese children also stressed the importance of peer choice:

"You really have to think about who do you want to hang out with. Because they can have big influence in your life and affect the direction you go."

—13 year-old boy from Guangdong

Regarding peer choice, some Chinese children expressed some negative attitudes towards specific student groups, mostly African Americans and White Americans. However, instead of suggesting avoidance, some students gave more specific strategies that range from reciprocity to specific advice on how to deal with certain groups, usually based on stereotypes.

"I would tell them [co-nationals] that they will get along with many people very easily. But if you don't treat them well, they will not treat you well. I would tell them to be extra careful because the Black students might beat them."

—11 year-old girl from Guangdong

"Think twice before you come. Schools in the U.S. are not as good as you thought. Don't offend people, specially the Vietnamese. They are specially tough and cruel."

—15 year-old boy from Hong Kong

A Chinese boy advises not to fight with specific student groups, not including the co-national group. This young man attends a diverse school.

"Don't fight with the blacks and whites, because if you fight for three times you will be punished. You may be suspended for a few days in a month."

—15 year-old boy from Guangdong

As in other categories (e.g., academic), Chinese messages seem to be very instrumental and strategic (e.g., advising specific behaviors). Peer Messages upon entry reflected not only perceptions of peers, but also advice regarding specific behaviors on "how to" interact with peers.

Positive messages about peers usually referred to:

- Co-national peers as being friendly and supportive
- The importance of establishing selective friendships in the school.

Surprisingly, most of the Peer Messages were positive, depicting friends as nice and helpful:

"Friends are nice to you. They listen to your problems and try to help you. Classmates are very nice if you have questions about the class. They can help you answer the questions."

—13 year-old boy from Guangdong

"In general, people don't know Chinese. [But] there are quite a number of Chinese in the schools. They will play with you. If you don't know something in the school, the Chinese friends will help you. You can call your Chinese friends and ask questions."

—15 year-old boy from Guangdong

"I don't want to tell them [co-nationals] about the fighting and cursing at school because they will tell my parents and my parents will scold me. Classmates are very nice to me, not very selfish."

—Chinese girl from Fujian (no age data)

Many children expressed that it was easy to make friends in the U.S. However, peer choice data shows that most of these children have co-national friends. Therefore, many of the positive messages about peers may refer to the co-national peers, rather than peers in other groups. Some children also give advice to potential co-nationals about how to select their friends and the importance of making friends in school.

"You should get a lot of friends, classmates. Things to do, you should hang out with people, like play with others and things to avoid is like don't let people tease you, make fun of you"

—13 year-old boy from Inner Mongolia

An interesting finding is that most of the children that shared positive perceptions of peers had parents with college education or high school. This is a different pattern from the children who had negative messages about peers whose most parents had no post-elementary education. It is interesting that of these children, about half attended mostly-White schools, and the other half attended mostly-Asian schools or diverse schools. This indicates that regardless of the density of the co-national group in the school, these children perceived their co-nationals as a positive group to associate with because they were friendly and willing to provide support to the newcomer. However, the link between parental educational level and school type may indicate some socioeconomic issues regarding peer interactions within the same class (e.g., middle-class) as less confrontational. This raises questions about class issues. For example, are immigrant children in middle-class contexts more accepted by their (middle-class) peers, regardless of ethnic or racial backgrounds, than are immigrant children from working class backgrounds in low-income communities?

Mexican Messages: Peers as a Threat and Careful Choices

Mexican messages about peers were almost equally distributed between negative and positive messages (Appendix D). Negative Peer Messages were equally distributed by gender. These negative messages referred to:

- Negative peer behaviors within the school context (e.g., bullying, cutting classes)
- Peers involved in gang activities
- Negative perceptions towards specific student groups (e.g., African American and Asian students)
- The need to avoid "bad" peers (by behavior and ethnicity).

Among Mexican children, negative perceptions of peer behaviors included both school and gang related behaviors.

"Schools are good. Some peers are nice but others play too much. I would tell him to study. I would tell him not to hang out with Cholos gang members."
—15 year-old boy from Guerrero

Some children gave specific advice to the potential newcomers about gang markers and behaviors.

"First, not to wear baggy clothes or wear blue or red [gang related colors]. At first, he [co-national cousin] should not act out. Second, he should not hang out with those who wear caps [gang related]. At first, [I would advise] he should calm down, behave calmly [but] then if he wants to act out ... then I would have to say good bye [not hang out with him]. I would still talk to him but not in the same way."
—14 year-old boy from Jalisco

This boy's answer reflects a realization about the acculturation process that take place with the newcomers when they assimilate into peer groups that are perceived as gang-related. He advises about not wearing "gang" colors and presents his position about his "hypothetical cousin" becoming acculturated into bad behaviors—"acting out." Other children also spoke of negative peer influences and the need to avoid "bad kids":

> "I would tell my cousin not to hang out with [students' names]. I had friends who were troublemakers. If he came to this school, I would tell him that I hanged out with those boys but I do not anymore because they are troublemakers. I would advise him that if the troublemakers sought him to hang out with them, he shouldn't hang out with them. They were going to get him in trouble. That sometimes because of their fault, he could even go to jail, if he gets into gangs or fights other boys. They [peers] will get him in trouble, [invite him] to do something that is not good."
>
> —14 year-old boy from Jalisco

Some children articulated messages about the importance of choosing friends, not only in term of behavior but also in terms of ethnicity, establishing racial differentiation in peer choice.

> "Hang out with Mexicans, so he can understand better. Teachers get angry, so he needs to listen. Pay attention. Don't cut classes. Don't fight. Run when he sees Blacks. Stay away from Blacks."
>
> —13 year-old boy from Guerrero

The answer from this particular child regarding African American peers echoes the messages that he received from his co-nationals when he entered an American school for the first time as a fifth grader:

> "[Co-nationals told me] 'don't hang out with Blacks because they fight.' They told me the classes were easy."

This child entered an elementary school in the community of San Patricio. According to some documents from community meetings, the issue of gangs and violence in schools, especially at the local high school, is a major concern for community officials and law enforcement agencies. In a community meeting, a meeting report summarized:

One of the main problems of gang life seemed to be that the teenagers had nothing to do, and they are bored. As a result they hang out and smoke weed, drink, and cause trouble for fun. They argued that if they could build somewhere [some place] for the teenagers to go there would be less crime on the streets.

School context seems to be a key element in the construction of perceptions of peers among immigrant children. Of course, children will talk about what they experience. But again, I ask if there are ways in which communities, families, and schools can contribute to the breaking of these cycles, especially regarding the lack of positive interaction among peers from different backgrounds in the school.

One interesting fact about the Mexican students who received negative messages about peers is that most of these children have lived in the country more than four years. In the Chinese case it is mostly recent immigrants who held negative perceptions of their peers. This raises issues about the permanency of these stereotypical views of inter-cultural relations in the Mexican group.

It is important to note that most of these Mexican children had parents with less than some post-elementary education, that is, the parents did not complete high school. If there is a connection between education and income, this may indicate the parents' need to be relocated to poor areas of the U.S. (where housing is more affordable) like the community of San Patricio—with high density and poverty levels, where ethnic conflicts and gang activity may occur. Also, the majority of the children (9 out of 10) who expressed negative Peer Messages attend schools in San Patricio and the vicinity (e.g., the local high school is not located in San Patricio, but it is the only high school available for San Patricio students). Four of these children who stated negative perceptions of peers also heard such messages from co-nationals when they entered American schools. That is, for these four children (all attending San Patricio schools), the Welcoming Messages are reflected in their Current Messages about peers.

Positive messages among Mexicans related to:

- Positive perceptions towards peers' personalities
- Perceptions of peers who behave nicely

- Supportive peers who offer friendship and support to co-nationals
- Encouraging selective peer choice by behavior.

These messages were also balanced by gender (Appendix D).

"[I would tell my cousin] that they [schools] are very good for learning, teachers are helpful and that students behave well."
— 13 year-old boy from Michoacan

Mexican children who stated positive messages about peers usually expressed a distinction between "good" and "bad" peers, noticing that some kids are good and some are bad, and encouraging newcomers to socialize with the "good" kids.

"Some classmates are jerks but others are very cool. I would tell her to do the homework, do all the class work and not to cut classes."
— 13 year-old girl from Jalisco

"Classmates are good. I'd tell her to hang out with people that are not rude and don't fight."
— 14 year-old girl from Michoacan

Positive Peer Messages did not generalize about a particular group of students being good. Advice on how to choose peers who are "good" usually was based on behaviors rather than ethnicity.

Chinese–Mexican Comparison of Peer Messages

From analyzing the Peer Messages that immigrant children articulated, it is clear that they revealed the existence of racial separation. Usually, both Mexican and Chinese children talked about "other" student groups (e.g., African Americans, Whites, Asian) in negative terms. The "other" students were the students that fight, the ones who bullied and discriminated against the immigrant children. Most of the children established positive messages about their own ethnic group. However, there is an important distinction in the Mexican group. Some Mexican children made negative references to "Cholos." While Cholos (Latino gang members) share the same ethnic identification as Mexican immigrants (e.g., Hispanic, Latino), Mexican immigrants do not consider them as "Mexican" per se.

While Chinese Peer Messages often revealed strategies for assimilation and interaction with the "other," Mexican Peer Messages often use avoidance as the way to "deal" with conflicting peers. In the Mexican group co-national peers recommend avoiding peers by ethnicity. That is, among Mexican children, it was clear that they identified specific ethnic student groups as the "bad" children. However, when choosing children that were good or nice, Mexican children did not categorize any particular ethnic group as "good," encouraging newcomers to choose good peers by behavior, not necessarily by ethnicity.

An important finding in Peer Messages is that some of these messages may be reproducing themselves from the socialization with co-nationals. For example, the Mexican children's impression that children in American schools are involved in gangs and violent activities is a message that has been repeated through time—in Prior, Welcoming, and Current Messages. While Peer Messages represented less than 15% of the messages in each group, I think they do reveal important indications of social and inter-cultural relations in the school site and how these interactions are being shaped and influenced by the messages received in the co-national space. Specifically, because Mexican children often suggest "avoidance" of other ethnic groups (e.g., African American) as a way to deal with inter-racial conflict, I wonder if these negative perceptions are the product of actual interactions with other groups or from "rumors" that promote negative perceptions of other students groups among co-nationals.

SCHOOL MESSAGES: SERVICES AND OPPORTUNITIES

School Messages continued being an important category of transnational messages for both Chinese and Mexican children (see Table 7.1). School Messages were more predominant among Chinese females than among males. In the Mexican sample, School Messages were equally distributed by gender (Appendix D.).

Chinese Messages: Learning to Live in the American School

The majority of the Chinese children had positive messages regarding school issues. Negative Chinese messages about schools were focused on schedules.

> "You don't have a lot of breaks. In China, you have 10-minute breaks between classes."
>
> —16 year-old boy from Guangdong

> "You don't get as much vacation as you do in China."
>
> —13 year-old girl from Guangdong

In terms of positive School Messages, most children constructed these messages as advice for the newcomer and descriptions of U.S. schools' characteristics. The themes in Current School Messages included:

- Orientation to school rules, routines, and classroom behaviors
- Orientation to importance of socialization within school
- Positive perceptions towards less restrictive schedules and school routines
- Awareness of free services and materials in U.S. schools
- Awareness of the quality of services in school (e.g., sports programs).

Some advice was geared to orientation about school rules, routines, and classroom behaviors.

> "During recess, don't play with stones. Don't climb out of the fence. Don't get out of school campus."
>
> —15 year-old boy from Guangdong

> "School is quite good. The environment is quite good, very quiet with a lot of equipment. You usually don't get that much homework, unless you are in the 8th grade. Speak up and speak out in class, don't be too quiet."
>
> —13 year-old boy from Guangdong

Some children gave specific advice about how to socially navigate in the school environment:

> "Nothing much in particular. It is kind of the same in China. School is easier here. You have to do everything you do in China. You should communicate with your friends more. You should consider more about the overall performance of the whole group when presenting group projects. You should also participate in one sport so you will get to know people more easily."
>
> —15 year-old boy from Shangdong

This child has parents who have professional degrees. However, most Chinese children, regardless of parent education, provided School Messages about following the rules of school.

> "You have to finish all your homework. Don't skip school. Don't talk when teacher is teaching. If you do, you will be punished. You will need to copy things several times as a punishment. Communicate with your friends and schoolmates."
>
> —16 year-old girl from Guangdong

It is interesting to note that many of the Chinese children emphasized the issue of communicating with others within the school context.

Some Chinese students also communicated messages about the fact that American schools provide free services and materials including free tuition, buses, school supplies, and meals. Nevertheless, most of the messages were regarding orientation to school life and the organization of the American school. While advice messages regarding assimilation into the school life are present across all groups of parent education and school type, there are some differences in the messages regarding school services.

Children whose parents had professional degrees did not include themes regarding free services in the school. They mostly referred to information about school environment (less restrictive) or organization (e.g., schedule). They also included some messages regarding the quality of facilities and availability of programs (e.g., bilingual programs, and sports facilities). On the other hand, most of the children who stated messages regarding free services and materials offered in the school had fathers with less than elementary education. All of these children had mothers with elementary education.

This indicates that the types of messages and the emphasis that students place on different aspects of the school environment—programs, facilities, or free services—may be related to socioeconomic factors. Children of parents with limited formal education may also have lower income levels. Therefore, any services that the American school provides that reduce the cost of education for these families can become more salient for them than for families that are more privileged economically. However, it is clear that for the children in this sample, information about school rules and organization was one of the most important kinds of messages they would provide to Chinese newcomers.

Mexican Messages: Co-Nationals Providing a Comfort Zone

For the Mexican group, the School Messages also comprised the second largest category of Current Messages. Interestingly, this category also represented the most common message category for Prior and Welcoming Messages. Now that the Mexican children had experienced the American schools, the Academic Messages were more prevalent than School Messages. Most messages were positive (Appendix D). Negative School Messages referred to:

- Schedules and the difficulty of having to change classrooms and teachers
- Dissatisfaction with the facilities, especially regarding the physical outlook of the buildings.

A Mexican boy states his dissatisfaction with the overall appearance of school buildings:

"The truth is that schools are better in Mexico. There's no graffiti in the school in Mexico."
                                                    —14 year-old boy from Jalisco

The positive School Messages were concentrated in three major categories.

- Orientation to school campus
- Positive perceptions towards the presence of co-nationals in the school
- Awareness of the quality of services and materials in school (e.g., computers in the classroom).

Just like in the Chinese sample, most children offered to orient the newcomer to school life, specifically about school rules, schedules, and campus orientation:

"I would advise her on the classes she should take."
—17 year-old girl from Jalisco

Another major category was about advising the newcomer that there are co-nationals in the school.

"There are many bilingual teachers to help you. And there are lots of Latino students. Fifty-eight percent in this school."
—16 year-old girl from Veracruz

The recognition of diversity in the school was another theme in the Current Messages for potential co-nationals. Mexican students revealed that while there is diversity in the school, there are still many Mexicans in the school, therefore, newcomers should not worry. The Mexicans in the school become the group to hang out with, which speaks the same language and can help them.

"There are a lot of Blacks and Chinese. It is bad here but there are a lot of Mexicans as well who can help you."
—17 year-old boy from Jalisco

Other themes in the messages were regarding the quality of facilities and the services that school provided. Mexican children referred to how big the American schools were, about the different classes that they offered (e.g., music, computers), and the availability of equipment (e.g., computers).

"If you put your part, put in effort, it is a good school. There
are more opportunities. Here the teachers lend books but in
Mexico you have to buy them. Here you can take books out of
the library."
                                        —Mexican girl from Colima (no age data)

Free tuition and free services were also mentioned, especially free
meals in school. But only two children mentioned this. The lack of
emphasis on free services and materials may indicate a shift in
priorities for children—from school services to more academic
orientation. A few children also mentioned a less restrictive school
environment in terms of discipline in general.

Chinese–Mexican Comparison of School Messages

School Messages were an important theme that both the Chinese and
the Mexican children would share with a potential newcomer from their
country. These messages usually were given in terms of advice, which
reveals the potential instrumental value that the established co-national
in the school can provide for the newcomer in terms of information that
can orient the newcomer to the American school. This is an important
consideration because it shows that co-nationals are a source of
information and support to the newcomer in the U.S. school. Also, for
both groups, co-nationals are encouraged to socialize with other co-
nationals.

Also, an interesting perception is the quality of "school programs."
While some Chinese and Mexican children spoke of low quality of
instruction and less demanding academic standards in the U.S., others
seem to appreciate the non-academic programs that American schools
can offer such as music, art, or sports. This also raise questions about
whether these programs are available in the country of origin and how
the more diversified school activities can promote positive perceptions
towards American schools in immigrant children. That is, how do
immigrant children prioritize what is important or more appealing to
them in American schools? Are non-academic issues and programs a
more important aspect of immigrant children's lives in American
schools?

SOCIAL MESSAGES: THE SCHOOL SOCIAL CONTEXT

Social Messages were a category that emerged in Welcoming Messages and continues being present in Current Messages. These messages, rather than speaking of interactions with peers and teachers (those are discussed under their specific categories), revealed an understanding of some macro issues regarding the perception of these children about the American social context and their position within the society. Social Messages also depict socialization issues within the school context in general, rather than in perceptions of peer groups in the schools.

In Current Messages, Social Messages become a sizeable category (see Table 7.1). In the Chinese sample, the gender distribution in Social Messages was balanced, but in the Mexican sample these messages were predominantly male (Appendix D).

Chinese Messages: Learning How to Socialize in America

Negative Social Messages among the Chinese group referred to:

- The difficulty of handling cultural differences in the U.S.
- The existence of discrimination.

These messages reflected perceptions of discrimination against the Chinese in general. The children who expressed these messages were older children (15 and older). This may indicate that there are some developmental issues regarding ethnic identity and awareness of social issues such as discrimination that may not be so present in younger children. Most of these children came from families that are not highly educated (some post-elementary), yet attend schools where only a minority of students are either English language learners or qualified to participate in free/reduced lunch programs. These feelings of discrimination may also be a reflection of class-difference issues at play in the social relations with people in the United States.

Most of the Chinese children who gave positive Social Messages often referred to:

- Positive perceptions of freedom and equality in the U.S.
- The importance of socialization in the school in order to succeed.

Some Chinese children expressed positive attitudes towards the more liberal environment in the U.S. However, the main topic of Social Messages was the importance of socialization. According to Chinese Social Messages, learning how to socialize is pivotal in order to secure support from others who most likely would not offer it. For example, a girl whose parents both have elementary education explained what she would say to a potential newcomer:

> "Actually, the U.S. is a very independent place. Men and women are equal. That is why you first have to know how to work. That is, being nice to people, don't be straightforward, because you might offend people. And you have to be nice to your friends. The most important thing is better yourself. Try your best on whatever you are doing. The most important thing is to be able to reflect. Also, I will share with my cousin my feelings when I first came here. I will also tell him/her that here no one helps you. You have to learn to be open to get help. You have to communicate with people. The most crucial thing is to be nice to people, then people will be nice to you."
>
> —16 year-old girl from Fujian

This girl's message reveals a clear instrumental value towards socialization. In her answer, she affirms that "nobody helps you" but that "you have to learn to be open to get help." She also reflects on some of the issues that she considers important in American society, such as independence and gender equality. Socialization within the school context seems to be an important issue for the Chinese children. In fact, most of the positive messages about social issues referred to strategies to establish social relations in the school context (12 out of 15). Some of the answers also reveal difference in the role of social relations in the school context.

> "Socializing is more important than schools are. You need friends more than your grades. However, it also depends on which grade you are in. If you are a senior, grades are more important. If you are freshmen, you should hang out more with your friends."
>
> —16 year-old boy from Beijing

For the Chinese children, establishing relationships in school is important to succeed and participate in school. Socializing with other children provides a support system that is needed in order to participate in the U.S. school. Also, there is a perception in the Chinese children of the value of social relations in American society (e.g., it is important to establish social relations). However, Chinese students urge the newcomer to be selective in peer choice.

> "Schools are very good. If you want to make friends, make sure you know if they are studying or not. Consider whether or not your friendships with him/her may affect his/her study."
> —15 year-old girl from Hong Kong

The children who gave positive Social Messages attend predominately White or diverse schools. While this is a distribution that mirrors the general distribution of the overall Chinese group, it may also indicate the emphasis on cultural differences and the need for assimilation. If the children attend highly diverse schools, it is logical that they are aware of the cultural differences played out in the school context. On the other hand, children who attend predominately White schools would be exposed to American middle-class societal norms that they seem to reflect on. Also, remember that some of the school advice from Chinese in predominately White schools refers to the importance of learning behaviors and adopting fashions in order to fit into the American mainstream culture. Chinese students seem to be aware of cultural differences and opt for assimilation and cultural learning (U.S. mainstream) as tools for enhancing participation in the school context.

Mexican Messages: Good Behaviors and Solidarity

Rather than being classified positive or negative, Mexican Social Messages seemed to focus on providing advice about:

- Adopting positive social behaviors (e.g., being good)
- Showing solidarity to co-nationals
- Becoming aware of different people in the U.S. (good and bad)

For example, one boy reflects on the need to help other co-nationals:

> "Remember those who helped him when he arrived, so later on, he can help others. He needs to watch out for others, beware of others."
>
> —15 year-old boy from Guerrero

> "[I would tell my cousin] to come prepared. [Life in the U.S.] is very different than over there."
>
> —14 year-old boy from Jalisco

> "That she's [co-national] better [off] watching whom she hangs out with, find people that treat her with respect. Here in the U.S., there is every kind of people, some are kind of good people but others are not."
>
> —13 year-old girl from Sinaloa

Most of the Social Messages refer to general statements about being a good child and being aware of the importance of socializing with nice people. These messages advised co-nationals "to be good." While these messages may be related to School Messages (e.g., school rules), they were classified as Social Messages because children did not specify that these behaviors were part of the school rules or teacher expectations, and they were not related to academic behaviors (e.g., do your homework). These messages seemed to be the result of the Mexican children's understanding of the moral duty to be a "well-behaved" child. More boys gave Social Messages than girls did (Appendix D).

Chinese–Mexican Comparison of Social Messages

Social Messages seemed to be more salient in the Chinese sample. In the case of the Mexican sample, the Social Messages were a bit too general to carry a deep meaning—people are different in the U.S. from Mexico and "be good." While Chinese children expressed ideas about socialization in American society, Mexican children gave advice about adopting general social behaviors that seem to reflect an appreciation for children who behave well, perhaps within a Mexican context, rather than the new social context they may experience in the U.S. That is, it is possible that the Mexican children's advice on being good is a reflection of Mexican societal views about how children should behave, rather than a suggestion that in order to function socially in the U.S. children need to behave nicely. For those Mexican children who stated messages regarding American society, the concern seems to be around about differences in the "kinds of people" between Mexico and the U.S., but no strategies were offered about how to react to these differences—other than being careful about with whom to socialize.

On the other hand, in the Chinese sample, the social advice is clearly given in terms of how to function in the new U.S. context. Some children reflected on the differences in American society that were salient (e.g., independence, gender issues). But most importantly they constructed the "need" for socialization in terms of adaptation to the American school, as they implied that socialization is important in American schools (the role of socialization in the school context). Socialization became instrumental in order to ensure participation in the school context.

Chinese children seemed to be aware of the problematic nature of cultural differences and how this might affect their participation, in the social context of the school and society at large. The Chinese children seemed to strategize more about how to overcome these barriers. They viewed the need to socialize as more pivotal than the Mexican children in this sample did, in part because of the types of school most of them attend—White, middle-class schools. That is, Chinese children have exposure to mainstream American culture in the school and therefore can perceive a need for socialization in order to fit into the majority culture in the school.

For Mexican children who attend mostly-Latino, inner-city schools, the model of mainstream American culture may not be present in the school site nor within the peer culture. Because Mexican children socialize in school sites where the co-nationals in the school represent the majority of the school population, socializing strategies within the peer group may not be salient because it is understood that the newcomer already knows how to socialize with other Mexicans. Therefore, the advice regarding social behaviors was important in terms of good behavior. While most Chinese students do socialize with co-nationals, even when this group is not predominant in the school, the exposure of the mainstream culture (most children attend predominately White schools) in the school may influence the children's perception of the need for social integration.

The Social Messages can also be linked to the availability of the co-nationals as a support group (Peer Messages). In the Chinese sample, this support was given in terms of "acculturation" into the American school and the mainstream culture. On the other hand, the social support from the Mexican co-national peer was more in terms of a reinforcement of their own culture, language, and national identity. The Mexican co-nationals become the peers of choice because it is the group that speaks the language and understands the Mexican social norms. Also, the solidarity towards co-nationals based on a reciprocal relationship seemed to be more salient in the Mexican group. While Chinese children also referred to the co-nationals in the school as a source of support (see Peer Messages), the relationship seemed to be more instrumental than reciprocal.

Further, the lack of concern about cultural differences in the Mexican sample may be linked to the cultural isolation that these children may experience in school without exposure to the mainstream society. In my ethnographic experiences with schools where the predominant group is Latino, in Northern California, the children were often highly segregated, especially in relation to immigrant, non-English speaking Latino students.

For example, schools in San Patricio usually placed Latino, non-English proficient children, especially at the middle and high school levels, into "bilingual" cohorts that segregated students from any academic involvement with any other group but with Spanish speaking, Latino children. Further, in an attempt to provide a more culturally sensitive and linguistic match in the curriculum, Latino teachers were usually hired (many of them nationals of Latin American countries and Spain, often on emergency credentials) to serve these students. While these bilingual programs aimed to provide the academic support in the first language with teachers that may understand the culture, these programs attempted to solve one problem perhaps by creating another. The isolation of Latino English learners seemed to create problems in inter-cultural relations because these children had limited opportunities to interact within an academic context with children from different cultural backgrounds.

I am not suggesting that it is wrong or inappropriate to have these bilingual cohorts. I think it is important for students to develop a strong academic foundation in their own language and capitalize on the richness of their home culture and continue promoting it. However, the lack of meaningful interactions within school with children from other groups may indeed reinforce the negative attitudes that immigrant children have of other ethnic groups. As these immigrant children lack actual positive experiences with children from other groups within the academic context, they often resort to stereotypical images of other ethnic students that are being promoted by other co-nationals. Could these bilingual cohorts promote bi-culturalism, rather than cultural isolation, and integrate instructional activities that involve participation with children of other cultural groups?

TEACHER MESSAGES: PERSONALITY MATTERS

Teacher Messages were not particularly important in the Prior and Welcoming Messages. However, as these children have been assimilated into the schools for a number of years, Teacher Messages become more prevalent (see Table 7.1). More Chinese girls gave Teacher Messages than boys. The distribution by gender in the Mexican sample was balanced (Appendix D).

Chinese Messages: Nice but Incompetent Teachers

As in Prior and Welcoming Messages, most Teacher Messages in the Current category were positive. Negative messages among the Chinese participants referred to:

- Low teacher quality
- Lack of teachers' ability to implement discipline and classroom management
- Negative references to the teachers' personalities (e.g., teachers are mean).

Chinese children became critical of teachers' instructional and discipline styles when sharing their perceptions:

"Teachers use many lessons to teach one thing. One topic is taught for several days. [It is] just a waste of time. Teachers, then just try to get by in school. If they can't finish the topic today, they will simple leave that for tomorrow. They don't lose anything for teaching slow. Just the students suffer for learning fewer things."

—16 year-old girl from Hong Kong

Other negative perceptions of teachers usually included comments such as "teachers are mean," but another negative opinion from the Chinese children was the lack of control that some teachers seem to exercise over their students.

"In some public schools some teacher can't control the students, can't manage the students."

—15 year-old girl from Guangdong

Some Chinese children gave specific advice about teacher choice, suggesting that becoming aware of "teacher quality" is important.

"Teachers. Always at the end of the year, always call or write to the school, asking about nice and good teachers for the next year. Otherwise they will give you any teacher. We did that for 5th grade. I got an extremely good teacher."

—13 year-old boy from Inner Mongolia

However, it is important to note that this child attends a school in a Boston suburb, where 85% of the student population is White, only 8% are in free/reduced lunch programs, and less than 2% are English language learners. Also, this boy's parents had graduate and professional degrees. These characteristics may indicate some issues of social capital regarding the utilization of the school system to ensure the academic development of this child.

Most of the students who gave negative messages about teachers were female, ages 15–17. This may indicate that as children are in high school and are more conscious about academic requirements for college, they may be more critical of the quality of instruction. The profile of Chinese children who articulated these messages shows that even within middle-class, suburban schools where we might expect higher academic standards and more instructional resources, Chinese children were critical of teacher preparation and disciplinary control.

However, most of the Teacher Messages in the Chinese group were positive. More girls articulated positive Teacher Messages (Appendix D). While some students were critical of the lack of discipline displayed by some teachers in U.S. schools, some Chinese children perceived the lack of discipline as a positive attribute of the teachers in American schools. Positive Teacher Messages among the Chinese included:

- Less restrictive and less severe disciplinary styles among teachers in the U.S.
- Academic support that teachers provide to students in the U.S.
- Positive perceptions towards teachers' personalities that facilitate cordial students-teacher relations.

Chinese children seem to appreciate the less restrictive nature of the teachers in the U.S. and the less severe punishments in the schools.

"Teachers are much nicer than in China. The treat everyone equally. Teachers won't punish you if you don't finish homework. They will just tell you to finish your homework. You can go to the bathroom between classes. They give you less homework than in China."
— 13 year-old girl from Fujian

"It is fairly easy, not very strict. Teachers are really causal. You don't have to sit all day that straight. Homework is easy."
— 13 year-old girl from Sichuan

"The teachers here don't punish you as hard as in Hong Kong."
— 12 year-old girl from Hong Kong

Another teacher quality Chinese children mentioned was the academic support that teachers in the U.S. provided to students.

"Teachers in the U.S. are very nice. If you don't know something, they will teach you."
— 15 year-old boy from Guangdong

"Teachers are helpful. They can help you with things that you don't understand. They can answer your questions. School is quite good."

—13 year-old boy from Guangdong

However, the majority of the positive messages regarding teachers refer to positive perceptions of Chinese students towards their teachers' personalities. Children referred to teachers' personality and how this improved student-teacher relationships. Chinese children often referred their teachers as being "nice," "sympathetic" and treating them with respect, fairness, and equality.

Most of the Chinese children who gave positive messages about teachers tended to be younger children. This may indicate that due to maturity issues and less emphasis on academic demands (compared to high school students) they place more value on the student-teacher relations and the "nice" personality of their teachers. Also, these children are relatively recent immigrants; therefore, they may still have a vivid image of the rigorous and disciplinary style of the teachers in China. For children who articulated positive Teacher Messages, parent education is distributed across different backgrounds—from post-elementary to graduate/professional. One interesting aspect of the Teacher Messages is that for Chinese children, the teachers in the U.S. are not necessarily less disciplinary, but more liberal, fair, and less restrictive.

"They [teachers] are easier and pretty liberal about things. Teachers are not very strict, usually sympathetic."

—15 year-old boy from Beijing

"Teachers here will treat you very nicely."

—15 year-old boy from Guangdong

Just like in the Academic Messages where Chinese children tended to compare American standards to Chinese practices, the teacher in the U.S. school provided a less stressful, more comfortable environment that Chinese children seemed to appreciate.

Mexican Messages: Mixed Feelings about Teachers' Personalities

More Mexican children gave positive messages about teachers than the Chinese children did. However, some of their negative views of teachers in the U.S. included:

- Teachers' personalities and treatment towards students
- Teachers' instructional practices (e.g., boring)
- Lack of teachers' ability to implement discipline and classroom management
- Teachers' apathy towards reinforcing school rules and academic expectations.

Negative messages in the Mexican sample referred mostly to personality factors—teachers were mean to students.

> "Teachers get angry, so he needs to listen. Pay attention. Don't cut classes."
> —13-year-old boy from Guerrero

Other children also commented teachers were "boring" in the U.S., making references to the quality of instruction. A few children also express discontent with the low academic demands that some teachers in the U.S. have for students.

> "In Mexico teachers are very strict. Here [it] is like if you want to bring the homework, you may bring it, if you don't want to, don't bring it. Here, they [teachers] ask you for the homework once in a while, some teachers don't [even] ask for it. There, in Mexico you have to bring all your work neatly. Here U.S., there are some students that bring their homework in their pockets, like they [teachers] don't care as long as you bring the homework, that's it. In Mexico they are very strict, you have to bring your books with covers, neatly. If you have a little spot, they tell you it is not well done and they give it back to you."
> —15 year-old girl from the State of Mexico

Negative messages in the Mexican sample reflect some of the same themes as in the Chinese group—low quality of instruction, lack of discipline, and bad teacher personalities. Girls reported most of the negative messages. Also, all of these children have attended the same middle and high schools in San Patricio. The fact that the negative messages about teachers in the U.S. come from children who have attended these two schools (out of 32 schools in the study) is an interesting pattern that reveal some concerns about quality of instruction in the schools in this particular community. However, it is important to note that these messages, indeed, are a minority. Furthermore, students' perceptions are highly contextualized by the individual relationships they have with their teachers.

Positive messages about teachers represented the majority of the messages among the Mexican group. Positive Teacher Messages included:

- Positive perceptions towards teachers' personalities as "nice" and "caring"
- Reciprocal students-teacher relations
- Academic support teachers provide to students in the U.S.
- Lack of corporal punishment

The most predominant message about teachers was about positive perceptions of teachers' personalities and the relationship with their students. Just like the Chinese students, most Mexican children said that they would communicate to their co-nationals that teachers in the U.S. were "nice." However, many Mexican children constructed the personality of teachers in the U.S. in terms of "caring" for children:

"It was a good opportunity. He will enjoy school. The teachers are caring."

—17 year-old boy from Colima

"[I would tell my co-national cousin] that it is pretty with good teachers that care about us. That they dedicate a lot of time to them"

—11 year-old boy from the State of Mexico

One interesting aspect of the idea that "teachers are nice" is that for some students this is based on a reciprocity factor. Some Mexican children expressed that teachers are nice, if students are nice to them. That is, teachers care and pay attention to children that are well behaved. For example, a boy who attends a predominately Latino middle school in Northern California shared his perspective on teachers:

> "[I would tell my co-national cousin] that the teachers behave great with me. If you behave you won't get in trouble."
>
> —14 year-old boy from Mexico City

Another boy who attends the local middle school in San Patricio also shared a similar pattern in the dynamics of student-teacher relations:

> "I would tell him [my cousin] about teachers. That depending on how one behaves, the teacher responds to you in the same way."
>
> —14 year-old boy from Jalisco

The relationships between teachers and students based on students' behavior is an important one, especially because many teachers in these schools where student discipline is a problem tend to reward children for their good behavior with good grades and attention. In my ethnographic work in the local middle school in San Patricio, I have observed the classrooms of five teachers in the last three years, and have conversed with about 15 teachers about immigrant children. These teachers tended to pay attention and invest in children who behave well. In other words, teachers tended to ignore and sanction children who presented discipline problems. Children who did not present a discipline problem for the teacher usually gained the teacher's attention and support over time. Further, in this middle school it has become a common rule that children perceived that students get good grades if they behave well. In one of my conversations with a teacher she complained that a Latino child was surprised that he received a low grade in the mid-year evaluation. When the teacher explained that the child had not turned in all of the homework assignments, the child replied, "but I have behaved well all the time. I always get good grades if I behave well."

This pattern is influenced by the violence and discipline problems that prevail in San Patricio schools, especially at the middle and high school levels. Teachers feel threatened and wish to get by during the school day with the fewest disciplinary problems possible. By rewarding children for good behavior with good grades, they aim to promote good behavior in the classroom. I have been informed by a teacher in the bilingual cohort that classroom behavior is an important factor in her grade assignment. A science teacher and an ESL teacher in this middle school commented that they usually gave higher grades to students who are well behaved in their classes. This may be a bit problematic if teachers are inflating grades to reward good behavior, and the grade does not really reflect the academic ability of the student. Further, teachers in San Patricio not only rewarded well-behaved children with good grades, but also with their time and support. Teachers usually felt more willing to invest and "care" about children that were well behaved, coaching them to pursue their academic goals. This may explain the fact that some Mexican children qualified teachers in the U.S. as "caring."

Another important theme in the Teacher Messages was the issue of academic support. Many Mexican children spoke of "helpful teachers" and "teachers will help you."

"Teachers are always helping you with homework."
—14 year-old girl from Baja California Norte

Finally, Mexican children also appreciated the less strict discipline displayed in the U.S., specifically the lack of corporal punishment.
"That is good. Here teachers don't hit you like in Mexico."
—14 year-old boy from Sonora

Chinese–Mexican Comparison of Teacher Messages

Teacher Messages is one of the categories that show more similarities between the two groups—Chinese and Mexican. Negative Teacher Messages are a minority for both groups. Both Chinese and Mexican children seemed to recognize some teachers' lack of preparation and classroom control in U.S. schools. However, Mexican children seemed to emphasize the "personality" factor as a negative treat in teachers.

Most of the Teacher Messages for both groups communicated a general positive perception of the teachers in the U.S. to potential newcomers. Both Chinese and Mexican children have a positive attitude towards their teachers, considering them respectful, if not very well prepared, yet nice and caring. Also, some children actually expressed positive perceptions towards teachers' disposition to help their students academically.

The fact that Mexican children articulate student-teacher relationships as reciprocal indicates the power of teachers to selectively distribute their support and dedication among different students. Some of this selective distribution of attention and support may be the product of the teachers' agency, but it may also be a reflection of the limited amount of resources (including time) that teachers in public schools may have to reach out to all of their students. If teachers could get the necessary support to "serve" all children, not just the well-behaved, the teacher could be a very significant player to provide social capital necessary to achieve in school, become a positive role model, and provide opportunities for meaningful and positive inter-cultural relations among peers.

Also, the fact that many of these children may indeed have co-national teachers is an important consideration in inquiring how well-prepared these co-national teachers are to provide social capital that reflects the needs of the immigrant children in their new social context—the U.S. Do co-national teachers have the necessary ability to understand the "know-how" of academic and social participation within the American school system? While I recognized the enormous contribution that these co-national teachers may have in the education of immigrant children, I wonder if these teachers have the necessary social capital to transmit to their students about the academic pipeline that could lead these students to higher education in the United States. I wonder if these teachers somehow reproduce the cultural constructions of schooling from their countries of origin (e.g., same instructional and disciplinary styles as in China or Mexico) and how this reproduction may affect immigrant children participation in American schools.

TRANSNATIONAL MESSAGES OVER TIME

In general, the construction of positive and negative messages about the U.S. schools over time confirms that many of the messages that children in 2000 were willing to share with their potential co-nationals in the school reflect what they heard in Prior and Welcoming Messages. This indicates that over time, immigrant children tend to focus on the same issues—academic, school, peers, and teachers. But also, as they experience American schools, the nature of their perceptions about the same themes change, and sometimes new themes emerge (e.g., social). Table 7.2 depicts a general distribution of the messages over time.

Table 7.2.
Transnational Messages over Time

Type of Message	Prior Immigration		Welcoming		Current	
	Chinese	Mexican	Chinese	Mexican	Chinese	Mexican
Academic	23%	14%	12%	21%	24%	21%
English	3%	7%	1%	4%	5%	8%
General	9%	14%	3%	12%	9%	17%
No answer	38%	32%	53%	22%	1%	4%
Peers	5%	12%	4%	15%	15%	10%
School	12%	16%	9%	14%	20%	15%
Social	0%	0%	4%	4%	9%	10%
Teachers	10%	5%	6%	8%	17%	15%
No co-nationals	0%	0%	8%	0%	0%	0%
Total	100%	100%	100%	100%	100%	100%

As in the case of construction of students' perceptions over time about the U.S. school, the distribution of Prior, Welcoming, and Current Messages also shows some emphasis on the same themes over time. Let us explore some of these issues.

Frequency of Messages

Immigrant children receive more messages from co-nationals prior to immigration than from co-nationals in the school upon entry to the U.S. Chinese and Mexican students received more messages prior to immigration than upon entry to the U.S. schools. However, more Mexican children than Chinese received messages upon entry. In the Chinese sample, there are fewer Welcoming Messages across all categories than Prior Messages. This finding need to be contextualized in terms of the characteristics of the receiving school site. For the Chinese students, most assimilate into mostly-White schools where the presence of the co-nationals in the school is less predominant. Eight percent of the Chinese children indicated that there were no co-nationals in the schools they attended upon arrival to the U.S. Therefore, the incidence of the messages from co-nationals may be less significant than in the Mexican group, which overwhelmingly assimilated into mostly-Latino schools. Also, the fact that children receive more messages prior to immigration rather than upon entry to the school may indicate that the co-nationals in the schools may not be a significant "source" of information about the U.S. school. However, this does not necessarily mean that the co-national in the school is not a significant player in the assimilation of the newcomers into the school life. It just indicates that most children—perhaps for developmental reasons—do not articulate "messages" about the American school.

Sources of Messages

Interpersonal relations are the major source of information about the U.S. school. Prior to immigration, most of these messages come from relatives who either live in the U.S. (Chinese sample) or transnational relatives (Mexican sample) rather than from parents. I think the reason for this is not that parents are not interested in their children's education or are not willing to share information. I think what this finding reflects is the lack of information that parents may have about American schools. Since the relatives who "talk" about the U.S. schools are people who have resided in the U.S., they become the major source of information because they have such information. Some of these relatives are minors who have attended American schools or parents of children who have been in the U.S. system. Unfortunately, because these messages come from personal experiences, they are highly influenced by the type of schools these children and their parents have exposure to or experience with.

Types of Messages

Over time, some themes seemed to continue being the focus of the transnational messages, while others changed. Let us explore some of these issues.

Academic Messages

Academic Messages are overall the top category of the Chinese messages over time. This indicates that issues of an academic nature (e.g., curriculum, instruction, assessment, etc.) are salient themes in the conversation of immigrant children across time. Over time, Academic Messages for the Chinese group emphasize one issue—a less demanding academic life in the U.S. This in turn seems to indicate a perception of a more attainable academic excellence in the U.S. without the pressure of the Chinese educational system. Over time, as children experience the American school, some Chinese children seem to become critical and disappointed about the "less demanding" nature of the school curriculum. However, most of them still express the fact that an educational experience in China may provide a competitive edge to the Chinese immigrant student who competes with less academically engaged American students. Academic Messages are present in equal proportions in the Prior and Current Messages. As mentioned before, Welcoming Messages were less frequent in the Chinese group, reflecting that children may not talk about school with their co-nationals. However, the fact that across time, most Chinese co-nationals articulated Academic Messages raises questions about the cultural construction of school. That is, it seems like Chinese people seem to construct "school" images mostly around academic issues. This may indicate a construction of the goals of the school to be mostly academic, rather than social. Therefore, when children are asked about "schools," they delineate the domain of school ideas about academic issues. An interesting "change" over time was that prior to immigration, Academic Messages emphasized the availability of educational opportunities in the U.S.—mainly higher education. As these messages are constructed once the children immigrate, they tend to emphasize more "practical" issues regarding curriculum, instruction, and academic engagement.

For the Mexican students, Academic Messages became increasingly salient over time. While Academic Messages were second to the top category of messages prior to immigration, over time the proportion of Academic Messages increased. One of the reasons for this may be attributed to the fact that more Mexican children heard messages about U.S. upon entry to the U.S. (78%) than prior to immigrating to the U.S. (67%). Also, most of the Welcoming Messages and Current Messages were constructed as "academic advice"—what to do in the American school. As with the Chinese sample, Academic Messages also emphasized the idea of a less demanding academic environment—schools in the U.S. are "easy." However, the responses in the Mexican group did not clearly indicate the significance of schools being easy in the U.S. Another interesting distinction in the Academic Messages in the Mexican group was the construction of "educational opportunities" around issues of cost of education and continuation of basic education—secondary—due to the fact that schools in the U.S. are more affordable than in Mexico (free materials and tuition).

English Messages

English Messages over time was a not very relevant category among the transnational messages. Overall, English Messages comprised a minority of the transnational messages in both groups across time. For the Chinese group, most of the English Messages were less than five percent of the distribution. Most of these messages, across time, emphasized the need for proficiency and the opportunity to learn English. For the Mexican group some changes in the emphasis of English issues occurred over time. English Messages Prior to Immigration focused on the fact that English was spoken in the schools and that they could learn to speak English. Welcoming Messages spoke mostly of the language barrier that English imposed on the newcomers, and on the need for proficiency. However, Current Messages focused mostly on the difficulty of learning English. The English Messages over time in the Mexican sample changed. While prior to immigration the messages presented an optimistic look of learning a new language, the Welcoming Message focused on the need on proficiency. However, after a few years of experiencing the American school, the Mexican children presented a less optimistic view of English language acquisition—it is difficult to learn English.

Peer Messages

Peer Messages in the Chinese group became more salient in the Current Messages. This indicates that prior to immigration and upon entry to the U.S., Chinese children do not receive many messages about peers. However, as they become participants in the school context, peer issues may become more salient for the co-nationals to share with potential newcomers. Further, children received most of their messages prior to immigration from relatives—transnational and U.S. residents. Many of these relatives were adults (uncles and aunts) who may not share specific messages about peers.

In the Chinese group, Peer Messages Prior and Welcoming remained constant, with an increase in the Current Message. Chinese messages prior and upon entry emphasized negative messages regarding peers behaving badly and negative perceptions of specific student groups (no positive messages mentioned). After a few years in the U.S., while Chinese children continue the pattern of having negative perceptions about student groups, Chinese children also articulated positive messages about their co-national peers. In the Mexican case, Peer Messages were more salient across time, and showed consistent proportions (10–15%) across time. For the Mexican group, messages regarding violent behaviors, gang involvement, and negative racial attitudes towards peers prevailed across all categories of transnational messages—Prior, Welcoming, and Current.

School Messages

In the Chinese group, School Messages became less salient in the Welcoming Messages. However, this may be because about 8% of the Chinese children indicated that there were no co-nationals in the school. In the Chinese group, children received messages prior to immigration regarding facilities and free services, with an emphasis on free tuition. Welcoming and Current Messages in the Chinese group emphasized orientation to school life—both received from and given to the co-national.

School Messages in the Mexican sample presented a consistent pattern—between 14–16% over time. However the emphasis of these messages changed a little bit. Prior to immigration, most Mexican messages concentrated on issues about the facilities and free services and materials (mostly meals and school supplies) offered in the U.S. school. Welcoming and Current Messages emphasize a more involved role of the co-national in the school providing orientation to the newcomers. In Welcoming Messages, the participants received orientation and guidance into school life from co-nationals in the school. In Current Messages, the participants took this role, offering advice and orientation to the potential newcomer. This indicates a sense of social responsibility on the Mexican group to help the co-nationals in the school. In general, both Chinese and Mexican children emphasized the same topics in School Messages.

Social Messages

Social Messages were a category that emerged in the Welcoming and Current Messages only. For the Chinese group, this took form in terms of the realization of the importance of socialization in the U.S. In the Mexican group, Social Messages took form in terms of adopting good social behaviors (behaving well) and seeking support from co-nationals. The fact that Social Messages were not present in the Prior Messages indicates that immigrant children do become aware of social issues in the school, and also the importance of socialization. This may also indicate that as children grow older, the social environment of the school may become more salient as children start to face issues of identity development in adolescence and try to seek a reference group in the school.

Teacher Messages

Teacher Messages over time showed some changes. In the Chinese sample, Teacher Messages were more salient prior to immigration and after a few years in the U.S. Also, the nature of the Teacher Messages changes over time. Messages prior to immigration were all positive messages towards teachers—mostly regarding the less restrictive nature of their disciplinary style and nicer personalities. Welcoming and Current Messages in the Chinese group emphasized the nice personality of teachers and improved student-teacher relations. However, in Current Messages, Chinese children became more critical of teachers in terms of the quality of their instruction.

Mexican messages regarding teachers were not very prevalent in Prior and Welcoming Messages. Most of these messages Prior to immigration and upon entry to the U.S. school, talked about less disciplinary teachers with nice personalities. Some messages also reported negative messages about the teacher in terms of disciplinary actions (more strict) and mean personalities. However, it is clear that for Mexican children, they received messages regarding teachers' disciplinary style and personality, not really about academic standards or instruction issues. Current Messages, however, started to include issues regarding academic behaviors. For example, negative teachers' messages reflected disappointment with the quality of instruction. Most children, however, gave positive messages about teachers. While the "nice" personality message continue to appear (mostly emphasizing "caring" teachers) some students also shared that teachers taught "well" and that they supported students academically.

This study has shown that for these Chinese and Mexican immigrant children, along their journey of immigration, the co-nationals have served as sources of information about U.S. school. Now, what is the role of these transnational messages in the academic life of immigrant children? How do these messages reveal the school life of these children and their potential for academic success?

CHAPTER 8

Lessons from Transnational Messages

This study represented a journey towards an understanding of the participation of immigrant children in transnational social spaces. It showed how perceptions of U.S. schools were constructed among transnational human collectivities of co-nationals and how these messages reflected specific values or expectations that Chinese and Mexican immigrant children came to have with respect to American schooling. This study demonstrated that most immigrant children heard messages prior to immigration and continued to receive messages as they socialized with co-national peers in the school. It also showed how some of the major themes that children constructed over time reproduced the transnational messages' conceptualizations of American schools. But what does this information provide for educators and policy makers regarding educational services for immigrant children? Also, what do these messages reveal about the impact of these immigrant children on American schools?

One of the most important implications in these findings relates to how these messages reflected sources of vulnerabilities and resources (using Portes' labels) in the receiving community and school experiences. Further, these messages can indeed become sources of vulnerabilities and resources within the transnational social space when the co-nationals share messages that can reinforce and promote attitudes and behaviors that can either support or marginalize co-nationals in the school.

VULNERABILITIES AND RESOURCES IN TRANSNATIONAL SOCIAL SPACES

As explained in chapter 2, Portes (1995) brought attention to the impact of the receiving community in the different kinds of assimilation patterns among different immigrant groups. My argument has been to expand this notion to include how transnational social spaces (via the interaction with co-nationals across multiple localities) can also be a source of vulnerabilities and resources. I have used "information" as one of the ways to explain how the transnational social space can promote resources or vulnerabilities by transmitting information that could be used to enhance or hinder the participation of immigrant students in the U.S. school. I now discuss how these transnational messages have illustrated the presence of some vulnerabilities and resources in the schooling experiences of immigrant children in American public schools.

Transnational Resources

Based on the analysis of transnational messages, it is clear that some messages revealed how immigrant children were aware of some resources in the school context and in their relationships with co-nationals.

Chinese Resources

In analyzing the Chinese Messages, five main resources are identified in the transnational messages:

1. The instrumental association with co-nationals in the school to learn to participate in the U.S. school (including assimilation into mainstream)
2. The perception of attainability of academic excellence
3. The promotion of positive perceptions of Chinese students' academic abilities
4. A more liberal and less restrictive school environment (as compared to China) that promotes positive attitudes towards the U.S. school

5. "Nice" teachers who establish more positive student-teacher relations (compared to those in China) which can promote positive attitudes towards school and academic achievement.

The Chinese Messages over time indicate that Chinese immigrants have received messages that have been instrumental in nature from the co-nationals in the school. Chinese Messages emphasized the need to make friends (Peer Messages), the importance of socializing with Americans and assimilating into the mainstream culture (Social Messages), and the dissemination of information that can help the newcomers to participate in the academic and social aspects of school (Academic and School Messages). Specifically, the co-national peer in Current Peer Messages was identified as a helpful friend who can provide support not only academically but also in terms of orientation to the school routines and rules. Most of the transnational messages in the Chinese group were expressed in strategic manner, "how-to" statements that could facilitate the participation of co-national newcomers in the school.

Another resource that can be identified as the result of the socialization with co-nationals is the fact that Chinese children expressed enthusiasm about the possibility of attaining academic excellence in the American school. The less demanding academic nature of the American school provided Chinese children with an optimistic perspective about their ability to achieve academic excellence. Chinese students perceived that their opportunities to get good grades without too much effort were enhanced in the American education system.

Also, co-nationals often advised newcomers of how advanced they were in terms of subject matter content, compared to American peers. By becoming aware of their "competitive edge" in many content areas (e.g., Math) because they were educated in schools with more rigorous academic standards, Chinese children were presented with a source of pride and self-esteem. Within the co-national social space, Chinese children expressed some sense of academic superiority over their American educated peers. This, in fact, may indicate the presence of a kind of socialization patterns among co-national peers that promotes academic excellence within the group, promoting activities that engage the newcomers in academic matters, including conversations about higher education.

Another resource that Chinese children seemed to identify within the American school is the more liberal climate that prevailed in these schools, as compared to Chinese schools. The fact that Chinese children appreciated American school being more liberal, less restrictive than in China, may promote positive attitudes towards schools; children enjoy more freedom and individuality within the context of American schools.

Finally, Chinese students overall received and articulated positive perceptions of teachers. While some were critical of the academic preparation of American teachers and instruction styles, most Chinese children appreciated the nice and relaxed personalities of teachers in U.S. schools. Most children framed this positive perception in terms of the improved teacher-student relations with American teachers. The fact that Chinese children perceived teachers as respectful of the students may reinforce positive attitudes towards school and learning.

Mexican Resources

In the Mexican sample, three major resources are identified in the transnational messages:

1. The appreciation of having co-nationals in the school who provide support and social comfort
2. The free services and materials offered in the U.S. school that can contribute to the lowering of the cost of education
3. Nice and caring teachers.

For Mexican children, also, the co-national in the school was a source of guidance and information. However, for the Mexican group, the co-national was also appreciated based on solidarity and affective ties. The co-national in the school became someone who they could relate to; who presented a more familiar environment that made the Mexican children more comfortable in school. While for the Chinese the co-national was viewed more in an instrumental perspective—someone who can help and support, the Mexican children also added the emotional and cultural dimension. They socialized with co-nationals because these children were socially and culturally like them. Further, Mexican Messages seldom were very specific in relation to strategies to participate in school life. Most of them were general statements and descriptions of school characteristics. The "how-to" element present in the Chinese group was not salient in the Mexican Messages.

Just like the Chinese Messages, Mexican Messages also suggested that co-nationals in the school could be instrumental by guiding the newcomers to get acquainted with school (School Messages) and appropriate classroom behaviors (Academic Messages). While Chinese children emphasized the *need* to make friends because they often provided support in schools, Mexican children did not construct this idea of peer socialization as instrumental. They socialized with co-nationals because they were friendly or because they shared the same language or the culture. Mexican children constructed the support from co-nationals more in terms of reciprocity rather than instrumentality—helping those who help you. Following Faist's typology (1998) of the transnational social space based on the kind of *ties* that sustained the flow of information within the human collectivities of co-nationals in the school, Mexican children created some kind of *transnational kinship group*, where information and support were exchanged based on reciprocity. Exchanges of information and support within the Chinese human collectivity in the school seemed to resemble the ties of *transnational networks*, where the link between co-nationals seemed to be based more on an instrumental social exchange than on reciprocity.

Another resource identified in the transnational messages within the Mexican group is the awareness of services and materials offered in the U.S. school and how these contributed to the lowering of the cost of education. That is, within the Mexican group, school resources did also include positive perceptions of what the school can provide to support children's needs. Especially from a parental perspective, free school resources and materials were considered as positive in the evaluation of American schools. While Chinese children and parents also mentioned issues regarding free services and materials, these categories were more salient in the Mexican sample, especially when they were newcomers (Prior and Welcoming Messages).

Finally, teachers can be viewed as a resource in the American schools for the Mexican group as well as for the Chinese group. While over time Mexican children in this study had mixed views towards teachers, the majority spoke of teachers as being nice and caring.

However, the Mexican Messages about teachers were slightly different from the Chinese sample. While Chinese children emphasized the teacher-student relation and the nice personality of teachers, Mexican students emphasize the "caring" nature of teachers. Teachers were not only nice, but also supportive and caring of their students. This indicates that Mexican children perceived teachers as adults that "care for them". This raises important issues about the enormous potential that teachers have in the Mexican children to become significant adults in the lives of these immigrant children. The fact that over time, most Mexican children had positive attitudes toward teachers indicate that these can be considered a "resource" for Mexican children in the school—somebody who cares and is nice to them.

Transnational Vulnerabilities

The transnational messages also revealed vulnerabilities in the school context. Moreover, transnational messages can be a source of vulnerabilities for immigrant students as they participate in these transnational social spaces and receive information from co-nationals that potentially lead them to a marginalized participation in the school.

One of the interesting findings about the transnational messages is that overall, most of the messages were positive, indicating that immigrant children viewed the American school with appreciative lenses. However, some of the negative messages indeed revealed some factors that can be considered vulnerabilities. Even though some of these vulnerabilities may reveal the voice of the minority, they are important to discuss because of the impact that these messages may eventually have in the socialization of future generations of immigrants. Further, both the Chinese and the Mexican group shared many of these vulnerabilities.

Chinese Vulnerabilities

The transnational messages revealed three main vulnerabilities that the Chinese group recognized in the school context:

1. Negative perceptions of peers that reproduce negative racial attitudes towards other student groups in the school in terms of behavior and academic performance.

2. Fewer academic demands that may translate into low quality
   .education
3. Negative perceptions of teachers as lacking academic
   preparation and classroom management skills.

The most significant vulnerability—because it prevailed across time—was the negative perception of peers along racial and ethnic lines. Chinese students often had positive perceptions of co-national peers, but negative perceptions of peers from other racial and ethnic groups. While negative perceptions towards non-Chinese peers mainly implied some bullying behaviors and classroom disruptions, the fact that most of the Chinese students spoke of perceptions of students by groups (stereotypical perceptions) raises the need to increase opportunities for inter-group understanding.

One interesting aspect of these negative perceptions of other peer groups within the Chinese group is that they often articulated the perceptions in terms of becoming aware of these cultural differences and assimilating into the mainstream social patterns of the school life. In other words, the stereotypical perceptions of other groups did not necessarily mean that the Chinese actively avoided these groups. But rather, Chinese students attempted to conform to the majority group and learn about how to navigate the school social space by learning from co-nationals how to react and behave towards other students groups. However, it seemed like the White, middle-class group, was considered the most desirable group to assimilate into.

Another vulnerability reflected in the Chinese Messages was the awareness of the negative impact of the lower academic demands in American schools. This negative impact was reflected in the children's realization of lack of learning opportunities. Along with these perceptions, Chinese children also become aware of the lack of preparation of teachers—often recognizing the nice personalities of teachers but with inability to teach or control the classroom. Also, Chinese children shared negative perceptions of teachers in reference to their seeing less qualified teachers in the U.S. than in China.

Mexican Vulnerabilities

From the Mexican responses, the transnational messages also revealed three vulnerabilities. These are the same as the Chinese vulnerabilities

1 and 2 (negative racial attitudes and lower academic demands), but the construction of the messages was a little bit different. Further, the Mexican children had another vulnerability not present in the Chinese sample—the issue of learning English. The vulnerabilities identified in the Mexican transnational messages include:

1. Negative perceptions of peers that reproduce negative racial attitudes towards other student groups in the school and threaten children's perception of safety in the school (e.g., gangs)
2. Fewer academic demands that translate into low-quality education and dissolution of aspirations to achieve an education in the U.S.
3. Negative perceptions towards English language acquisition that promotes frustration towards the process.

As in the Chinese sample, the most significant vulnerability reflected in the transnational messages (consistent over time) is the negative perceptions towards peer groups. However, there are some important differences in the way Mexican children constructed these perceptions. First, they included one issue that the Chinese children did not articulate—gangs. Over time, Mexican children (mostly females) expressed concern about the existence of gangs in the school, making these children feel unsafe in the school. That is, while negative peer perceptions in the Chinese group usually referred to bullying and classroom disruptions, Mexican children are aware of the danger of gangs in the school, threatening the sense of well being and safety of immigrant children in American public schools. Chinese children focused their attention on how negative peer behaviors within classroom interactions can hinder their academic and social participation, but Mexican children were more aware of safety issues.

Second, while Chinese Messages also emphasized negative perceptions about other groups, for the Mexican group, the negative perceptions were mostly about one particular group—the African American peers. This raises questions about the sources of the messages and how these are reinforced by the socialization with other co-nationals. How is the subject brought into these transnational conversations? To what extent are these messages the result of actual interactions? My concern is that the reproduction of negative images seems to be the product of word-of-mouth, rather than of actual interactions with African Americans. Because transnational messages sometimes suggested to co-nationals not to socialize with African Americans, it is likely that these negative perceptions were not the result of direct interaction with this group, but of stereotypical constructions about African Americans.

Third, in the Mexican group, avoidance rather than integration was the strategy to cope with conflictive inter-racial interactions. While the Chinese children opted to learn about cultural differences and adopt some of the majority school culture, Mexican children opted to advise co-nationals just to avoid African Americans and "Cholos" (gang members). It is important to understand that this isolation may not be the result of personal choice in the Mexican immigrant children. Indeed, many of the participants in this study attended schools that place them in bilingual cohorts that limit their interactions with other non-Latino, non-English language learners within an academic context. Most of the Chinese participants attended predominantly White schools and might have felt the need to integrate, not only because of their minority status in the school, but also in the recognition of the instrumentality of assimilating into the White, middle-class culture.

The literature has identified that the issue of racism may negatively affect the self-confidence and self-efficacy of minority students, resulting in the students' withdrawal from academic participation (Gandara, 2001). This study has found that co-national peers communicated messages that indeed promoted and reinforced negative racial views of different ethnic groups in the U.S. This finding needs to be considered because if racist perspectives hinder the academic achievement of minorities, it is clear that some transnational messages that carry negative racial attitudes may adversely affect the academic achievement of immigrant children and others. Moreover, the transnational messages not only carried the image of the immigrant group as a target of discrimination, but also immigrant children came to the U.S. and continued to transmit to others negative perceptions of other ethnic and majority groups in the school. That is, these students participated in the reproduction of negative racial attitudes and stereotypes within the transnational social space.

Just like the Chinese group, Mexican immigrant children had negative perceptions about the quality of education in the United States. For some Mexican children, frustration built up when they realized they were not learning anything new beyond what they already knew in Mexico. This could be a serious vulnerability that can translate into apathy and negative attitudes towards school. It may also create frustration about the possibilities of higher education that these children may have when they feel unprepared academically.

Finally, one kind of vulnerability in the Mexican sample (not dominant in the Chinese sample) is the perception of Mexican children towards English language acquisition. While English Messages were not very dominant in either sample, in the Mexican case, more children expressed negative perceptions about the English language. Mexican immigrant children were told by co-nationals how difficult English language acquisition could be. The fact that Mexican children heard from and continued to share with co-nationals about how hard it was to learn the English language may promote pessimistic attitudes towards the process. Perhaps these pessimistic perspectives reflect low self-efficacy among Mexican children in this domain, but they also speak of the perception of low quality of instruction in English language development programs available to these language learners.

The Balance of Resources and Vulnerabilities

My findings on transnational messages indicate that indeed co-national peers are a source of information for immigrant children, a guiding agent that helps newcomers to integrate to the American school. These immigrant children do experience American school in the context of a transnational social space—a human collectivity of co-nationals in the school—rather than in the social space of the mainstream group in school. This means that, depending upon the academic and social position of the co-national group within the school context, the co-national peers and the messages they share can foster or hinder academic engagement in newcomers. It is important that educators are aware of the balance between the resources and vulnerabilities that the socialization with co-nationals in the school, in the community, and even in the countries of origin, presents to the immigrant children.

The results of the study indicate that most immigrant children indeed communicate positive messages about school. Even when these messages promote positive attitudes towards academic engagement, obviously this may not be enough to ensure an adequate academic and personal development in immigrant children. As explained in chapter 2, the agency that immigrants may have in transnational social spaces may not be sufficient to overcome contextual factors that marginalize immigrants in society (e.g., prejudice or less than optimal school and community contexts). Further, the socialization with co-nationals may also lead to added vulnerabilities when the co-national group lacks the social capital to share information that can help immigrant students to succeed in school. In fact, some of the information that transnational messages promote can actually perpetuate the marginalized experiences of the co-national group in the school (e.g., promoting inter-cultural conflict).

While both Chinese and Mexican children have expressed that their co-nationals can provide support, this support may not compensate for the vulnerabilities that the school context and the co-national group present to newcomers. Moreover, different immigrant groups experience different mixes of vulnerabilities and resources. For example, it is clear that for the Chinese group, most of the resources facilitate academic engagement. On the other hand, the resources that the co-nationals and their messages provide to the Mexican group relate more to social support from peers, appreciation for positive social relations with peers and teachers, and services received in the American schools.

The differences in the constructions of transnational messages by the Chinese and the Mexican sample seem to be the result not only of cultural differences, but they are also clearly the products of the context in which these children experience the American school. This study has established some ground in the study of immigrant students' assimilation in American school in relation to the influence of transnational social spaces when children socialize with co-nationals. However, there are more questions to be answered. Some of these questions are key to enhancing our understanding of how the co-nationals may influence the assimilation of immigrants into different paths.

AN AGENDA FOR FUTURE RESEARCH

One of the interesting findings of this study is that children received some messages about American schools that tended to be consistent over time. While most of these messages were positive, they often did not reflect values that could foster more academic achievement (e.g., low academic expectations, nice but unprepared teachers, negative peer perceptions). Given the nature, content, and context of the construction of the transnational messages, as revealed by this study, educational researchers need to recognize and continue researching five major areas that may influence the participation of immigrant children into the U.S. school.

The Educational System in the Country of Origin

Transnational messages about U.S. schools were often constructed under a comparative framework between the U.S. school and the school in the country of origin. While many of these messages often spoke of pragmatic school characteristics e.g., such as infrastructure and organization, in my analysis of the data I found that many of these messages reveal some cultural constructions about the notion of school's role and place in a child's life.

The predominant Chinese Message was regarding the less stressful academic life. This reveals that some Chinese children came with the understanding that school was about study, working hard, and not having fun. When they came to the U.S. and faced a more liberal and less stressful academic life, they still seemed to root the idea of school as a place to work and study—often speaking of the slow American kids and "those White devils" who distracted the teacher. The high academic demands in elementary schools in China (the level that most of these immigrant children had experienced) and the competitive environment of academic assessment represent a system where only a few excel academically.

As explained in chapter 4, Mexican elementary education is mostly focused on civil responsibility and developing skills that can be used to efficiently perform everyday tasks, especially language development. As in the Chinese education system, the Mexican system operates by a process of elimination. But this elimination sometimes is not only marked by the academic achievement of students, but also by the limited availability of institutions of secondary education in many rural areas and by the financial limitations of parents to continue supporting their children's education in terms of tuition and materials. Because higher education is limited, education in Mexico aims to give a comprehensive education at each level, to ensure that even those Mexican nationals with limited education are able to function as citizens and in the labor market. Civil responsibility and good interpersonal skills are often emphasized in Mexican elementary education. Mexican children coming to the U.S. know that in school they are expected to act civilly and get along with everyone, including the teacher. Therefore, in the transnational messages they continued to advise the newcomers to "behave" nicely and avoid trouble. Social Messages, for example, overwhelmingly reflected this notion of the responsibility of being a "good kid". More research needs to be done in understanding how philosophies of education in different sending countries contribute to the socialization of children and their expectations of school participation.

Also, the social constructions of school across different countries are an area worthy of being explored. In the Chinese sample, it is clear that when children were asked about "school," most of the responses focused on academic issues. This may indicate an emphasis on the academic aspects of school in the Chinese children (academics as a priority). But it may also indicate differences in how the concept of *school* is constructed among Chinese children. It may be the case that in the cognitive map of Chinese children, "school" includes only academic issues, even if Chinese children are exposed and aware of other factors (e.g., gangs) in the school. But because they are not "academic" issues, Chinese children do not view these as part of the school experience.

Culturally Established Expectations of Schooling and Academic Achievement in the Family and the Ethnic Community

Another important area of investigation is the role of family expectations and the parents' constructions of the role of the school in their children's lives. Immigrant children come with established ideas about the role and goals of the school as delineated by the educational systems in their country of origin. However, culturally established expectations of children in regards to school and academic achievement are also established in the household and sometimes in the ethnic community. It is important to understand the constructions that parents have of the role of the school in their children lives.

This kind of investigation needs to go beyond asking parents if they think school is important in their children's lives. The data demonstrate that most parents will assent to this. However, what is not clear is the role of academic achievement and higher education in the family dynamics. For example, family expectations regarding academic achievement are very prevalent in Chinese families because of the status that academic excellence brings to the family within the community (Chuang, 1985). However, in Mexican families, because of the emphasis on civil responsibility in schools, it may be likely that Mexican families also value their children's good behavior over academic achievement. That is, it is important to conduct more research that investigates the relationship between philosophies of education in the education systems of sending countries and the family values regarding academic achievement. Do parents become socialized in the country of origin to reinforce the goals of the school as delineated by the school system of the country of origin? Do these parents continue using the same paradigm as in the country of origin to participate in their children's educational life in the United States?

Other interesting areas of inquiry include issues relating to the following questions: Do parents from different immigrant groups value other aspects of children's behavior (e.g., good behavior, decency) over academic achievement? Do certain immigrant parents place academic achievement as the only testimony of their children's success?

Parental expectations also need to be investigated within the context of assimilation/acculturation and how different immigrant groups are socialized into an immigrant culture that promotes specific kinds of achievement and success in the U.S. (e.g., via higher education vs. work).

Social Capital and Cultural/Class Integration in the School

It is clear that there are certain issues that the transnational messages reveal about some of the vulnerabilities in the school context—e.g., segregation, negative racial attitudes, and low quality of instruction. These issues need to be the focus of sound reforms.

First, it is clear that schools often reflect the vulnerabilities and resources in the community. Schools in communities like San Patricio face the same social problems as the community at large—interracial conflict, violence, crime, and gang involvement. Transnational messages clearly reflected some of these community issues regarding peers' behavior. Schools need to take a more proactive role of providing images other than the ones that the community can reflect.

Instead of reproducing in school what the community reflects, perhaps there are ways that schools can influence the community. Further, is it possible to expand the scope of schools beyond the community in which they are located? Could schools bring models from other communities to increase exposure and interactions with other cultural and class models in such a way that the inner-city children could see these as attainable?

This idea is based on Min Zhou's research with Chinatowns in Los Angeles (Zhou et al., 2000). In their research, Zhou and others have found that the role of the middle-class Chinese Americans in the Chinatown (usually a low-income community) has brought a source of social and cultural capital for less privileged Chinese youth. That is, the involvement of the Chinese middle-class as patrons in Chinatown presents an attainable model of success for less privileged residents of Chinatown—attainable because of the ethnic identification with these middle-class Chinese. Further, middle-class Chinese are often seen as sources of information to strategize success in the U.S.

Borrowing from this idea, schools could take a more active role in bringing diverse cultural and class models in a systematic way that could serve as sources of the so-needed social and cultural capital to attain academic achievement (Gandara, 2001). These class role models need to include models from the same ethnic community as the children. But they also need to include models from other ethnic communities that could assist in the promotion of positive experiences with diversity for immigrant children—moving toward the elimination of the negative perceptions of certain groups in the U.S.

However, class and cultural models need to be carefully introduced in an additive rather than subtractive fashion. The goal is not the eradication of the home culture of the immigrant children as it has been in the past. I am not suggesting or advocating a revised model of the cultural deprivation theory (Johnson, 1966; Riessman, 1962). The cultural deprivation theory held that minority students from cultures other than middle-class Anglo backgrounds were not able to participate in the dominant culture because they lacked the know-how of the dominant culture. (Carter, 1970). Therefore, perceived deficits in the minority students' culture were considered the primary cause of the disadvantaged minority child's lack of success in school (Riessman, 1962). This theory proposed that school was the primary agent providing these culturally different students with exposure to the dominant culture (Carter, 1970). The negative impact of this model was that it assumed that the children's home values and culture were not the appropriate ones to ensure adequate participation in the school system. Further, this perspective narrowly blurred class and cultural differences.

My proposition of bringing different class models into school is based on a "class-integration" model, not class substitution. I am not suggesting that children need to be stripped from their home and community cultures and be taught to adopt middle-class values that may not reflect their present reality. As a former educator of children often labeled "at risk," I learned that the challenges and vulnerabilities these children experience in their daily lives are also a source of social capital that allows them to survive in these environments. In fact, I believe that people from middle-class and different ethnic backgrounds could benefit from expanding their knowledge base about immigrant and other minority children in school and community settings that are different from middle-class (e.g., working class minorities).

I suggest offering alternative models for children, beyond what their communities can offer, without implying that their communities have nothing of value to offer, because they do. I am suggesting the implementation of programs that not only expose children to multiple "cultures" but also multiple "classes" and models of different classes within cultures. Programs that provide tangible avenues for social mobility, rather than social reproduction in minority student populations, could be implemented to disseminate information that reflects the social capital needed to attain academic achievement. Of course, any intervention model needs to be grounded in research.

The reality is that if we aim to increase the academic attainment of minority children, we must acknowledge that schools and society still function under a mainstream paradigm. Research has identified that the lack of social capital impedes minority children's access to education (Gandara, 2001). If schools could provide these sources of social capital, minority children could have a chance to reach higher educational goals. However, if schools are mere reflections of their communities, then children in privileged communities will continue enjoying educational advantages over children in communities such as San Patricio. Further, these programs where mutual understanding and learning take place may promote diversity integration and become the beginning of the transformation of the dominant mainstream discourse to include multiple voices from people of different ethnic, class, and other diverse backgrounds.

Teachers as Sources of Social Capital

In the transnational messages, most children revealed positive attitudes towards their teachers. These positive perceptions are not constructed in terms of teacher preparation or quality of instruction, but in terms of personality and student-teacher relations. Teachers are seen as "approachable". This places the teachers in a key position to influence children's lives—to become significant adults and potential sources of social capital for immigrant children. More research is needed to assess the nature of teacher-student relations in order to determine if these relationships can evolve in ways so that teachers can become a source of social and cultural capital.

Promoting Positive Experiences with Diversity

Finally, I think that an area that critically needs to be researched is the formation and reproduction of negative perceptions of other groups and the conflicting nature of inter-cultural relations in the school. However, because many of these messages are being reproduced in transnational contexts, it is important that this research involves investigations in the countries of origin regarding inter-cultural perspectives and construction of social positions of different groups in American society.

Regarding segregation, schools also need to investigate ways to break the pattern of "cultural isolation" where children participate in a social context within the school that is determined by ethnic, linguistic, or racial lines. Schools need to reconsider their choices of curricula, placement, and school organization in order to educate and promote positive intercultural reactions, instead of promoting cultural isolation.

Obviously, more research needs to be done before developing any sound program. I hope that the identification of the transnational messages, and the vulnerabilities and resources that these reflect, may help educators and policy makers to realize the potential powerful influence of the co-nationals in the school in the lives of immigrant children within American schools.

I also hope that the educational community reconsiders the effects of segmented assimilation in schools that are segregated by ethnicity and language. We need to realize that the "assimilation" of immigrant children in American schools is not taking place within the mainstream social space. Many immigrant children do not assimilate into the mainstream, middle-class, but rather into a transnational social space where the co-nationals in the school share their experiences, reproducing messages that sometimes carry very discouraging pictures of the social position of the immigrant populations in this country.

While the transnational social spaces provide comfort and a form of social capital for immigrant children, their benefits alone are not sufficient to ensure that these children achieve academically, unless some of the vulnerabilities within the school and community contexts are eliminated.

Transnational Messages Questionnaire

1. Sometimes people hear about how life is in the U.S. even before they move here. When you lived in your country, what did you hear about schools in the U.S.? *[Prompt: subjects, social climate, difficulty, etc.]*

[IF CHILD HAD NOT HEARD ANYTHING -- GO TO QUESTION 70]

2a. How did you hear these things about American schools? (Q1)

[IF CHILD DOES NOT MENTION MEDIA, THEN ASK:]

2b. Did you hear anything about U.S. school on TV, radio, newspapers, magazines, or Internet?

3. How did you feel after hearing these things about U.S. schools knowing that you might be attending a school in the U.S.?

4. I am going to ask you to try to remember all the schools you have attended here in the U.S. Please tell me in which grade you were when you started school in the U.S.

Circle GRADE OF ENTRY. Then ask the child if there were any students from C/O in the school, starting at the GRADE OF ENTRY. For example, if GRADE OF ENTRY IS FIRST GRADE, ask: **Were there any students from C/O when you were in 1ˢᵗ grade?** Repeat question for subsequent grades (2ⁿᵈ 3ʳᵈ, etc). THEN CHECK THE APPROPRIATE BOX.

GRADE	CO-NATIONALS IN THE SCHOOL?		NAME OF THE SCHOOL (OPTIONAL)
	YES	NO	
K			
1ˢᵀ			
2ᴺᴰ			
3ᴿᴰ			
4ᵀᴴ			
5ᵀᴴ			
6ᵀᴴ			
7ᵀᴴ			
8ᵀᴴ			
9ᵀᴴ			
10ᵀᴴ			

PLEASE REFER TO THE ANSWERS IN THE TABLE TO DETERMINE NEXT QUESTION

- *If the child found no-conationals in any of their grades* ⑧ SKIP TO QUESTION 6
- *Otherwise, continue*

5a. Think about when you arrived in the U.S. and you found students from [your COUNTRY OF ORIGIN] in the school. What kinds of things did they tell you about U.S. schools? *[Prompt: suggestions, advice, tips, anecdotes]*

5b. Do you think these comments helped you in anyway?
❏ YES   ❏ NO

5c. How?

6. You may know that schools are different in every country. Imagine that you are calling your cousin on the phone. He/she and his/her family are moving to the U.S. next month. Your cousin wants to know about your experience in schools in the U.S. He/She wants to know as much as you can tell him/her -- about teachers, friends, classmates, the school, homework, things to do, things to avoid, etc. What would you tell him/her about U.S. schools?

Sample Profile

STUDENT PROFILE

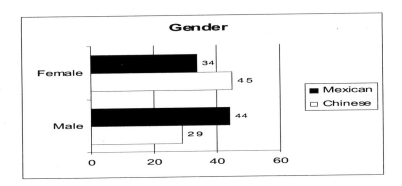

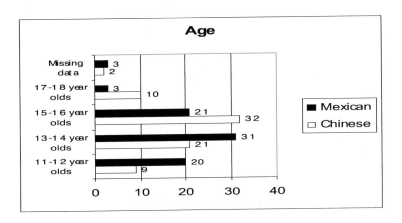

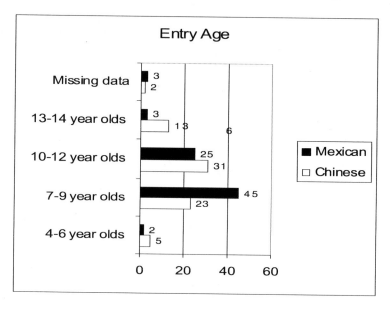

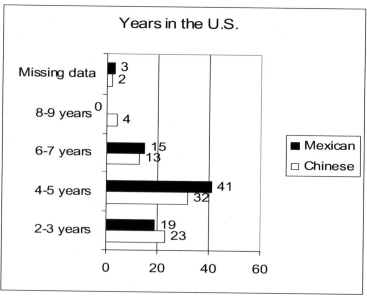

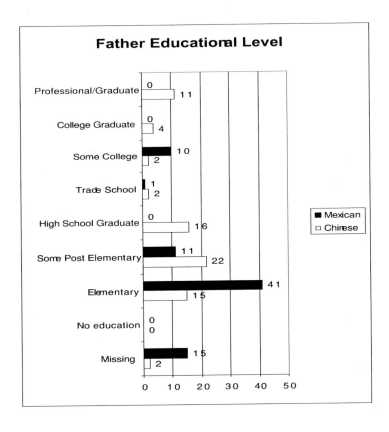

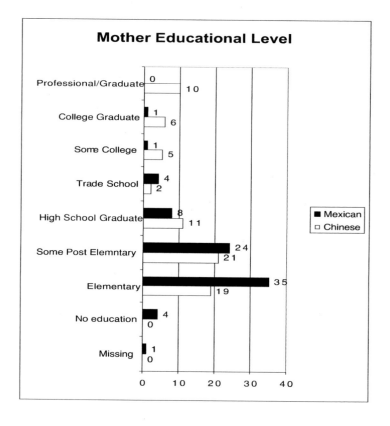

Mother Educational Level

Category	Mexican	Chinese
Professional/Graduate	0	10
College Graduate	1	6
Some College	1	5
Trade School	4	2
High School Graduate	8	11
Some Post Elemntary	24	21
Elementary	35	19
No education	4	0
Missing	1	0

■ Mexican
□ Chinese

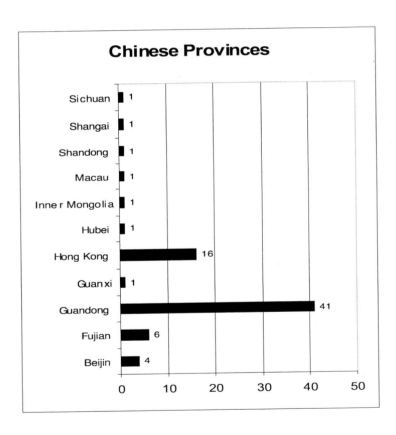

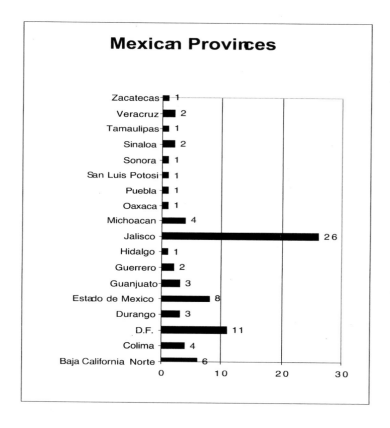

SCHOOL CHARACTERISTICS

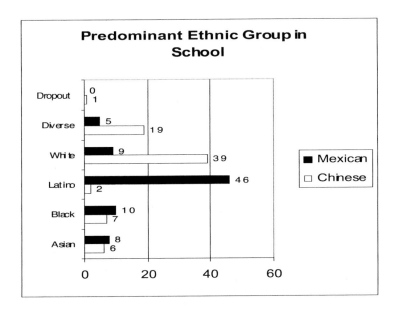

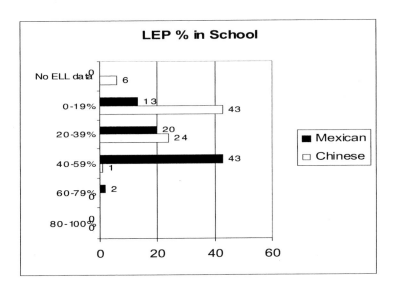

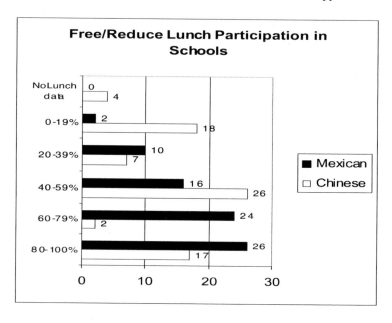

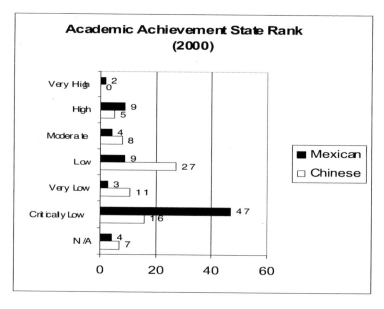

1995 College Graduates in Selected Mexican Provinces

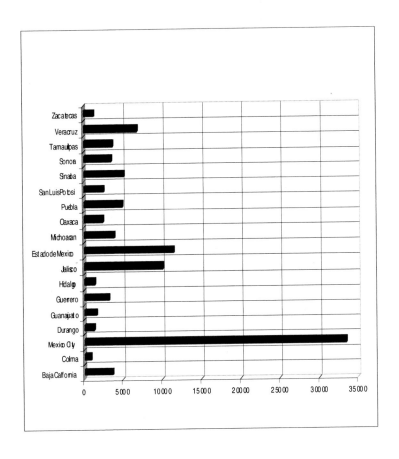

Source: **http://www.anuies.mx/estadisticas**

Positive and Negative Transnational Messages
Distribution by Gender

PRIOR MESSAGES

ACADEMIC MESSAGES	Chinese (N=24)				Mexican (N=15)			
	Negative (17%)*		Positive (83%)*		Negative (40%)*		Positive (60%)*	
	N	%	N	%	N	%	N	%
Females	4	100%	16	80%	4	67%	4	44%
Males	0	0%	4	20%	2	33%	5	56%
Total	4	100%	20	100%	6	100%	9	100%

ENGLISH MESSAGES	Chinese (N=3)				Mexican (N=8)**			
	Negative (67%)*		Positive (33%)*		Negative (50%)*		Positive (25%)*	
	N	%	N	%	N	%	N	%
Females	2	100%	1	100%	2	50%	0	0
Males	0	0%	0	0%	2	50%	2	100%
Total	2	100%	1	100%	4	100%	2	100%

** Two Mexican children (boy and girl) gave a neutral response towards English issues

* Negative and Positive Percentage figure corresponds to the proportion that Negative and Positive Messages represents out of the major messages category (e.g. Academic, English, etc.)

PEERS MESSAGES	Chinese (N=5)				Mexican (N=13)			
	Negative (80%)*		Positive (20%)*		Negative (100%)*		Positive (0%)*	
	N	%	N	%	N	%	N	%
Females	2	50%	1	100%	10	77%	0	0%
Males	2	50%	0	0%	3	23%	0	0%
Total	4	0%	1	100%	13	100%	0	0%

SCHOOL MESSAGES	Chinese (N=13)				Mexican (N=17)			
	Negative (0%)*		Positive (100%)*		Negative (12%)*		Positive (88%)*	
	N	%	N	%	N	%	N	%
Females	0	0%	7	54%	1	50%	6	40%
Males	0	0%	6	46%	1	50%	9	60%
Total	0	0%	13	100%	2	100%	15	100%

TEACHERS MESSAGES	Chinese (N=10)				Mexican (N=5)			
	Negative (0%)*		Positive (100%)*		Negative (40%)*		Positive (60%)*	
	N	%	N	%	N	%	N	%
Females	0	0%	8	80%	2	100%	2	67%
Males	0	0%	2	20%	0	0	1	33%
Total	0	0%	10	100%	2	100%	3	100%

* Negative and Positive Percentage figure corresponds to the proportion that Negative and Positive Messages represents out of the major messages category (e.g. Academic, English, etc.)

WELCOMING MESSAGES

ACADEMIC MESSAGES	Chinese (N=11)				Mexican (N=24)			
	Negative (27%)*		Positive (73%)*		Negative (25%)*		Positive (75%)*	
	N	%	N	%	N	%	N	%
Females	3	100%	3	38%	4	67%	11	61%
Males	0	0%	5	62%	2	33%	7	39%
Total	3	100%	8	100%	6	100%	18	100%

ENGLISH MESSAGES	Chinese (N=1)				Mexican (N=4)			
	Negative (0%)*		Positive (100%)*		Negative (100%)*		Positive (0%)*	
	N	%	N	%	N	%	N	%
Females	0	0%	1	100%	1	25%	0	0%
Males	0	0%	0	0%	3	75%	0	0%
Total	0	0%	1	100%	4	100%	0	0%

PEERS MESSAGES	Chinese (N=4)				Mexican (N=17)			
	Negative (50%)*		Positive (50%)*		Negative (76%)*		Positive (24%)*	
	N	%	N	%	N	%	N	%
Females	1	50%	1	50%	6	46%	3	75%
Males	1	50%	1	50%	7	54%	1	25%
Total	2	100%	2	100%	13	100%	4	100%

* Negative and Positive Percentage figure corresponds to the proportion that Negative and Positive Messages represents out of the major messages category (e.g. Academic, English, etc.)

SCHOOL MESSAGES	Chinese (N=8)				Mexican (N=16)			
	Negative (0%)*		Positive (100%)*		Negative (0%)*		Positive (100%)*	
	N	%	N	%	N	%	N	%
Females	0	0%	5	62%	0	0%	9	56%
Males	0	0%	3	38%	0	0%	7	44%
Total	0	0%	8	100%	0	0%	16	100%

SOCIAL MESSAGES	Chinese (N=4)				Mexican (N=4)			
	Negative (50%)*		Positive (50%)*		Negative (0%)*		Positive (100%)*	
	N	%	N	%	N	%	N	%
Females	1	50%	2	100%	0	0%	2	50%
Males	1	50%	0	0%	0	0%	2	50%
Total	2	100%	2	100%	0	0%	4	100%

TEACHERS MESSAGES	Chinese (N=6)				Mexican (N=9)			
	Negative (0%)*		Positive (100%)*		Negative (67%)*		Positive (33%)*	
	N	%	N	%	N	%	N	%
Females	0	0%	5	83%	5	83%	2	67%
Males	0	0%	1	17%	1	17%	1	33%
Total	0	0%	6	100%	6	100%	3	100%

* Negative and Positive Percentage figure corresponds to the proportion that Negative and Positive Messages represents out of the major messages category (e.g. Academic, English, etc.)

CURRENT MESSAGES

ACADEMIC MESSAGES	Chinese (N=53)				Mexican (N=47)			
	Negative (19%)*		Positive (81%)*		Negative (23%)*		Positive (77%)*	
	N	%	N	%	N	%	N	%
Females	5	50%	23	53%	5	45%	17	47%
Males	5	50%	20	47%	6	55%	19	53%
Total	10	100%	43	20%	11	100%	36	100%

ENGLISH MESSAGES	Chinese (N=13)				Mexican (N=18)**			
	Negative (62%)*		Positive (38%)*		Negative (44%)*		Positive (17%)***	
	N	%	N	%	N	%	N	%
Females	7	88%	3	60%	4	50%	1	33%
Males	1	12%	2	40%	4	50%	2	67%
Total	8	100%	5	100%	8	100%	3	100%

** Seven Mexican children (3 boys and 4 girls gave a neutral response towards English issues)

PEERS MESSAGES	Chinese (N=33)				Mexican (N=22)			
	Negative (39%)*		Positive (61%)*		Negative (45%)*		Positive (55%)*	
	N	%	N	%	N	%	N	%
Females	9	69%	12	60%	5	50%	6	50%
Males	4	31%	8	40%	5	50%	6	50%
Total	13	100%	20	100%	10	100%	12	100%

* Negative and Positive Percentage figure corresponds to the proportion that Negative and Positive Messages represents out of the major messages category (e.g. Academic, English, etc.)

SCHOOL MESSAGES	Chinese (N=44)				Mexican (N=32)			
	Negative (7%)*		Positive (93%)*		Negative (9%)*		Positive (91%)*	
	N	%	N	%	N	%	N	%
Females	2	67%	25	61%	1	33%	16	55%
Males	1	33%	16	39%	2	67%	13	45%
Total	3	100%	41	100%	3	100%	29	100%

SOCIAL MESSAGES	Chinese (N=20)				Mexican (N=22)			
	Negative (17%)*		Positive (83%)*		Negative (0%)*		Positive (100%)*	
	N	%	N	%	N	%	N	%
Females	3	60%	8	53%	0	0%	8	36%
Males	2	40%	7	47%	0	0%	14	64%
Total	5	100%	15	100%	0	0%	22	100%

TEACHERS MESSAGES	Chinese (N=38)				Mexican (N=33)			
	Negative (24%)*		Positive (76%)*		Negative (12%)*		Positive (88%*	
	N	%	N	%	N	%	N	%
Females	6	67%	18	62%	3	75%	12	41%
Males	3	33%	11	38%	1	25%	17	59%
Total	9	100%	29	100%	4	100%	29	100%

* Negative and Positive Percentage figure corresponds to the proportion that Negative and Positive Messages represents out of the major messages category (e.g. Academic, English, etc.)

References

Alder, R. H. (2000). Human agency in international migration: The maintenance of transnational social fields by Yucatecan migrants in a southwestern city. *Mexican Studies-Estudios Mexicanos, 16*(1), 165–185.

Albrow, M. (1998, May). *Frames and transformations in transnational studies*. Paper presented at the Economic and Social Research Council (ESRC) Transnational Community Programme Seminar, Oxford, England.

Alvarez, S. E. (1998). Latin American feminism 'go global': Trends of the 1990's and challenges for the new millennium. In S. E. Alvarez, E. Dagnino, & A. Escobar (Eds.), *Cultures of politics, politics of cultures: Re-visioning Latin American social movements,* Boulder, CO: Westview.

Anderson, B. (1991). *Imagined communities: Reflections on the origins and spread of nationalism.* New York: Verso.

Appadurai, A. (1996). *Modernity at large: Cultural dimensions of globalization.* Minneapolis, MN: University of Minnesota Press.

Apple, M. W. (1996). *Cultural politics and education.* New York: Teachers' College Press, University of Columbia.

Apple, M. W. (1997). *Education and power.* (2nd ed.). New York: Routledge.

Armstrong, W. (1998, March). *Belonging, ethnic diversity and everyday experience: Co-existing identities on the Italo-Slovene frontier.* Paper presented at the Economic and Social Research Council (ESRC) Transnational Community Programme Seminar, Oxford, England.

Aurbach, L., Jr. (1999, December). *Recent U.S. Immigration: Geography, assimilation, and neighborhoods,* [on-line]. Available: http://users.erols.com/ljaurbach/ImmigrantGeography.htm

Basch, L., Glick-Schiller, N., & Blanc, S. (1994). *Nations unbound: Transnational projects, postcolonial predicaments, and deterritorialized nation-states.* Basel: Gordon & Breach.

Bean, F. D., & Tienda, M. (1987). *The Hispanic population of the United States.* New York: Russell Sage Foundation.

Bernal, M. E., & Martinelli, P. C. (1993). *Mexican American identity.* Encino, CA: Floricanto Press.

Besserer, F. (1998, May). *A space of view: Transnational spaces and perspectives.* Paper presented at the International Centre for Contemporary Cultural Research (ICCCR) International Conference on Transnationalism, Manchester, England.

Browing, H. L., & De la Garza, R. (Eds.) (1986). *Mexican immigrants and Mexican Americans: An evolving relation.* Austin, TX: CMAS Publications.

Burma, J. H. (1970). *Mexican Americans in the United States: A reader.* Cambridge, MA: Schenkman.

Carnoy, M. (1989). Education, state and culture in American society. In H. Giroux & P. McLaren, (Eds.), *Critical pedagogy, the state and cultural struggle.* (pp. 3–23). New York: State University of New York Press.

Carter, T. (1970). *Mexican Americans in school: A history of educational neglect.* New York: College Entrance Examination Board.

Caplan, L. (1998, May). *Colonial and contemporary transnationalisms: Traversing Anglo-Indian boundaries of the mind.* Paper presented at the International Centre for Contemporary Cultural Research (ICCCR) International Conference on Transnationalism, Manchester, England.

Cassagnol-Chierici, R. M. (1991). *Demele: "Making It""—Migration and adaptation among Haitian boat people in the United States.* New York: AMS Press, Inc.

Castells, M. (1997). *The information age: Economy, society and culture. Vol. II: The Power of Identity.* Malden, MA: Blackwell.

Castles, S. (1998, June). *New migrations, ethnicity, and nationalism in Southeast and East Asia.* Paper presented at the Economic and Social Research Council (ESRC) Transnational Community Programme Seminar, Oxford, England.

Castles, S., & Miller, M. J. (1998). *The age of migration: International populations movements in the modern world.* New York: The Guilford Press.

Chen, K. (1996). Not yet the postcolonial era: The (super) nation-state and transnationalism of cultural studies: Response to Ang and Stratton. *Cultural Studies, 10*(1), 37–70.

Cheng, J. Y. S. (2000). Guandong's challenges: Organizational streamlining, economical restructuring, and anti-corruption. *Pacific Affairs 73*(1), 9–35.

Chin, K. (1999). *Smuggled Chinese: Clandestine immigration to the United States.* Philadelphia, PA: Temple University Press.

Chinatown Coalition. (1994, February). *The Chinatown Coalition Needs Assessment Report.* Boston, MA.

Chuang, S. W. (1985). *Perceived usefulness of higher education: Major choices and life goal values among Chinese-American students.* Doctoral dissertation, California School of Professional Psychology, Los Angeles.

Cohen, R. (1998, June). *Transnational social movements: An assessment.* Paper presented at the Economic and Social Research Council (ESRC) Transnational Community Programme Seminar, Oxford, England.

Collins, G. (1996, May 14). Advertising information resources takes aim at the ethnic market, and Nielsen. *New York Times,* 3/3.

Cornelius, W. A. (1995). Educating California's immigrant children: Introduction and overview. In R. G. Rumbaut & W. A. Cornelius (Eds.), *California's immigrant children: Theory, research, and implications for educational policy,* (pp.1–16). San Diego: Center for U.S.-Mexican Studies, University of California.

Cornelius, W. A. (1998). The structural embeddedness of demand for Mexican immigrant labor: New evidence from California. In M. Suarez-Orozco (Ed.). *Crossings: Mexican immigration in interdisciplinary perspectives.* Cambridge, MA: Harvard University Press.

Cornelius, W. A., & Bustamante, J. A. (Eds.). (1989). *Mexican immigration to the United States: Origins, consequences, and policy options.* San Diego: Center for U.S.-Mexican Studies, University of California.

Cornelius, W. A., Chavez, L. R., & Castro, J. G. (1982). *Mexican immigrants and Southern California: A summary of current knowledge.* (Research Report Series No. 36). San Diego: University of California, Center of U.S.-Mexican Studies.

Cornell, S., & Hartmann, D. (1998). *Ethnicity and race: Making identities in a changing world.* Pine Forge Press: Thousand Oaks, CA.

Crisp, J. (1998, June). *Policy changes of the new diasporas: Migrant networks and their impact on asylum flows and regimes.* Paper presented at the Economic and Social Research Council (ESRC) Transnational Community Programme Seminar, Oxford, England.

Dirlik, A. (1996). Asians on the rim: Transnational capital and local community in the making of contemporary Asian America. *Amerasia Journal, 22*(3), 1–24.

Donald, S. (1998). Mapping China: Considering the presentation of statistical and cultural data for large readerships. [On-line]. Available: *www.sshe.murdoch.edu.au*

Durand, J., & Massey, D. S. (1992). Mexican migration to the United States: A critical review. *Latin American Research Review, 27*(2), 3–42.

Durand, J., Massey, D. S., & Parrado, E. A. (2000). *The new era of Mexican migration to the United States,* [on-line]. Available: *http://www.indiana.edu/~jah/mexico/jdurand.html*

England, S. (1999). Negotiating race and place in the Garifuna diaspora: Identity formation and transnational grassroots politics in New York City and Honduras. *Identities.* (forthcoming).

Espenshade, T. J. (Ed.). (1997). *Keys to successful immigration: Implications of the New Jersey experience.* Washington, DC: The Urban Institute Press.

Faist, T. (1998, May). *Transnationalization in international migration: Implications for the study of citizenship and culture.* Paper presented at the Economic and Social Research Council (ESRC) Transnational Community Programme Seminar, Oxford, England.

Gandara, P. with D. Bial (2001). *Paving the Way to Higher Education: K-12 Intervention Programs for Underrepresented Youth.* Washington, DC: National Center for Education Statistics.

Gibson, M. A. (1995). Additive acculturation as a strategy for school improvement. In R. Rumbaut & W. Cornelius (Eds.), *California Immigrant Children: Theory Research and Implications for Educational Policy.* (pp.77–106). San Diego: University of California.

Giroux, H. (1993). Literacy and the politics of difference. In C. Lankshear & P. McLaren (Eds.), *Critical Literacy: Politics, praxis and the postmodern,* (pp. 367–378). New York: State University of New York Press.

Giroux, H., & McLaren, P. (Eds.) (1989). *Critical Pedagogy, the state and cultural struggle.* New York: State University of New York Press.

Glendhill, J. (1998, May). *Thinking about states, subalterns, and power relations in a world of flows.* Paper presented at the International Centre for Contemporary Cultural Research (ICCCR) International Conference on Transnationalism, Manchester, England.

Glick-Schiller, N., Basch, L., & Szanton, B. (1994). From immigrants to transmigrants: Theorizing transnational migration. *Anthropological Quarterly, 68*(1), 48–63.

Glick-Schiller, N., & Fouron, G. E. (1999). Terrains of blood and nation: Haitian transnational social fields. *Ethnic and racial studies, 22*(2), 340–366.

Grescoe, T. (1994, Winter). Hot type. *Vancouver, 81,* 114–118.

Guarnizo, L. E. (1998). The rise of transnational social formations: Mexican and Dominican state responses to transnational migration. In *Political power and social theory, vol.12* (p. 45–49), JAI Press, Inc.

Hall, J. R., & Neitz, M. J. (1993). *Culture: Sociological perspectives.* Englewood Cliffs, NJ: Prentice Hall.

Hall, S. (1990). Cultural identity and diaspora. *Identity: Community, culture, difference.* pp. 222–236.

Hamel, R. (1993). No job, no home, no English. Now what? *American Demographics*, 6. 42–43.

Hannerz, U. (1996). *Transnational connections: Culture, people, places.* London: Routledge.

Horton, J. (1996). The Chinese suburban immigration and political diversity in Monterey Park, California. *Social Justice, 23*(3), 100–111.

Hunt, J. F. (1990). *The social dynamics of schooling: Participants, priorities and strategies.* London: The Falmer Press.

Itzigsohn, J., Dore-Cabral, C. B., Hernandez-Medina, E., & Vazquez, O. (1999). Mapping Dominican transnationalism: narrow and broad transnational practices. *Ethnic and racial studies, 22*(2), 316–339.

Jasso, G., & Rosenweig, M. R. (1990). *The new chosen people: Immigrants in the United States.* New York, NY: Russell Sage Foundation.

Johnson, K. R. (1966). *Teaching the culturally disadvantaged pupils.* Chicago, IL: Science Research Associates, Inc.

Joppke, C. (1999). *Immigration and the Nation-State: The United States, Germany, and Greta Brittain.* Oxford, England: Oxford University Press.

Karim, K. H. (1998, June). *From ethnic media to global media: Transnational communication networks among diasporic communities.* Paper presented at the Economic and Social Research Council (ESRC) Transnational Community Programme Seminar, Oxford, England.

Kastoryano, R. (1998, June). *Transnational participation and citizenship: Immigrants in European Union.* Paper presented at the Economic and Social Research Council (ESRC) Transnational Community Programme Seminar, Oxford, England.

Keefe, S. E., & Padilla, A. M. (1987). *Chicano ethnicity.* Albuquerque: University of New Mexico Press.

Kloss, H. (1977). *The American bilingual tradition.* Rowley, MA: Newbury House.

Landolt, P., Autler, L, & Baires, S. (1999). From Hermano Lejano to Hermano Mayor: The dialectics of Salvadoran transnationalism. *Ethnic and racial studies, 22*(2), 290–315.

Leong, A. (1996). The struggle over Parcel C: How Boston's Chinatown won a victory in the fight against institutional expansion and environmental racism. *Amerasia Journal, 21*(3), 99–119.

Levitt, P. (1998). Local-level global religion: The case of U.S.-Dominican Migration. *Journal for the Scientific Study of Religion, 37*(1), 74–89.

Lowe, L. (1992). Chinese immigrant workers and community-based labor organizing in Boston: Paving the way. *Amerasia Journal, 18*(1), 39–48.

Mahler, S. J. (1998). Theoretical and empirical contributions toward a research agenda for transnationalism. In M. P. Smith & L. E. Guarnizo (Eds.), *Transnationalism from below* (pp. 64–102). New Brumswick, NJ: Transaction Publishers.

Malkin, V. (1998, May). *Gender, status, and modernity in a transnational migrant circuit.* Paper presented at the International Centre for Contemporary Cultural Research (ICCCR) International Conference on Transnationalism, Manchester, England.

Marcia, J. (1966). Development and validation of ego-identity status. *Journal of personality and social psychology, 3,* 551–558.

McCarthy, K. F., & Vernez, G. (1997). *Immigration in a changing economy: California's experience.* Santa Monica, CA: RAND.

McLaren, P. (1988). Culture or canon? Critical pedagogy and the politics of literacy. *Harvard educational review, 58,* 211–234.

Menjivar, C. (1997). Immigrant kinship networks: Vietnamese, Salvadorans, and Mexicans in comparative perception. *Journal of comparative Family Studies, 28*(1), 1–24.

Merterns, D. M. (1998). *Research methods in education and psychology: Integrating diversity with quantitative and qualitative approaches.* Thousand Oaks, CA: SAGE Publications.

Miller Matthei, L., & Smith, D. A. (1998). Belizean ""Boyz 'n the Hood""? Garifuna labor migration and transnational identity. In M. P. Smith & L. E. Guarnizo, (Eds.), *Transnationalism from below* (pp. 270–290). New Brumswick, NJ: Transaction Publishers.

Mitra, A. (1997). Virtual commonality: Looking for India on the Internet. In S. G. Jones (Ed.). *Virtual culture: Identity and communication in cybersociety*, (pp. 55–79). London: Thousand Oaks.

Myers, W. H. III (1997). Of Qinqing, Qinshu, Guanxi, and Shetou: The dynamic elements of Chinese irregular populations movement. In P. J. Smith, *Human smuggling: Chinese migrant trafficking and the challenge to America's immigration tradition,* (pp. 93–133). Washington, DC: The Center for Strategic and International Studies.

Ogbu, J. U., & Matute-Bianchi, M. E. (1986). In Bilingual Education Office, California State Department of Education, *Beyond language : social and cultural factors in schooling language minority students.* (pp. 73–142) Los Angeles: Evaluation, Dissemination, and Assessment Center, California State University.

Olsen, L. (1997). *Made in America: Immigrant Students in Our Public Schools.* New York: The New Press.

Olsen, L. (1988). *Crossing the Schoolhouse Border: Immigrant Students and the California Public Schools.* San Francisco: California Tomorrow.

Ong, A. (1995). Writing Chinese women out of context. In R. Behar & D. Gordon,. *Women writing culture.* University of California Press.

Ong, A., & Nonini, D. (1997). Toward a cultural politics of diaspora and transnationalism. In A. Ong & D. Nonini (Eds.), *Underground empires: The cultural politics of modern Chinese transnationalism,* (pp. 323–332). London: Routledge.

Osborne, E. H., Fu, Y., & Men, Z. (2000). Entering the Chinese market: A guide for U.S. small business. [On-line]. Available: *www.sbaer.uca.edu*

Pan, L. (Ed.) (1999). *The Encyclopedia of Chinese Overseas.* Cambridge, MA: Harvard University Press.

Peshkin, A. (1991). *The color of strangers, the color of friends: The play of ethnicity in school and community.* Chicago, IL: The University of Chicago Press.

Pessar, P. (1994). Sweatshop workers and domestic ideologies: Dominican women in New York's apparel industry. *International journal of urban and regional research, 18*, (1), 127–142.

Pessar, P. (1996, January). *The role of gender, households, and social networks in the migration process: A review and appraisal.* Paper presented at the Social Science Research Council Conference - Becoming American/American Becoming: International Migration to the United States, New York.

Popkin, E. (1999). Guatemalan Mayan migration to Los Angeles: Constructing transnational linkages in the context of the settlement process. *Ethnic and racial studies, 22*(2), 267–289.

Portes, A. (1995). Segmented assimilation among new immigrant youth: A conceptual framework. In R. G. Rumbaut & W. A. Cornelius (Eds.), *California's immigrant children: Theory, research, and implications for educational policy,* (pp.71–76). San Diego, CA: Center for U.S.-Mexican Studies, University of California.

Portes, A. (1996a). Global Villagers: The rise of transnational communities. *The American prospect, 25,* (pp. 74–77).

Portes, A. (1996b). Globalization from Below: The rise of transnational communities. In W. P. Smith & R. P. Korczenwicz (Eds.), *Latin America in the world economy,* (pp. 151–168). Westport, CN: Greenwood Press.

Portes, A. (1999). Towards a New World—the origins and effects of transnational activities. *Ethnic and racial studies, 22*(2), 463–477.

Portes, A., & Bach, R. L. (1985). *Latin journey: Cuban and Mexican immigrants in the United States.* Berkeley: University of California Press.

Portes, A., Guarnizo, L. E., & Landolt, P. (1999). The study of transnationalism: Pitfalls and promise of an emergent research field. *Ethnic and racial studies, 22*(2), 217–237.

Portes, A., MacLeod, S. A., & Parker, R. N. (1978). Immigrant aspirations. *Sociology of education, 51*(4), 241–260.

Portes, A., & Zhou, M. (1990, April). *Divergent destinies: Immigration, poverty, and entrepreneurship in the United States.* Paper written for the project on Poverty, Inequality, and the Crisis of Social Policy, Joint Center for Political and Economic Studies, Washington, DC.

Power, C. (1998, May 11). Good riddance and good luck. For most of China's political exiles there is not helping hand in America. *Newsweek, 131*(19), 44–46.

Rheingold, H. (1993). *The virtual community: Homesteading on the electronic frontier.* Reading, MA: Addison-Wesley.

Ribeiro, G. L. (1998). Cybercultural politics: Political activism at a distance in a transnational world. In S. E. Alvarez, E. Dagnino, & A. Escobar (Eds.), *Cultures of politics, politics of cultures: Re-Visioning Latin American social movements,* (pp. 325–352). Westview.

Riessman, F. (1962). *The culturally deprived child.* New York: Harper & Row Publishers.

Roberts, B. R., Frank, R., & Lozano-Ascencio, F. (1999). Transnational migrant communities and Mexican migration to the U.S. *Ethnic and racial studies, 22*(2), 238–266.

Rose, P. I. (1997). *They and We: Racial ethnic relations in the United States.* New York: McGraw-Hill.

Rothstein, S. W. (1996). *Schools and society: New Perspectives in American education.* Englewood Cliffs, NJ: Prentice-Hall.

Rouse, R. (1991). Mexican migration and the social space of postmodernism. *Diaspora, 1*(1), 83–95.

Rumbaut, R. (1995). The New Californians: Comparative research findings on the educational progress of immigrant children. In R. Rumbaut & W. Cornelius (Eds.), *California Immigrant Children: Theory Research and Implications for Educational Policy.* (pp. 17–70). San Diego: University of California.

Rumbaut, R. G., & Cornelius, W. A. (Eds.). *California's immigrant children: Theory, research, and implications for educational policy.* San Diego: Center for U.S.-Mexican Studies, University of California.

Sagara, C., & Kiang, P. (Eds.). (1992, February). *Recognizing poverty in Boston's Asian American community.* Paper presented in the Asian American Resource Workshop, Boston, MA.

Schein, L. (1998). Forged transnationality and oppositional cosmopolitanism. In M. P. Smith, & L. E. Guarnizo (Eds.), *Transnationalism from below* (pp. 291–313). New Brumswick, NJ: Transaction Publishers.

Schuck, P., & Münz, R., (Eds.). (1998). *Paths to inclusion: The integration of migrants in the United States and Germany.* New York: Berghahn Books.

Sklair, L. (1998, May). *Transnational practices and the analysis of the global system.* Paper presented at the Economic and Social Research Council (ESRC) Transnational Community Programme Seminar, Oxford, England.

Smith, M. P. (1994). Can you imagine? Transnational migration and the globalization of grassroots politics. *Social Text*, pp. 15–33.

Smith, M. P., & Guarnizo, L. E. (Eds.) (1998). *Transnationalism from below.* New Brumswick, NJ: Transaction Publishers.

Smith, R. C. (1998a). Transnational localities: Community, technology, and the politics of membership within the context of Mexico and U.S. migration. . In M. P. Smith & L. E. Guarnizo (Eds.), *Transnationalism from below* (pp. 196–240). New Brumswick, NJ: Transaction Publishers.

Smith, R. C. (May, 1998b). *Transnational public spheres and changing practices of citizenship, membership, and nation: Comparative insights from the Mexican and Italian cases.* Paper presented at the International Centre for Contemporary Cultural Research (ICCCR) International Conference on Transnationalism, Manchester, England.

Smolowe, J. (1993, June 21). Where is the promise land? Illegal Chinese aliens. *Time, 141*(25), 29–31.

Spindler, G., & Spindler, L. (1990). *The American cultural dialogue and its transmission.* London: The Falmer Press.

Stivens, M. (1998, May). *Gendering the global and the anti-global: Asian modernities, "Asian values," and the "Asian family."* Paper presented at the International Centre for Contemporary Cultural Research (ICCCR) International Conference on Transnationalism, Manchester, England.

Strauss, A. L. (1996). *Qualitative analysis for social scientists.* New York: Cambridge University Press.

Suarez-Orozco, C. (2000). Identities under siege: immigration stress and social mirroring among the children of immigrants. In C. G. M. Robben & M. Suarez-Orozco, (Eds.), *Cultures under siege: Collective violence and trauma.* (pp. 194–226). New York: Cambridge University Press.

Suarez-Orozco, M., & Suarez-Orozco, C. (1995). Transformations: Immigration, family life, and achievement motivation among Latino adolescents. Stanford, CA: Stanford University Press.

Torres-Saillant, S., & Hernandez, R. (1998). *The Dominican Americans.* Westport, CT: Greenwood Press.

Valdes, G. (1996). *Con Respeto: Bridging the distances between culturally diverse families and schools.* An Ethnographic portrait. New York, NY: Teacher College Press.

Vertovec, S. (1999). Conceiving and researching transnationalism. *Ethnic and racial studies, 22*(2), 447–462.

Vlach, N. (1992). *The Quetzal in flight: Guatemalan refugee families in the United States*. Westport, CT: Praeger.

Walhbeck, O. (1998, August). *Transnationalism and diasporas: The Kurdish example*. Paper presented at the International Sociological Association XIV World Congress of Sociology, Montreal, Canada.

Waters, M. (1995). *Globalization*. London: Routledge.

Welch, O. M., & Hodges, C. R. (1997). *Standing outside on the inside: Black adolescents and the construction of academic identity*.

Wong, B. (1998). *Ethnicity and entrepreneurship: The new Chinese immigrants in the San Francisco Bay area*. Boston, MA: Allyn & Bacon.

Wu, K. B. (1997). Education politics in Taiwan (China) and Hong Kong. In W. K. Cummings & P. G. Altback, (Eds.), *The challenge of Eastern Asian education: Implications for America*, (pp. 189–203). Albany: State University of New York.

Zhou, M. (1997). Social capital in Chinatown: The role of community-based organization and families in the adaptation of the younger generation. In M. Seller & L. Weis (Eds.), *Beyond black and white*, (pp. 181–205). Albany, NY: State University of New York Press.

Zhou, M, Adefuin, J. Y., Chung, A., & Roach, E. (February, 2000). *How does community matter for immigrant children? Structural supports and constraints in inner city neighborhoods*. Paper presented at the Sociology of Education Association Conference, Pacific Grove, California.

Index